The British Political Process

✦

HORIZONS IN
RATIVE POLITICS

The British Political Process

Concentrated Power Versus Accountability

JORGEN S. RASMUSSEN
Iowa State University

Wadsworth Publishing Company
Belmont, California
A Division of Wadsworth, Inc.

Political Science Editor: Kris Clerkin
Editorial Assistant: SoEun Park
Production Editor: Angela Mann
Designer: Andrew Ogus
Print Buyer: Barbara Britton
Art Editor: Kelly Murphy
Permissions Editor: Peggy Meehan
Technical Illustrator: Precision Graphics
Cover Designer: Andrew Ogus
Cover Photograph: The griffin on the site of Temple Bar. Photograph by
Jorgen S. Rasmussen
Compositor: Thompson Type
Printer: Malloy Lithographing

*This book is printed on
acid-free recycled paper.*

Printed in the United States of America

1 2 3 4 5 6 7 8 9 10 — 97 96 95 94 93

Library of Congress Cataloging-in-Publication Data

Rasmussen, Jorgen Scott.
    The British political process : concentrated power versus accountability /
Jorgen S. Rasmussen.
        p.   cm.
    Includes index.
    ISBN 0-534-20064-8
    1. Great Britain — Politics and government.   I. Title.
JN318.R37   1993
320.941 — dc20   92-35681

Contents

CHAPTER 5
....

The Legislature 93

CHAPTER 6
....

The Judiciary 124

PART III ✦ POLITICAL STRUCTURES

CHAPTER 7
....

Elections 147

CHAPTER 8
. . . .

Parties   185

PART IV   ✦   CONCLUSION

CHAPTER 9
. . . .

Prospects for Stability
and Change   241

Foreword

✦

The Wadsworth series, New Horizons in Comparative Politics, seeks to present timely, readable, up-to-date books in that exciting and booming political science field. Convinced that other Comparative Politics series are outdated or no longer suitable for classroom use, Wadsworth launched this series to remedy the situation. The time is ripe for fresh perspectives in view of changing world events and new disciplinary approaches.

Books in the series may take one of several forms: country studies, regional studies, or studies of topical issues such as "Democracy in Comparative Perspective," "The New Europe," or "Corporatism in Comparative Perspective." The books in the series will be brief (in the neighborhood of 200 pages), readable, and designed for introductory and upper division courses in comparative politics. But it is hoped that more senior students and scholars will find their data and interpretations of interest as well. The goal of the series is to provide political science students with texts that are accessible, yet enhance their understanding of the vital themes, approaches, and analyses in comparative politics. So far as is feasible and to facilitate comparative analysis, parallel chapter outlines will be used for the country and area books in the series. Books for the series have already been commissioned and are underway on such topics as Great Britain (Jorgen Rasmussen), France (Ronald Tiersky), China and Japan (Peter Moody), and Eastern Europe (Ivan Volgyes). Other books that are a part of the series are *An Introduction to Comparative Politics* by Howard J. Wiarda and *Comparative Government and Politics* by John McCormick.

In launching this new series we have sought to get balanced scholars and lively, readable authors. We also made a conscious decision to move to a new generation of scholars who see things from a fresh perspective. Our goal is to provide short, versatile volumes that can be used in a myriad of comparative politics courses. We hope some of the excitement and enthusiasm that our authors feel for their subject areas is contagious.

We are especially pleased to begin the series with this excellent study of Britain by Jorgen S. Rasmussen. Professor of Political Science at Iowa State University, Dr. Rasmussen is recognized as one of the leading scholars on British politics in the United States.

There are sound pedagogical reasons for beginning a comparative politics series with a book on Britain. Among the great variety of political systems in the world, British politics are most like our own. Many American political precepts and institutions are derived from Great Britain. Professor Rasmussen presents the argument in his opening pages that one should study Britain in order to better understand the United States. That certainly is true, but there is a second pedagogical lesson here: An understanding of British politics also provides a good introduction to the comprehension of other political systems that are unlike our own. My experience in teaching comparative politics over twenty-five years is that it is best to start with the familiar or at least the semifamiliar, and then go on to the less familiar. That is an argument, I believe, for beginning students of comparative politics to study Britain first, then continental Europe (the typical introductory course), and only then move on to more unfamiliar and difficult areas like Asia, Africa, Latin America, or the Middle East.

Professor Rasmussen has done a marvelous job of introducing us to British politics — and of launching our series. His book is serious, balanced, well informed, well written — and witty. The book covers all the requisite subject areas: the political culture, social structure, and history of Britain; interest groups, political parties, and elections; government institutions (executive, legislature, judiciary); and public policy. He wrestles with the issue of how and where British politics is very similar to that of the United States — and how it is very much different. In this way, he not only enables us to understand Britain, but he adds a unique perspective on American politics, about which most of us already have quite a bit of information, and also serves to introduce us to the general field of comparative politics as well as to other, even more challenging political systems quite different from our own.

HOWARD J. WIARDA

Preface

I hope this text will help American students to understand British politics. Britain may be the United States' closest ally. Certainly the United States shares many basic values with Britain, and many American governmental institutions are rooted there. It is well worth knowing about this country. I also hope that through this text students will come to understand how one studies comparative politics and why it is worth doing. And, finally, I hope that this text will lead students to see American government in a new perspective, to have a fuller, more objective understanding of it for having studied the British system.

In a brief Introduction I set forth the basic theme of the crucial problem in democratic government of limiting power sufficiently to prevent its abuse while not rendering it ineffective. This may be the most fundamental concern of political science. Every country must grapple with this problem; therefore, those students who go on to study other foreign countries can focus then on the same issues as are being raised here. I explain how the British response has taken the form of a search for a balance between concentrated power and accountability. The Introduction, like much of the rest of the book, is about, but not limited to, Britain. Perhaps the most basic idea I'd like this book to communicate to students is that governing is about making choices — choices not between good and bad, but between shades of gray; whatever is chosen, there ain't no free lunch. Every choice has a cost that someone must pay.

The main sections of the book are the setting, the government, and politics. Each chapter in these sections begins with a brief statement of a central problem or issue serving as the focal point for the material included. Each ends with a brief summary of the discussion. For the most part this is a concise recapitulation of the argument, but at times requires making explicit ideas only implicit in a chapter itself.

Chapter 1 summarizes the key events of British history and explains how they have affected the balance between power and accountability. Contemporary problems of balance get special emphasis. In Chapter 2 I've not tried to provide comprehensive information on all aspects of British life and society. For example, I've included little about the British economy. I preferred to concentrate on the diversity/homogeneity of Britain, to examine those social divisions that can produce tensions requiring action by the political system. The basic principles of the British Constitution and how they relate to the country's value system are the focus of Chapter 3. These three chapters in Part I present the foundation of the British system and its flaws or, at least, the points of tension.

The threefold division of government into executive, legislative, and judicial branches is familiar to anyone who has taken American civics courses in school. Despite Britain's having a fusion, rather than a separation, of powers, I retained the familiar pattern to organize Part II. Rather atypically, Chapter 4 on the executive branch includes not only the Cabinet and the Prime Minister (obviously) and the monarch (not too surprising), but also the civil service (usually in a separate chapter). Given the book's basic theme, starting with the governmental institutions where power is concentrated seemed most logical. After that, Chapter 5 could focus on the structures entrusted with the job of calling power to account. Although this is primarily the task of the House of Commons, the chapter discusses the House of Lords, also. Much of the chapter deals with relations between the Commons and the Government (the Prime Minister and colleagues). Had I included this material in Chapter 4, much of it would have been unclear; only after I've examined separately the executive and the legislature can I discuss their relations. The judicial branch in Britain is not fused to the same degree as are the legislative and executive branches. Thus, Chapter 6 is a bit more autonomous. Nonetheless, the discussion of the role of judges in making British public policy helps to integrate this material into the rest of the text and indicates the extent to which they can provide a constraint on power.

Politics has not been absent from either Part I or Part II. Part III, however, does focus on what might most readily come to mind when someone mentions politics: elections and political parties. Chapter 7 devotes a good deal of space to the development of the British electoral system, because this is an excellent example of the British approach to reform. In addition, this information helps to provide perspective on current discussions about changing the electoral system. Finally, this chapter explains electioneering as currently practiced in Britain. As the opening portion of Chapter 8 indicates, the nature of the British party system is rather uncertain. Exactly what type is it? For reasons that will be made clear, I've chosen to concentrate almost entirely on the Conservative party, the Labour party, and the Liberal Democrats (the latter getting the least attention). Regional parties and national minor ones receive little mention. Admittedly, my treatment isn't complete, but it does reflect power realities. This is intended to be a readable textbook and Chapter 8 already is — most readers are likely to think — too long. For the three main parties, I've explained how they developed and are organized, what they stand for, who supports them, and what strength they have.

Finally, in Part IV's single chapter I try to integrate all this material in a synthesizing conclusion that provides an overview and an evaluation of the British system. The text's subtitle, directing attention to how concentrated power can be made accountable, is most explicitly discussed here. The question of reform of the British system is linked to the British tradition of fortuitous and imperceptible change. Comparison with the United States, particularly with reformist aims, is addressed again through the topic of transplanting institutions.

Anyone looking at the table of contents of this book may conclude that certain familiar topics have been ignored. Unlike many books, this one doesn't offer a separate chapter on policy. Such chapters strike me as afterthoughts, tacked on when the real business of the book is already finished. Policy is treated as though it were an autonomous area, having little to do with government and politics. I've preferred to incorporate policy concerns as appropriate throughout the book. The section of Chapter 2 on race and ethnicity has a good deal to say about race relations policy in Britain. Law and order — a major political issue in the United States — gets special attention in Chapter 6 on the judiciary. The great bulk of Chapters 7 (on elections) and 8 (on parties) deals with policies and issues. These are just some instances of the text's concern with policy making.

Similarly, the contents lists no separate chapter nor portion of one dealing with interest groups. This is because, for example, Chapter 4's discussion of Parliament devotes attention to the role of groups in legislative activity. The political role of trade unions and their important connection with the Labour party are significant topics in the recent history section of Chapter 1 and in the analysis of party development and organization in Chapter 8.

Most every topic that appears in traditional texts is included in this one, it's just that I've organized the material differently. After all, why write a new text if all you are going to do is follow the well-trodden path. Others have been down that way before and have done a good job of it. As they used to say on *Monty Python*, "And now for something completely different."

A couple of decades ago few British politics texts were available. Now the selection is better and some of them are quite good. None, however, provides all the features that I would like to offer the students in my British politics classes. Perhaps I'm not unique in seeking a different mix, another option. I didn't need, nor wish to write, an encyclopedic tome, a reference work for library shelves. As a text, this book contains a good bit of information. I don't want just to describe, however, but also to explain sufficiently to encourage understanding.

A text can't help students learn about a subject if the writing is so formal and dull that they dread reading it. I've tried to adopt almost a conversational tone. Some specialized terms have to be included (and should be defined when they are), but professional jargon isn't necessary. Nor is there any need to be pedantic and pompous. I favor a light touch. I agree with a prominent radio personality of several decades ago who used to ridicule his advertisers. His view was that if something was good enough it could stand a little kidding. Similarly, I think that only if you take a subject sufficiently seriously can you see its humorous aspects. If something strikes me as ridiculous, I see no reason for not pointing it out, in hopes that the reader will smile over the incongruity as well.

Another way of making a book readable is to break up page after page of solid text with illustrative material. This book has more such material than any other British politics text. I've included these illustrations not just for decoration. They are fully incorporated into the written material. They appear to *illustrate* a particular point. If one picture is worth a thousand words, then this material should have enabled me to keep several topics shorter than they otherwise would have been. This material should help to give students a greater sense of "feel" for Britain and its politics.

When I went to graduate school — a time that will seem to most readers of this book as remote as the Middle Ages — I knew that I wanted to specialize in comparative government, probably British politics. My reason for selecting this field within political science can be explained by the story of the chance meeting between two old friends. They had not run into each other since the one had served as the bridesmaid at the other's wedding. After updating each other on their activities in the interim, the former bridesmaid inquired, "How's your husband?" To which her friend replied, "Compared to what?"

Almost all Americans study American national government in high school. Many universities make introduction to American government a required course. Such extensive study can inculcate a lot of facts; understanding American government, however, requires comparing it with other systems. How do other cultures conceive of the role of government? How do they go about trying to implement that conception? What procedures are thought to be appropriate in making decisions that are binding on the entire society? How efficient and effective are other governments?

Even the most nationalistic American must recognize that one can't accept merely on faith the belief that American procedures are the only way or, indeed, the best way. If other countries do things differently, why is that so? To what extent does doing things differently produce more or less success than American methods? Only by comparing the American system with others is it possible to see what this country does well and what could be improved and to obtain some ideas about how to devise any improvements that are needed.

Yes, one could spend the equivalent amount of time in further study of American politics and, thereby, learn a great deal. What one would miss, however, would be perspective. The ability to see ourselves as others see us always is to be highly prized. Although this book is not about British views of the United States, it does reproduce the lens through which Britons view government and politics. Looking at the United States through this lens should help to bring into focus previously unseen sights.

Since this book is written for American students, I assume that the readers do know something about U.S. government and politics and that they are likely to be especially interested in British contrasts with the United States. So comparisons with the United States abound in this book. When I first began teaching British politics the purpose of such comparisons would have been to convince you that the United States should adopt many British procedures and institutions. I no longer think that. Each country does some things better and some things worse; each has its own particular set of problems. Even when problems are common to both, the details differ. For example, racism is a problem in each country, but in different ways and for different reasons. And the response of these two countries to racism has differed considerably. You should not think that you need to search in British race relations policies for specific programs or actions to improve American life. The aim instead is to sensitize you to another way of thinking, to help you see that others face similar problems but perceive and react to them differently. What's being offered is not specific solutions, but the stimulation to think in new ways that is essential to devising appropriate solutions.

Finally, I would like to thank reviewers James Alt, Harvard University; Forest Grieves, University of Montana; Henry Steck, SUNY–Cortland; and T. Phillip Wolf, Indiana University Southeast, for their helpful comments.

JORGEN S. RASMUSSEN

About the Author

✦

Jorgen S. Rasmussen received his Ph.D. in political science from the University of Wisconsin–Madison, following an A. B. with highest honors in Government from Indiana University. Currently he is Distinguished Professor of Political Science at Iowa State University, having served as chair of that department from 1972 to 1976. He also has taught at the University of Glasgow, Vanderbilt University, Columbia University, and the University of Arizona. One of the founders of the British Politics Group, he has been its Executive Secretary for more than a decade and a half. He has been a manuscript referee and a member of the editorial board for various scholarly journals. He has served as a member of the Fulbright area advisory committee for Britain and Ireland. From time to time he comments on American political developments for the BBC Scotland news broadcasts.

He is the sole author of two other books, one on the British Liberal party and another on the study of comparative politics. In addition, he is a joint author of *Major European Governments* (Wadsworth Publishing) and a contributor to several other books. His scholarly articles have been published in journals both in the United States and abroad, as have been many book reviews.

Introduction

✦

Concentrated Power and Declining Accountability

No political system has been as widely copied as the British system. Although Britain's legislature is not the world's oldest (that distinction goes to Iceland), the country long has been called the mother of parliaments. Many countries around the world have modeled their legislatures on the British Parliament. In the nineteenth century when parliamentary democracy was a radical, indeed, revolutionary idea, European reformers sought to establish in their countries the key features of Britain's system. When many Third World countries gained independence after World War II, they gave themselves the "Westminster model," although the home of that model — Britain — had been their colonial master for generations, if not centuries. Even in the United States, where a protracted war against Britain was once required for independence, most of those advocating reform of American government urge adoption of various features of British government. What has made Britain's system so attractive to so many for so long?

What Britain had managed to do over a period of about six centuries was to develop a system that successfully integrated two fundamental aspects of government: power and accountability. The American system fractionalizes power, not only between the legislature, the executive, and the judiciary at the national level, but also between the national government and the states. In contrast, the British system concentrates power. Britain wasn't unique in doing so; autocratic governments through the ages had done the same. The innovation of the British system was to constrain this power to prevent its abuse. British citizens, unlike so many on the European continent, did not need to fear that their government would arbitrarily imprison them. Should they be charged with a crime, various procedural protections helped to ensure a fair trial. They could read newspapers and books that criticized the government and criticize it themselves if they wished. They could join others to form groups seeking changes in public policy.

Britons were free to an extent envied by European reformers not because a basic framework document like the American Constitution guaranteed them such rights. As I'll explain in Chapter 3, Britain never—except about a decade some three and a half centuries ago—has had a written constitution. Instead, accountability was the key constraint on arbitrary government, the fundamental defense for Britons' liberty. Initially the judiciary had played a crucial role in limiting arbitrary government. Subsequently and even more significantly, the legislature gained the power to require the executive to answer for, to justify publicly, its actions. This procedure was effective in preventing abuse of power because a sanction backed it. The legislature also had developed the ability to remove the executive from office whenever it so desired.

This double-barreled accountability—justify or be removed from office— not only protected citizens from arbitrary power but also gave them concentrated power's benefits. Governmental power is *both* a threat *and* a boon. Government can provide many services and programs to enhance the life of citizens. A weak and ineffective government, however, can implement few of these. Concentrated power facilitates prompt, coherent action alleviating public problems and meeting public needs. Such action is likely, not just possible, because when power is concentrated so, too, is responsibility. Should government fail to act or take steps that are ill-advised, it is clear who to blame. The executive is at fault; it can't pass the buck. It possessed the power to remedy the problem and didn't do so. Britain's system of accountable concentrated power helped to protect its citizens from the abuse of bad government and to deliver the benefits of good government.

The irony is that only a tiny political elite could wield this crucial power of accountability. Despite being the model for European democrats, Britain denied the right to vote to most men, to say nothing of women, until the last decade and a half of the nineteenth century. Throughout that century the United States, which few countries regarded as a model system, was much more democratic than Britain. Britain had solved the problem of controlling power by making it accountable; what it had not yet done was to establish broad-based accountability. Britain had not extended to the people, as distinct from the elite, the ability to call governmental power to account. Chapter 7 discusses in detail how Britain tried to institute popular accountability. Unfortunately, despite Britain's cautious advance, the process was complex and beset with unforeseen side effects. The impact of broadening accountability on parties and, in turn, on the legislature was counterproductive. At the end of the nineteenth century power was more democratically accountable — many more people could vote — but less constrained than it had been earlier.

These trends continued in the twentieth century. By mid-century many commentators on British government had become concerned about the ineffectiveness of the British Parliament. Although it was the key link in the chain of accountability, it seemed to have lost most of its ability to require the executive to justify its actions. No longer could it be said to constrain concentrated power. A prominent politician, Lord Hailsham (the son of a leading politician, a contender for leadership of the Conservative party, and, eventually, the head of the British judicial system), warned that Britain was developing an elective dictatorship. Clearly, something had gone drastically wrong. Reversing what had been the pattern, British reformers began looking to the United States for governmental institutions and procedures to remedy the defects in the British system. The British system no longer was the model.

The *Financial Times* (FT), one of Britain's "quality" newspapers (the British distinguish between tabloids and "quality" newspapers), saw the balance between power and accountability as penetrating to the heart of the 1992 election campaign.[1] The FT's editors noted that the traditional stance of both major parties failed "to cultivate successfully . . . those public services upon which a modern economy is heavily dependent," such as education, local government, and industrial affairs. The common theme of these and other key issues the FT recognized "is broadly that of governance." As one example the FT queried, "What do we think local government is for: an agency for delivering central government programmes or an expression of democratically accountable civil will?" Keep this question in mind as you read Chapter 2. The greater Britain's diversity, the more relevant it becomes. If Britain is a homogeneous society, then national policies produced by concentrated power are appropriate. If it is a highly pluralistic society, then concentrated power may provide insufficient scope for diversity in public policy.

The FT asserted that Britain had "an urgent need for stable, efficient policy delivery mechanisms, locally accountable and unbeholden to producer interests." The editors clearly recognized that power had to be concentrated sufficiently to be effective, but also wanted accountability to constrain it. The

---

1. "An election that matters," *Financial Times*, 12 March 1992, p. 14.

relevance of the last few words about interests will become much clearer after you read Chapter 1. Remember this comment as you read about the problems of both the Labour and the Conservative Governments in the late 1960s and early 1970s and the issues of "Who Governs?" and "the winter of discontent." That portion of Chapter 1 will tell you how Britain went from consensus to conviction politics. The FT hoped that the result of the 1992 election would be to return to the former. It advocated regional devolution and proportional representation in elections because "the processes involved [in these] offer the best hope of the sort of true consensus-building needed for Britain to re-discover stable and accountable institutions. An elective dictatorship in London is incapable of imagining what is needed, let alone delivering."

This text offers a good deal of information about British government and politics. The theme underlying these many facts is a crucial dilemma in political philosophy: How can power be sufficiently concentrated to enable government to provide society the benefits of collective or community action without being so strong that it invites and facilitates abuse of citizens' rights? How can power be called to account? Why did seeking to involve the public in this process in Britain attenuate accountability? What is the balance between power and accountability in Britain in the last decade of the twentieth century and how is this balance likely to affect the evolution of British government? Thus, although this information concerns only one country in the world, the implications of this information relate to government and politics everywhere.

Part I

✦

The British Setting

Photo on previous page: Victoria Tower and the Union Jack.

1
✦
Power and Accountability Through the Years

As I noted in the Introduction, Britain managed over several centuries both to concentrate and constrain governmental power. This unique achievement was unlike developments on the European continent. Therefore, a brief historical summary explaining how this occurred is useful. The first part of this chapter covers the highlights through the start of this century. The remainder of the chapter summarizes key events following World War II to the present. The aim is to provide both a feel for recent political events and personalities in Britain and to examine the difficulty that Britain has experienced in maintaining a satisfactory balance between concentrated power and accountability in recent years.

The Importance of Being Ancient

If ever a country valued historical tradition — stressed the importance of being ancient — it is Britain. It projects an image of centuries of ordered, proper behavior, of stable placidity. As so often is true, the stereotype is only partially valid. Before the nineteenth century, Europeans regarded the English as a volatile nation of brawlers. European sports fans may still hold such a view. English soccer fans have become infamous for hooliganism; at times the country's teams have been banned from international competition for fear their supporters would maim and kill fans from other countries.

In the nineteenth century lawlessness in Britain was at a level we now find hard to believe. Today when the House of Commons ends its business each night, the police officers on duty pass through the building shouting the traditional cry, "Who goes home?" What seems a quaint custom (the police are not intending to hail taxis for the Members) has a serious origin. As recently as a century and a half ago one was so likely to be mugged on the London streets at night that police escorts had to be formed to get Members of Parliament home safely.

What of political, as distinct from criminal, violence? An accidental fire destroyed the Houses of Parliament in 1834. According to a leading political figure of the day, Robert Peel, one reason that they were rebuilt in the same location was "the facility which the [River] Thames offered for escaping from inflamed mobs."[1] At the start of the 1830s incidents of violence and riots accompanied the campaign to expand the right to vote. The violence practiced both by and upon the women suffragists in Britain early in the twentieth century far exceeded that which occurred in the United States. In 1990 opposition to the new poll tax erupted into riots in London.

How did such a people get a reputation for being sedate, or, as the British would say, unflappable? The British response to two major historical events that occurred within about a half century of each other is the answer. When France was convulsed by a revolution toward the close of the eighteenth century—a revolution that claimed to be advancing the cause of the oppressed everywhere without regard to national boundaries—British society and its political system remained intact and unaltered. An analogy would be if Canada had a bloody communist revolution and Americans hardly noticed. Similarly, in the middle of the nineteenth century, revolutions swept the Continent but created little turmoil in Britain. Out of such tranquil responses grew the British reputation for political stability and decorum. Given Britain's checkered past, a summary of the key historical events that have shaped governmental institutions is instructive.

Charles de Gaulle, the illustrious French leader, liked to express his disdain for Britons and Americans by lumping them together as "the Anglo-Saxons." Like many other observers of the United Kingdom, he overlooked entirely the importance of the Celts. Two and a half millennia ago in the mists of early history, various Celtic groups invaded the British isles from the Continent; one of these was the forerunner of the Scots, another of the

---

1. Quoted in M. H. Port, ed., *The House of Parliament* (New Haven, Conn.: Yale University Press, 1976), p. 20.

Welsh, and a third of the Irish. When the Romans invaded in A.D. 43, the Britons they attacked were ethnically Celts. The civilized Romans defeated these barbarians and included Britain in their empire for nearly four centuries.

The Romans extensively settled what is now England — building villas with central heating, constructing temples to Roman deities, developing ports and marketplaces, and living very much as they did back in Italy. In the north and west, however, the rugged countryside prevented them from controlling the entire island. In what is now northern England and southern Scotland, they simply built walls stretching across the countryside from one body of water to the other to protect themselves from attack from the areas they didn't dominate. In the west, the Romans occupied what is now Wales, but their presence was little more than a system of forts linked by good roads, and in the mountainous areas their control was even more tenuous. The same was true for the bulk of the peninsula jutting out into the Atlantic. These differences in Roman control are the origin of the regional contrasts I'll discuss in Chapter 2. Thus, control by the Romans affected what eventually became the United Kingdom. What's surprising, however, is how little four centuries of Roman rule influenced modern British governmental institutions.

When their empire began to crumble under the pressure of various barbarian invasions, the Romans had to withdraw all military forces from the British Isles; they left the population to see to its own defenses around 410. These people — mainly Romanized Celts — were known as Britons. Since the Roman legions had gone, the more militant, less civilized Celts could surge back from the fringe areas into which they had been driven. (The outer periphery of Scotland, Northern Ireland, Wales, and west England is known even today as the Celtic fringe.) The Britons hired the Saxons, people living in what is now northern Germany, to help defend against this threat. The resultant upheavals — civil war among the Britons, rebellion by the Saxon mercenaries, and resurgence of the Celts — destroyed the culture that Roman rule had established. Even before the Romans withdrew, Germanic raiders had been attacking along the British coasts. These people (Angles, Saxons, and Jutes), capitalizing on the political chaos, gained control by around 600 of virtually the same areas that the Romans had dominated. The Britons retired in disarray to the fringe areas of the British Isles as the last remnants of Roman civilization were destroyed.

Why should you be concerned with struggles that are so obscure, indeed legendary (was there really a King Arthur?), that even historians don't know exactly what happened? Whatever the detailed events of this period, their cumulative impact was to eradicate any basis for the Roman law tradition that prevails on the Continent. Instead, because of what happened in Britain's "Dark Ages," the country eventually developed the common law system. This

© King Features. Reprinted with permission of King Features Syndicate Inc.

gave both Britain and the United States (which inherited the system from Britain) very different legal and judicial procedures from those existing in such countries as France and Germany. (I'll explain the contrast in more detail in Chapter 6.) So, about the only lasting contribution of the Romans to British life was a network of roads; few new ones were built in Britain until fourteen centuries after the Romans' departure.

The Germanic invaders proved to be more than just raiders, because they began to settle in the country. From them comes the ethnic stock of most people now living in the United Kingdom. That is, the Anglo-Saxons became what we now call English, while the Celtic Britons became the Welsh, Scots, and Irish. But this was not the end of diverse ethnic influx. Perhaps Britain, like the United States, should be seen as a melting pot of a variety of peoples.

Next to come were the Vikings, or Norsemen. They began raiding Britain before 800 and in less than a century controlled a considerable portion of what now is northeast England. At Jorvik (now called York) they established a thriving commercial center. The struggles between the Saxons and the Danes surged back and forth — the Danes ruled the entire country from 1016 to 1042. This contest remained unresolved when another group of Norsemen intervened in 1066. Viking raiders had been terrorizing the Continent as well as the British Isles. They were given territory in what is now France (called Normandy in recognition of their being north-men) in an effort to buy them off. These Normans crossed the Channel in 1066 to defeat the English at the Battle of Hastings.

One of the reasons that William the Conqueror, the Norman leader, was able to establish his rule was that the population of England and Wales was only 1.75 million — less than that of Minneapolis-St. Paul today. The importance of the Norman Conquest lies first in that it eliminated the several different dukedoms that formerly comprised the country to produce a united entity. William's centralized rule was a major step in the essential process of nation building. The Conquest's other important effect was introducing the feudal system into Britain. Under feudalism the rights, as well as the duties, of the nobility were specified. Although obligated to render certain services

© King Features. Reprinted with permission of King Features Syndicate Inc.

in exchange for the lands the king granted them, nobles also were to enjoy certain rights as long as they remained loyal subjects. Disputes concerning the exact nature of these rights and duties were to be settled by a council of the king and his leading lords. These practices were the foundation on which constitutionalism and parliamentary government gradually were constructed.

The gains made under William's rule were nearly lost in the virtual anarchy following his death. Eventually, however, central control was again established. Over the next several centuries the country balanced between feudal anarchy and tyrannical kingship; at any given moment one or the other might be ascendant. But equilibrium was maintained much more consistently than in any other European country. This balance was not so much the product of wise rulers' purposeful policies as it was the serendipitous result of variously motivated actions. For example, in the twelfth century the Crown developed a policy of sending judges throughout the kingdom to settle disputes without resort to arms. The aim was to help unify the country and to increase central revenues by collecting legal fees. Unintentionally, it laid the foundation for the common law, one of Britain's major contributions to constitutional government. In deciding the controversies presented to them, the itinerant judges tended to rely more on tradition, the customs of the local people, and precedent than on formal edicts or statutes. This practice gave rise to the idea that the judges were bit by bit elaborating a "higher law," more valid than that embodied in any written legal code. This in turn suggested that The Law was above the monarch; any rules he or she made that clashed with it were unjust and invalid. The concept of limited, or constitutional, government developed from such thinking.

Besides the courts, the other governmental structure that played an important role in controlling royal power was Parliament. Lacking sufficient revenue to finance his policies, King John decided in 1213 to tax the lower nobility, who previously hadn't had to bear this burden. Since they were too numerous for all to be summoned to the Great Council that was to approve the tax, John ordered that a few knights be chosen to speak for the many holding such a title. Unknowingly, John had taken the first step toward representative government; previously those who participated in the decision-making process were included because of their personal eminence and spoke only for themselves. Later in the same century the brief Parliament of the rebel Simon de Montfort called representatives of the townspeople, as well as of the knights. This practice was legitimized when in 1295 a legal ruler, Edward I, repeated it.

From these feeble, fortuitous beginnings a body of representatives known as Parliament was established. It had very little authority, was not popularly elected, and met only when the monarch called it. Sometimes several years passed between meetings. Moreover, it was not really a legislature but served as a kind of high court of justice concerned with judicial and administrative matters. The commoners from the counties and the boroughs were not permitted to meet with the monarch and nobles to take direct part in making decisions. In time the representatives of the commoners were allowed to present grievances to the monarch. But it was not until the fourteenth century that they were told to elect a speaker (to communicate their collective decisions to the monarch) and not until the reign of Henry V (1413–1422) that they began putting their petitions in the form in which they wished them enacted, thus initiating a crude legislative process.

Parliament had not been intended to be a means of controlling the monarch's government. Gradually, however, this is what it came to do. This development was furthered as the House of Commons acquired the right of originating all bills for raising or disbursing revenue. This right made the support of the Commons essential to the Crown. Nonetheless, Charles I attempted to rule without Parliamentary support and declined to call Parliament into session from 1629 to 1640. Such high-handed government—characterized as well by illegal taxation, martial law, and arbitrary imprisonment—combined with religious conflict between Protestants and Anglicans to culminate in a civil war during the 1640s. The king was executed, and the monarchy was replaced by a republic, which tended to be an autocracy under General Oliver Cromwell. With Cromwell's death the regime disintegrated because of factional conflict within the army, and the monarchy was restored. This period of little over a decade more than three centuries ago is the only experience Britain has had with republican government or a written constitution. The dearth of achievements during that time, along with the solemn and joyless quality of life imposed on the people, helps explain the restoration of the monarchy.

The rule of James II raised again the questions, Was Britain to be a Catholic or a Protestant country? and Was ultimate power to reside with the monarch or with Parliament? In 1688 James was driven from the throne in a bloodless revolution, and Parliament invited his Protestant daughter Mary and her husband William to become monarchs. Since Mary was not the immediate heir to the throne, Parliament had demonstrated its power to determine who the monarch would be. By accepting Parliament's offer, William and Mary were acknowledging its supremacy.

Thus, when continental European feudal kingdoms were turning into absolute monarchies, feudal limitations on the royal prerogative in Britain were developing into parliamentary restrictions on the exercise of the powers of the Crown. The crucial question was whether the monarch could make laws on his or her own without approval by Parliament. The Civil War in the 1640s confirmed that the monarch was not above the law and that the common law could be amended only in Parliament. Since 1689 no monarch has challenged the supremacy of Parliament. This doesn't mean that after 1689 the monarch lost all governmental influence. On the contrary, several subsequent British monarchs were powerful. They had to depend on Parliament, however, for funds and for determining what was law. Nonetheless, the evolution of the monarchy since 1689 has been a peaceful decline in power and influence.

Parliamentary supremacy meant that the monarch had to govern through political leaders, known as ministers, who were acceptable to Parliament. William sought to reduce opposition from Parliament during a conflict with France (which was supporting the deposed James II) by giving some principal governmental offices to four leaders with a sizable following in the House of Commons. In time, such maneuvering developed into the practice of selecting chief ministers exclusively from that alliance of leaders able to control the Commons. Although these ministers were supposed to assist the monarch, the advice they could give was affected by the views of their legislative follow-ers. Until these groups developed into formal political parties, the monarch could try playing one faction against another but could not prevail against a united majority in Parliament.

The monarch's small group of chief advisors became known as the Cabi-net. During the eighteenth century the monarch stopped meeting with them as a group.[2] Although this temporarily reduced the power of the Cabinet, the ministers remained significant. Because the ministers as well as the monarch had to sign all official acts, they came to be regarded as responsible for those acts. The Cabinet became, in effect, the executive committee of the party that held a majority in Parliament. As the power of the House of Lords declined during the second half of the nineteenth century and through the twentieth, the political situation in the House of Commons became the more important one. The Cabinet's policies had to be those that could command support there. Cabinets advised the monarch what actions their party would accept. The monarch couldn't pursue a contrary policy since he or she would lack majority support in Parliament; the result would be a constitutional crisis — like the one that led to revolution in 1688 — of monarch defying Parliament.

At the same time as power within Parliament shifted from the Lords to the Commons, the Commons also became more democratic. Beginning in 1832 in a process that went on for almost a century (which I'll recount in Chapter 7), Britain permitted more and more of the population to choose the members of the Commons. Thus, the country's political leadership became more accountable to the people. Political parties developed along with the expansion of voting rights. The Whigs and Tories of the seventeenth century can be called parties only in the loosest sense, since they were little more than factions based primarily on personal connections rather than on shared policy preferences. But the process of developing the unified leadership and definite principles that were to characterize their successors started with them. Not until the nineteenth century did a modern party system, built upon an exten-sive grass-roots organization and coherent programs of policies, appear. The current pattern of partisan politics began to take shape at the start of the twentieth century when a Labour party, formally supported by the trade union movement and espousing socialist doctrine, was founded.

Although World War I was as traumatic for Britain as for other European nations, government and politics seemed to return to normal soon after hostilities ceased. Most people would have noted only two changes: (1) The

---

2. Historians have challenged the widely recounted story that George I refused to meet with the Cabinet because, coming from Germany, he couldn't speak or understand English well.

process of broadening accountability finally was taken to its logical conclusion as all adults, women as well as men, were given the right to vote; and (2) after a brief spell in a three-party configuration, the party system returned to its traditional two-party form. The once-great Liberal party declined to minor status, as Labour took its place; Labour and the Conservatives became the major parties.

At several points in this brief summary of British history, I've noted that a certain basic reform occurred gradually, in stages, without the change being consciously planned. Such an evolutionary process has been immensely significant in providing continuity to Britain's political development and giving it a durable political system. In nearly a millennium since the last time the country was successfully invaded, the only real break in its history has been the English Civil War and the republican form of government it produced. This break proved to be only a brief hiatus with little lasting effect. The restoration of the Tudor monarchy did nothing to resolve the fundamental power struggle between the monarch and the Parliament for political supremacy; concentrated power had not yet been made accountable. The Glorious Revolution of 1688, the chief watershed in British history, was needed to settle the issue. In the mid-seventeenth century, then, the course of British political development was disrupted. After some experimentation and false steps, Britain got back on track in less than a half century and resumed organic, evolutionary change into the twentieth century.

In Britain, in contrast to many other nations, reforms have been neither sharp nor sudden. As a result, they have won acceptance more readily and seldom have produced enduring extreme political cleavages. This has been the genius of British politics. British history exhibits a long-term trend — whatever the occasional periods of reversal or stagnation or of increased constraint on governmental power — toward greater responsibility or accountability of those holding power to those over whom it is exercised.

This trend can be traced until around the last quarter of the nineteenth century. Beginning then, changes in parliamentary procedure, legislative–executive relations, party organization, and electoral behavior significantly altered the British system. Contrary to appearances the system of 1920 differed fundamentally from that of 1870. The long-term process of constraining power through accountability had not only been halted but had been reversed. The issue no longer was control of the power of the monarch, but rather that of the Cabinet and the Prime Minister. That they were elected, not hereditary, rulers didn't make the problem any less serious.

Detailed discussion of the changes that reversed the evolution of British government must be reserved for the appropriate places in the following chapters. In the meantime, however, an understanding of the interplay between power and accountability in contemporary Britain and the problems associated with the new balance is essential.

From Consensus to Conviction Politics

As soon as World War II was over in Europe, Britain, which had not held elections for a decade, went to the polls. The results surprised many because the country's illustrious wartime leader, Winston Churchill, was driven from power. Unlike the United States with Franklin Roosevelt's reforming administrations, Britain during the 1930s had status quo government under the Conservatives. The British Government had been sufficiently powerful to try to alleviate the sufferings of the Depression but had regarded economic decline as an act of God and had done little. The country was determined to call the Conservatives to account even if it had to ditch Churchill to do so. The electorate insisted on the reformist Government it had not enjoyed a decade earlier.

For the first time in British history the Labour party won a majority of the seats in the House of Commons. (Lack of majority control of the legislature had hampered Labour during two previous periods in office.) Labour implemented a program of extensive economic reforms. Private owners were required to sell to the government their holdings in coal, gas, electricity, telecommunications, and transportation enterprises so that these could be owned and operated by the government. Nationalization or public ownership was to ensure that the "commanding heights" of the economy were run not for private gain but for public service.

Much more important for the average person, however, were the social reforms. Pensions were improved and the National Health Service (known as socialized medicine in the United States) was established. The NHS, perhaps the greatest social reform ever implemented in Britain, provided universal health care.

Despite such reforms, the late 1940s was a period of great privation and austerity in Britain. Fighting the war had exhausted Britain's financial resources. Bombing had destroyed or damaged many of its industries. Even if Britain had been able to produce as much as in the 1920s, the world economy had yet to adjust to peacetime and few countries could buy from Britain. As a result, rationing continued well into the postwar period and eventually came to include such staples as bread and potatoes. Government ownership of the coal mines failed to eliminate worker dissatisfaction, hampering production. During the harsh winter of 1946–1947 many people were unable to heat their homes adequately.

Labour seemed to be losing its sense of purpose. Government ownership of business enterprises was not a Labour innovation. Some commercial operations had been acquired by Conservative Governments during the interwar period. These and Labour's initial acquisitions could be justified on grounds of economic efficiency. Labour's later nationalizations, such as trucking and iron and steel, had less to do with practicalities, however, than with furthering a commitment to socialist ideology. Thus, Labour barely retained its hold on office in the 1950 election and, after staggering only for another year and a half, was voted out in 1951.

The Conservative party that returned to office differed dramatically from the one that the voters had repudiated only six years earlier. Although the party returned to private ownership some enterprises that Labour had nationalized, the Conservatives kept most of them in government ownership. Labour's social reforms, including the NHS, the Conservatives wholeheartedly embraced. The Conservative Government devoted considerable resources to expanding public housing — more than Labour had done. And it accepted Labour's position that unemployment must be kept to an absolute minimum.

In short, the 1950s saw the forging of a basic consensus in British politics. The two major parties weren't clones; they might disagree on details or means of achieving goals. But on the fundamentals of public policy they differed little. So great was the agreement that it is known as the time of "Butskellism." This term combined the names of Richard A. Butler, the number two man in the Conservative party, and Hugh Gaitskell, a prominent figure and eventual Leader of the Labour party. The idea was that economic policy in Britain would be essentially the same whether formulated by one or the other.

Nonetheless, the Conservatives did claim that they set the economy free by abolishing the remaining wartime regulations, thus giving the country thirteen years of growing prosperity. Although this action probably did help, the recovery of the world economy also was a major factor in Britain's revival. Whatever the reasons, most Britons did feel that they were living more comfortably than ever before. This feeling did not prevent growing dissatisfaction with the Conservatives. Like Labour before them, the Conservatives seemed to have lost their way and to have no goals other than maintaining themselves in office. That in itself need not have proved fatal to the party's electoral appeal. One of the Conservatives' strengths has been to present themselves as the party of government, the people who by training and experience (and perhaps even breeding) know how to run public affairs competently — better than that Labour lot can do. The Conservatives have appealed to the voters not so much on the merit of their policy promises as on the abilities of their leaders.

The performance of the Conservative Governments in the late 1950s and early 1960s began to call that claim into question. Foreign policy adventurism — colluding with the French and the Israelis to invade the Suez Canal — strained relations with the United States and demonstrated the vulnerability of both Britain's defense and its economy. A variety of domestic scandals (mainly sexual) involving Conservative politicians also made the party's claim to responsible leadership appear dubious.

Furthermore, despite the consensus of Butskellism, Labour was complaining of thirteen wasted years (dating back to the Conservative victory in 1951). Labour regarded the consumer boom that was fueling the economy as a waste of resources. The Conservatives were failing to invest in Britain's future. Insufficient public funds were being devoted to improving education, social services, and the economic infrastructure. By 1964 the Conservative party was being led by a traditional Scottish laird, Alec Douglas-Home (and one of the appeasers of Nazi Germany in the 1930s to boot), who freely admitted that he knew nothing about economics. The Labour Leader, Harold Wilson, was a trained economist and possessed something of the dynamic aura Americans associated with John Kennedy in 1960. Wilson enthused about the "white heat" of technology, about the need for government to invest in research and development to make Britain a leader for the remainder of the twentieth century.

Back in office for the middle and late 1960s, Labour presided over another period of extensive reform, although this time much more social than economic. Homosexual relations, abortion, divorce — the laws on each were liberalized. Although the Labour Government formally refrained from advocating reform on matters of conscience, its assistance to legislators seeking these measures was what made their enactment possible. An air of freedom and creativity seemed to permeate Britain; it was an exciting place to live. Perhaps the pace of reform was too rapid, however, for many Britons. Beyond that, some were becoming concerned about the economy and the power structure. The Labour Government seemed unable to deal with the trade unions. Strikes were growing at an alarming rate. Workers were demanding wage increases far in excess of productivity gains and thus were driving up inflation. British products were beginning to price themselves out of foreign markets.

Experts on British politics warned of the dangers of "pluralistic stagnation." Key economic groups had grown so powerful that they could determine economic policy. Despite the development of a system that concentrated power in its hands, the Government apparently was too weak to act effectively. By refusing to cooperate with government, interest groups could veto any policy they disliked. Power was gravitating to groups that couldn't be called to account by anyone.

Despite Britain's growing problems, Labour's loss of the 1970 election was unexpected. In contrast to their return to power in 1951, this time the Conservatives' period in office proved to be brief. The Conservatives under Edward Heath knew no more than had Labour how to reclaim Governmental power from the unions. The struggle reached a climax in a confrontation with the miners' union. At the end of 1973 lack of coal for electricity-generating plants forced the Government to limit most enterprises to operating only three days each week. A few months later, Prime Minister Heath called an election posing the central issue: "Who Governs?" It was incredible that such a question could be relevant in a system concentrating power as much as does the British system. Unfortunately for Heath, the British public long has had an affection for the miners. The danger and drudgery of their work has made them folk heroes, entitled to almost anything they want. The Conservatives lost the election.

Although Labour returned to office, it had not really won the election. It had a few more seats in Parliament than did the Conservatives, but lacked majority control. The year's second election, held only eight months after the first, did little to strengthen the Labour Government. Thus, from the middle of the 1970s to the end of the decade, the Government had less concentrated power than was typical in the British system. This decline in the capacity for effective action occurred at the worst possible time; economic problems — sluggish growth and high inflation — were becoming a crisis. Britain was consuming much more than it was producing, was buying much more from the rest of the world than it was able to sell to it. The Labour Government had to seek a huge loan from the International Monetary Fund, and the terms for getting the loan forced cutbacks on the program of social benefits that Labour's supporters had come to expect.

Furthermore, the Labour Government, like its predecessors formed by either major party, had no solution for labor unrest. Wage demands helped inflation to soar above 20 percent per annum. The unions seemed to be holding the country hostage. The climax came during 1978–1979, widely referred to as "the winter of discontent." The dustmen (trash collectors) were out on strike. In residential areas of London bags of trash and garbage began to pile up on the sidewalks outside houses. Many of the city's public squares became mountains of trash bags. But most traumatic was that funeral processions would arrive at the cemetery to find gates chained shut and entry prevented by striking gravediggers. Literally, Britons could not bury their dead.

More in frustration than in hope, the electorate turned again to the Conservatives, who had provided no evidence that they knew what to do during their period in office at the start of the 1970s. Once more, however, in only a few years the Conservatives had become a considerably different party. Now they were led by a woman, Margaret Thatcher, who, with the party's victory in 1979, became the first female Prime Minister in British history. (Of course, Britain already had had prominent female monarchs, such as Elizabeth I and Victoria, and when Thatcher became Prime Minister, Elizabeth II had been on the throne for more than a quarter of a century.) This election launched another period of Conservative dominance, which by 1992 had reached thirteen years.

In contrast to the previous thirteen years in the 1950s and early 1960s, however, this was not a time of bland prosperity and growing consensus. Thatcher was determined to turn her back on the entire postwar development of British politics. She labeled herself "a conviction politician" and, punning on the title of a well-known play about an accused witch by

Christopher Fry, proclaimed of herself, "The lady's not for turning." (In the title the word had been *burning*.) Welcoming confrontation with the trade unions, she so curtailed their power that they ceased to be a factor in the making of economic policy. Unemployment soared to more than 3.25 million — an astounding level, greater than the number out of work during the economic travail of the 1930s (although not as large a proportion of the labor force). Clearly the cross-party consensus on guaranteeing almost everyone employment had been repudiated; Butskellism was dead. Thatcher didn't deliberately seek to increase unemployment, but she was willing to accept it as a cost of creating a more efficient economy. She recognized that when many people were looking for jobs, unions would be much less militant — less likely to challenge Government policy — and more moderate in wage demands.

Determined to restore an enterprise culture to Britain, Thatcher sold back into private ownership many government enterprises such as telecommunications, gas, and even water. She could not really be called probusiness because she was unwilling to continue providing aid to those businesses that were poorly managed. Just as she did not flinch from rising unemployment, so she did not quail from the rising number of bankruptcies. Perhaps businesses that knew they could not expect a government handout would develop some backbone and stop caving in to excessive wage demands from unions.

Inflation did decline to a tolerable level and, eventually, unemployment returned to near traditional levels. British enterprises became more efficient as well, but the cost in terms of a constricted economy and weakened infrastructure was considerable. Some feared that Britain had been "deindustrialized" — that it would only be able to operate service industries, such as insurance and marketing, and would no longer be a major producer of manufactured goods.

Why were Britons willing to accept such harsh medicine, willing to reelect twice someone who broke so dramatically with the political consensus that had characterized the country's politics for three decades? Thatcher's popularity declined considerably during her early years in office. She might have been a one-term Prime Minister had it not been for the conflict with Argentina over the Falkland Islands. Her willingness to take such decisive action — dispatching a military force to retake the Islands — made her seem a stronger leader than her predecessors. And the success in defeating Argentina made her seem much more effective.

Nonetheless, Thatcher's decade in power was not so much a matter of her winning support as it was her opponents' failure to do so. The proportion of the electorate voting for the Conservatives during the Thatcher decade not only didn't increase but declined slightly. She continued in office because Labour was unable to mount an effective challenge. Following its loss of the 1979 election, the Labour party moved farther and farther to the left. It adopted such extreme and electorally unattractive policies as unilateral nuclear disarmament and huge increases in government ownership of enterprises. Like Thatcher, Labour, too, was breaking with the politics of Butskellist consensus. So far did it shift that in the early 1980s many of its moderate members broke away to found the Social Democratic Party (SDP). They claimed that they had not left Labour, but that the party had left them. Only by forming a new party could they remain true to Labour's traditional principles. The SDP soon formed a cooperative alliance with the Liberal party, thus giving the center of the political spectrum its greatest strength in half a century. This Alliance, however, proved even less able than the Labour party to drive Thatcher from power. In fact, the division of the anti-Thatcher vote between the Alliance and Labour only served to keep her in office. In the end only rebellion in her own party (as I'll discuss in Chapter 4) could remove her from power at the start of the 1990s.

One of the issues involved in Thatcher's downfall was Britain's relation with Europe. During the last couple of decades the British economy has been increasingly linked with the European Community (EC). When this organization was launched as the European Economic Community (EEC) in the 1950s, Britain held aloof. Britain doubted that the attempt at economic union would succeed and felt that its political traditions and governmental institutions were far superior to those of Continental countries. When Britain subsequently decided that to protect its traditional European export markets it would have to join, Charles de Gaulle, the French President, vetoed Britain's membership. Only after he had left office did Britain gain entry in 1973. The British government hoped that membership would strengthen British industry and, thus, the economy, by offering both an opportunity and a threat. Being inside the European Community meant, on the one hand, that British enterprises would benefit from the economies of scale involved in producing for a Continental-sized market. In addition, British manufacturers would face a competitive challenge since they would not have a tariff to protect them from the products produced by efficient German, and other European, enterprises.

Given that Britain didn't enter the EC on a wave of idealistic commitment to a United States of Europe whatever the cost, fluctuation in British opinion toward the EC is hardly surprising. Opposition to Britain's membership was so strong that a referendum had to be held on the issue — an unprecedented procedure in Britain. Of the two-thirds of those eligible who voted in 1975, support for membership outpolled opposition 2 to 1. Ten years later, however, an opinion poll found that only a third of Britons supported membership in the EC and more than two-thirds said they would be indifferent or relieved if the EC were to be terminated. As the EC moves toward tighter economic integration — the possible creation of a common currency, for example — and perhaps political union, the reluctance of many in Britain to give up any sovereignty is likely to make relations with Europe a political issue of continuing significance. Furthermore, the issue cuts across traditional party lines since both Labour and the Conservatives have their pro- and anti-EC factions.

Closer integration of Britain into the EC raises an interesting question of accountability: Insofar as crucial issues of economic and monetary policy are decided by the Community, then Britons, their Parliament, and even their Government have less ability to call power to account. Regardless of that development, accountability had already seemed weakened in Britain after World War II. The electorate could remove one party or the other from office, but could not seem to find any group of leaders who could remedy the country's ills. Concentrated power failed to produce effective government.

The American Founding Fathers had been willing to pay the price of less effective government to avoid the dangers of tyranny. They opted for fractionalized, rather than concentrated, power. Their choice was motivated by another consideration as well: They wanted subnational units of government to share in policy making. The United States was a diverse country and its governmental structure needed to reflect these differences by allowing policy to vary from one area to another. Fractionalized power corresponded to the geopolitical reality of the United States in the late eighteenth century. To what extent does concentrated power — the basic characteristic of the British political system — correspond to British society? Answering this question requires considering unity and division in Britain, as I do in Chapter 2.

2
✦
Unity and Divisions

Look at the back of one of the coins in your pocket or coin purse. *E Pluribus Unum* — "from out of many one." The motto of the United States admits that, like all countries, it has divisions — contrasts — that set segments of the population apart from the others. Yet it claims to have joined these many together into a single nation. During the nineteenth century when waves of immigrants swept into the United States, they were said to enter a melting pot that soon made each of them, whatever their origin, an American. In an era of heightened ethnicity, when everyone seems concerned with his or her roots, it is interesting to ask whether *E Pluribus Unum* remains a valid motto for the United States. Sometimes social differences go beyond mere divisions to become cleavages: contrasts so sharp that they threaten to disrupt the society. Nearly a century and a half ago the "United" States had to fight a war to determine whether regional cleavages had produced, in the words of Abraham Lincoln, "a house divided against itself," which, as he correctly pointed out, "cannot stand."

Region is just one of the societal differences that has produced conflict in many countries. Others of importance are religion, race, and social class.

Table 2 ✦ 1 Size of U.K. Component Nations

	Population (millions)	Area in Sq. Mi. (thousands)	Population Density per Sq. Mi.
England	47.3	50.4	938
Scotland	5.1	30.4	168
Wales	2.8	8.0	352
Northern Ireland	1.6	5.5	287
United Kingdom	56.8	94.2	603

This chapter discusses how greatly these four affect Britain. Like the United States, Britain claims to be a "United" Kingdom. Many Americans have felt that Britain had much the better claim to such a label. The country is small, thus, presumably, having little scope for regional differences. Communication by rail is easy. London newspapers circulate throughout the country and long ago became national news media. Immigration has been low; Britain lacks the large number of people from diverse cultural backgrounds that long has characterized the U.S. population. The British population is a native one, born into the national customs. Is Britain a closely knit, homogeneous country — that is to say fundamentally different from the United States? Or is it a pluralistic (perhaps, even divided) country? And, if so, do the key social divisions rank in the same order of importance as in the United States?

Region

Several years ago Lord Mabane, the head of the British Travel and Holidays Association, plaintively inquired in the House of Lords, "whether the correct official title for this country is Britain, or Great Britain, or the United Kingdom of Great Britain and Northern Ireland, or some other title; and whether a recent change of title has been announced, and if so, when?" Such uncertainty about how to refer to his country by the person responsible for trying to entice tourists to visit Britain says a great deal about Britain's history and diversity.

Americans are used to the political system coinciding with the nation. The Pledge of Allegiance asserts that the United States is ". . . one nation, under God, indivisible . . ." The country examined in this book, despite being only the size of Oregon and having only a quarter of the population of the United States, is composed of four nations: England, Scotland, Wales, and Northern

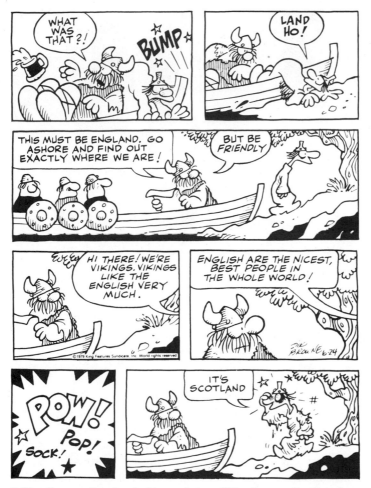

Ireland. As Figures 2.1 and 2.2 and Table 2.1 indicate, England is, by far, the dominant one. Should you, while visiting Birmingham or Manchester, refer to the entire country as England, no one will mind. Do not, however, do that in Glasgow, Scotland. As Hagar's buddy Eddie discovered, such a faux pas would be injurious to your well-being. Which brings us back to Lord Mabane's question. Britain, he was told, would suffice for semi-official purposes (and — although the formal reply didn't mention this — will not get you in trouble in Scotland).

For official purposes — that is, for international gatherings like the United Nations or for reference books containing data on the economic performance

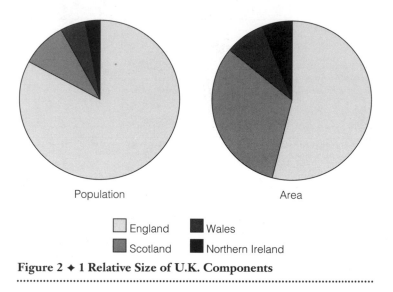

Population   Area

☐ England   ■ Wales
■ Scotland   ■ Northern Ireland

Figure 2 ✦ 1 Relative Size of U.K. Components

of the world's nations — the United Kingdom of Great Britain and Northern Ireland is used (abbreviated as U.K.). When asked where they come from, however, few people from the British Isles would reply, "The U.K." In any case, this solves only part of the problem because we are left with no word to refer to the people of this country. You can't call them English; based on residency alone, a sixth of them aren't that. Furthermore, as Richard Rose (an American political scientist transplanted to Scotland) wittily has observed, "There are no Ukes." "Briton" probably will suffice, although whether that includes those who live in Northern Ireland is questionable. Why does a relatively small country have such strongly felt internal contrasts and need such elaborate and confusing names and labels to avoid offending its citizens?

Centuries ago Wales was an independent country. England seized control of it late in the thirteenth century. For the next two and a half centuries, Wales remained an English possession until, early in the sixteenth century, it was incorporated into the English political system. Scotland has a considerably longer separate history. Not until the start of the eighteenth century did it accept union with England and Wales. Another century went by before Ireland was added. This late and large (Ireland's population was about half that of England, Scotland, and Wales combined) incorporation never was successful. Following decades of strife, the bulk of the Irish was permitted to secede in 1922 to form an independent country (now known as the Republic of Ireland or Eire). Thus, most of the smaller of the two main islands in Figure 2.2 is not part of the political system covered in this book. Only the portion in the upper right-hand corner of that island remains part of the United Kingdom.

Figure 2 ✦ 2 The United Kingdom of Great Britain and Northern Ireland

....

Most Britons (English, Scots, and Welsh) regard the people who live in Northern Ireland as Irish, not British. As for the people of Northern Ireland themselves, their views turn on their religious preference. About three-quarters of the Protestants in Northern Ireland think they are British, while an equal proportion of the Catholics considers themselves to be Irish. Three-fourths of the Catholics in Northern Ireland want the country to be united with the Catholic Republic of Ireland to the south, while an even larger proportion of the Protestants want it to remain part of the United Kingdom.

Separatist feelings among the Welsh are more a matter of culture and language than of religion. While only about a fifth of the people living in Wales can speak Welsh (most of them speak English, as well), the proportion increases as one moves into the rural areas. In western Wales about half the people speak Welsh and in the northwest nearly two-thirds do. In all parts of Wales many public notices, like road signs, are in Welsh. Furthermore, learning the language is becoming increasingly popular among young people. Many schools teach their classes in whatever subject mainly in Welsh.

The Welsh are regarded as a more excitable people than the English. They do not frown on public displays of emotion as do the English. They seem a warmer, more friendly people since they lack the reserve that often makes the English seem cold and aloof. Poetry and music long have been major elements in Welsh culture. Each year Wales celebrates what could be characterized as a national folklore gathering, at which the bards in flowing white robes sing and recite the nation's legendary tales.

Neither religion nor language is the source of Scottish distinctiveness. Only a handful of the Scots can speak Gaelic, although a few of the programs broadcast by Scottish regional TV are in that language (usually late at night). Nor can Scotland be said to have a unique culture in the way that Wales does. Nonetheless, the Scots have a well-developed sense of national identity, perhaps because of their long history as a separate, independent country. They would never call themselves English. While they would not claim to be as emotional as the Welsh, they, too, feel that they are more open and responsive than the English. Scottish feelings of separatism have been reinforced over the last couple of decades by an economic factor—North Sea oil. Those who want Scotland to be an independent nation have campaigned on the slogan: "It's Scotland's oil." That claim is by no means clear in international law. But were the revenues from this oil to go only to Scotland, instead of to the whole of the United Kingdom, the Scots would enjoy a greatly enhanced prosperity.

The United Kingdom thus is composed of four distinct nations—geographic concentrations of people with separate histories and contrasting ethnic backgrounds. Yet, surprisingly, the United Kingdom is a unitary system, not a federal one like the United States. As parts of the U.S. federal system, the states are guaranteed existence and considerable powers. As parts of a unitary system, the nations of the United Kingdom have only that status and power given them by the national government. When a separate, independent Irish state was established at the start of the 1920s, governmental institutions were created in Northern Ireland (the part remaining in the United Kingdom) to make decisions on matters of local interest without reference to the national government in London. A half century later, the national legislature abolished (technically suspended) the Northern Ireland government, because of the continuing violent religious conflict between Catholics and Protestants and instituted direct rule from London. For the U.S. Congress to abolish the government of an American state would be unthinkable and unconstitutional.

Whether language/culture or sense of identity combined with economics produces the stronger urge for separatism was tested in 1979. Referenda were held in Wales and Scotland to ascertain public preference regarding proposals for devolution: shifting some powers from the national government in London to governmental structures in the two nations. In Wales two-fifths of those eligible didn't even bother to vote and of those who did only 20 percent favored devolution. Every county in Wales had a majority *against* the proposed shift in powers. In Scotland six of twelve counties favored the shift and nationwide a bare majority approved devolution. Turnout, although slightly higher than in Wales, was still less than two-thirds. Members of the U.K. legislature who opposed devolution had included in the law authorizing the referendum a requirement that the proposals could be implemented only if supported by 40 percent of the *electorate* (all those eligible to vote). As a result the referendum lost in Scotland, as well as in Wales, and no shift in powers occurred.

Nonetheless, Scotland had shown considerably greater interest than had Wales in increasing its measure of self-government. The years since the referendum have done nothing to dampen this Scottish ardor. Efforts to found a Scottish Assembly that could wrest some powers of decision making away from the national government have continued unabated. The results of the 1987 election further fueled such sentiment. The Conservatives won a majority of the legislative seats in all the United Kingdom and thus controlled the national government. In Scotland, however, the party won only ten of the seventy-two seats; many Scots felt they were being governed by a party their nation had rejected. The 1992 election did little to alter such feelings, since the Conservatives increased by only one additional seat. An opinion poll at the start of the 1990s found that a third of the Scots favored independence, while half wanted Scottish governmental institutions to have greater power to tax and spend within the nation. Only a sixth were satisfied to leave things unchanged. Another poll at the end of 1991 found that a majority of Scots wanted complete independence. Although Britain doesn't want to lose Scotland, three-fifths of a national population sample agreed strongly or tended to agree that governmental power is too centralized in Britain. Some measure of devolution may have to be implemented in the next several years. This retreat from concentrated power would make the British governmental structure more reflective of geographic reality.

Being continental-sized and substantially settled by immigrants from all over the world has made the United States socially and politically diverse. Britain's small size and relatively limited immigration has led many Americans to think of it as homogeneous — life and politics in Britain were thought to be pretty much the same from one part of the country to another. Such a view may be due to the mistake of equating the United Kingdom with England. Contrasts within England itself aren't as fundamental as are those between England and the other three nations of the United Kingdom. Nonetheless, even within England differences in customs, speech, and food are notable from one area to another. Although many of these contrasts have little political impact, one that has been significant for some time is the north–south economic divide. Southern England has been much more prosperous than the North, with lower rates of unemployment. The impact this has on voting behavior and patterns of party strength I'll explain in Chapter 8. Whether one focuses on England only or on the country as a whole, significant regional variations have existed for generations, perhaps centuries. The *United* Kingdom is no more lacking in diversity than is the *United* States.

Religion

Regional contrasts are only one source of potential diversity within a country. Another factor often responsible for social divisions is religion. I've already noted how religion splits Northern Ireland. Discussing the role of religion in British life is difficult; when asked by pollsters, many people may be willing to express a religious preference even though they have not attended church for years. Despite that problem, few would deny that the importance of organized religion has been declining in Britain for some time. Formal church membership has fallen sharply in the last half century; probably less than half the adult population can be said to be actively involved in religious observances.

Secularism has grown even though Britain has an established church. The Church of England, also known as the Anglican Church, is the official denomination. North of the border, the Church of Scotland (a Presbyterian church), is the established denomination. Wales, on the other hand, has not had an established church throughout most of the twentieth century. Having an official church doesn't mean that Britain has abolished freedom of religion. People may belong to whatever church they wish, or to none at all. One evidence of religious establishment is inclusion among the monarch's titles of "defender of the faith." This has the practical result of empowering the Government to appoint the Church of England's clergy and requiring Parliament to approve changes in liturgy and worship aids, such as the prayer book.

Even more striking to Americans, familiar with the long controversy in the United States over prayer in the schools, is religious instruction. The curriculum for all tax-supported schools in Britain must include instruction in basic Christian beliefs. This is not just a matter of academic study, as would be a comparative religions course in the United States. Despite its preferred position, the Church of England's membership has fallen more rapidly in recent years than has that of other denominations, declining to less than half what it was a generation ago. Catholics now probably outnumber Anglicans.

Although Catholicism has lost fewer members than most other denominations in Britain, it remains a minority faith. The Protestant–Catholic balance favors Protestants in Britain. Few British politicians, unlike American ones, would spend much time worrying about the potential behavior of a Catholic bloc of voters.

For the most part in the United Kingdom, region and religion don't have much impact on one another. The notable exception is Northern Ireland. Elsewhere in the United Kingdom religious preference doesn't matter much. Support for Celtic or Rangers, Glasgow's two football (soccer) rivals, often correlates with religious preference, but no one would suggest that cheering for Celtic made you Catholic or vice versa. Around Liverpool in northwest England, being Orange (favoring the status quo in Northern Ireland) or Green (approving of a single country including *all* Irish) is likely to turn on religious affiliation; this area, however, is relatively small. Furthermore, these two examples are noteworthy mainly because they are so unusual.

Social status (which I discuss later in this chapter) correlates with religion more closely than does region. The Anglican Church tends to be middle or upper class. Since these groups are the core of the Conservative party's strength, the Anglican Church sometimes is said to be the Conservative party on its knees. *Nonconformists* (those, such as Baptists, not belonging to the Anglican Church; the term has nothing to do with weird behavior) tend to be lower middle and working class. In the nineteenth century, *chapel* (another term for nonconformists) tended to be linked with the Liberal party, especially in northern England and Wales. While that remains true, the relation between chapel and the Labour party became more significant in the second half of the twentieth century.

Non-Christian religious groups have been rare in Britain. Only about 1 percent of Britain's population is Jewish, considered as either a religious or an ethnic group. Furthermore, this handful is not sufficiently concentrated in geographic location or particular economic sector to wield much power. Politicians in some parts of the United States devote considerable time to courting the Jewish vote and the Israeli lobby is effective in the U.S. Congress. Neither is characteristic of British politics. Not only does anti-Semitism linger on in the English upper class, but Britain's historical links with various Arabic countries since the late nineteenth century have tended to generate considerable sympathy for Israel's enemies in the Middle East.

Although still a small group, Muslims are growing in importance in Britain. If you look out of your train window just before you arrive in downtown Glasgow, you might be surprised to see a sizable mosque. In central and northern England around such cities as Birmingham and Leeds, Labour party politicians for over a decade and a half have been cultivating relations with the leaders of the local Muslim community and speaking at their mosques during election campaigns.

Events in the late 1980s demonstrated that Muslim beliefs could raise a controversy considerably greater than the size of that community in Britain. Muslim religious leaders in Iran decreed that Salman Rushdie, a prominent author who had lived in London for many years, should be killed because his book, *The Satanic Verses*, was blasphemous and demeaned the Muslim faith. In effect, any Muslim living in Britain was given a license to kill. Most of the non-Muslim population of Britain regarded this decree as intolerable and recognized the serious freedom of speech problems that the controversy involved. On the other hand, many friends of the Muslim community could understand why *The Satanic Verses* was deeply offensive. To further complicate matters, Britain has a law on the books (although rarely enforced) that prohibits blasphemy—but apparently it applies only to the Christian God.

The government never acted, neither prosecuting Rushdie nor those threatening to kill him. The issue became moot because Rushdie went into hiding to protect his life. Almost no one knew where he lived and he would surface only unannounced for such events as TV interviews. This hardly was a satisfactory solution to the controversy. Differences in religious beliefs and cultures again had forced their way into the public arena. Religion is not the only factor in the distinctiveness of Muslims in Britain; ethnicity is at least as important and I'll examine that aspect in the next section of this chapter.

In summary, religion matters in Northern Ireland and can generate controversies for an ethnic group like Muslims. However, British life is quite secularized. Faith neither divides nor unites most Britons. While religion is not unrelated to region and social status, it generally does not exacerbate those divisions. Thus, for British society as a whole religion isn't a major cleavage.

Race and Ethnicity

As already mentioned, Muslims are a small but growing segment of British society. They are among those British residents that many Britons refer to as "coloured." Alternatively, Britons may term them "blacks," which is confusing to Americans, since the label covers not only people with roots in the West Indies or Africa, but also those from Pakistan or India. These Asians don't resemble African Americans at all. Even if these diverse people are lumped into a single category, they account for only about 5 percent of Britain's population. This is such a small proportion that you might conclude that Britain has escaped the traumas and injustices associated with race in American life. Unfortunately, you would be mistaken.

Many Britons can't believe that anyone with a darker skin color could possibly be British; he or she must be, based on appearance alone, a foreigner. Many "coloureds," however, are first or even second generation Britons; that is, they were born in Britain—it was their parents or grandparents who first immigrated there. The technicalities of the citizenship laws, however, matter little to many white Britons. If "coloureds" have managed to obtain some scarce, low-cost housing, hold even menial jobs when unemployment is high, and seem to be running all the small businesses like grocery stores and news agents shops, then some white Britons feel threatened and resentful. Opinion polls in the mid-1980s found that nearly two-thirds wanted less settlement in Britain by "coloureds." Some Britons support politicians who favor banning further "coloured" immigration into Britain or who propose that the government pay "coloureds" to "go back where they came from"—a ridiculous idea, especially since about half of them were born in Britain.

Compounding the problem is the younger average age for "coloureds" than for the rest of the population. As they marry and have families, their numbers will grow more rapidly than the white population. Furthermore, since unemployment in Britain is especially prevalent among those under twenty-five, the relative youth of the "coloured" population (without considering the effect of job discrimination) means that it has been particularly hard-hit. The potential for fear, resentment, and conflict is great.

Since the early 1960s, British policy concerning race relations has moved in two seemingly contradictory but in fact complementary directions. Immigration into Britain is now much more tightly restricted than it had been, and nonwhite residents in Britain are better protected from racial discrimination than formerly. The twin policies aim at assimilating nonwhites more easily and protecting their rights by keeping their numbers down.

The Conservative party began this process by restricting immigration. Although the regulations it introduced didn't discriminate against nonwhite immigrants as such, everyone knew this was the objective. The Labour party struck a high moral tone and denounced this action as racist. Then it discovered that its traditional supporters were among the most vociferous advocates of keeping "coloureds" out. Most of the immigrants had little money and lived in lower-class areas. They seemed to be competing with the working class for jobs and housing. If they did have funds, they often opened small shops in working-class areas; of necessity, these shops charged higher prices than supermarkets. Those few immigrants who had professional skills or who were well-off were likely to have had a Western education. They had adopted much of the British lifestyle and had abandoned many customs their poorer counterparts still practiced, customs that often offended lower-class Britons. Thus, the typical working-class Labour voter was a good deal more likely to favor limits on immigration than was the white collar Conservative supporter.

When Labour returned to power in 1964, it also tightened controls on immigration. In addition, however, it initiated the process of protecting nonwhites in Britain from various forms of discrimination. Both main political parties now agree in general on this double-barreled approach of holding down further nonwhite immigration into Britain while seeking fair treatment for resident nonwhites. Such consensus might seem a happy conclusion to the controversy, but the result frustrates many average Britons. They feel that the political elite lives in a different world and fails to understand everyday life. They want more government action to control immigration and keep "coloureds" out of their neighborhoods. However, few people in either of the main parties pay any attention to their concerns.

The importance of this emotional issue has varied considerably over time. Race was of some importance during the 1979 election, but of little significance in the elections of the 1980s. Early in 1990, however, the Government's proposal to permit some of Hong Kong's residents to emigrate to Britain caused controversy in Parliament. The idea was to provide a means of escape, if needed, from any persecution by Communists that might occur when this former British possession would be acquired by the People's Republic of China. Several right-wing Conservative legislators opposed their party's proposal to relax the immigration law, arguing that it might result in as many as a quarter of a million people coming from Hong Kong to Britain.

Gallup found in June 1988 that four-fifths of its respondents thought that people were discriminated against in Britain because of their color or race. Other surveys have reported that about two-fifths think there is more racial prejudice than there was five years earlier (only one-fifth think there is less), and about as many think there will be more discrimination five years in the future than there currently is. On the brighter side, two-thirds think discriminating against people based on race or color should be illegal and three-fourths claim they would not mind having "coloureds" for neighbors. In fact, when those surveyed listed the people they would *not* want to have as neighbors, heavy drinkers (45 percent) and left-wing extremists (38 percent) were more often rejected than were immigrants (21 percent).

Thus, although by American standards, Britain's population seems homogeneous, some racial and ethnic diversity does exist. And what does exist is sufficient to divide British society significantly. Furthermore, race relates to the social division of class status to a greater extent than do either region or religion. This compounding effect makes it a more potent cleavage than the other two.

Social Status

Class differences exist in the United States; some people obviously have a good deal more money and possess much more social prestige and influence than do others. Yet, were you to watch the people strolling through a shopping mall, you would have a hard time correctly guessing the social class to which each belonged. Distinguishing a farmer from a school teacher from a manual worker from a secretary from a doctor or a lawyer might well be difficult even if you talked with each shopper for awhile.

This isn't true in Britain. In discussing class differences, Anthony Crosland, a prominent British politician, cited "the most supremely unmistakable of all symbols of social standing — differences in accent and vocabulary. In no other country is it possible in the same way to assess a person's class standing the moment he opens his mouth."[1] Polls have found that nearly three-fourths of the British population think that people are very or quite aware of class differences. More than one-fourth say that they would be bothered if their child had a friend from another social class. Clearly, Britons are not just readily distinguishable by class, they are divided by it. Social class is a major cleavage in British society.

This distinction between the United States and Britain is not because of any radical difference in the structure of the work force between the two countries. In both, those engaged in agriculture account for only a couple of percentage points. And in both, most people are employed in service enterprises, rather than manufacturing. In the United States the ratio between these two sectors is about 2 to 1 toward services, while in Britain services are only about one-fourth larger. Although this is not a dramatic difference, it does help to explain why Britain is more heavily unionized than is the United States. Although union membership in Britain has fallen considerably during the last decade, its current level of about a quarter of the work force is nearly double the U.S. rate. Thus, Britain does differ somewhat from the United States in the structure and organization of the work force, but not sufficiently to account for a major contrast in the significance of social status.

Recently some students of British society have argued that the key occupational division falls between those who work for private enterprise and those who are employed by the government. In the United States less than a fifth of the work force is employed by government — national, state, or local. This proportion has increased very little in the past forty years. During this time public employment in most European countries has grown considerably. In Sweden close to two-fifths of the work force have government jobs. The proportion is not that high in Britain; nonetheless, with one-third in government employ, it is considerably greater than in the United States. The argument is that those who work for the government have a vested interest in expanding, or, at the very least, maintaining, its programs and services to ensure their continued employment. Thus their attitudes toward big government, huge budgets, and increased taxation are likely to differ from those of people working for private employers. Even if this hypothesis is valid, this

---

1. Anthony Crosland, *The Future of Socialism* (New York: Schocken Books, 1963; originally published in 1957), p. 111.

contrast in employment is too recent, historically speaking, to account for a fundamental social cleavage in Britain that sets it apart from the United States.

Money, of course, has something to do with social differences in Britain, but contrasts in income are not extreme, due to the redistributive effect of taxes and social programs. The initial or gross average income for the top fifth of British households is about 200 times that for the bottom fifth. However, after taxes, benefits in cash, and benefits in kind (free health care, for example), the top fifth averages only about four times the income of the bottom fifth. Wealth, however, is not as evenly distributed. The top 1 percent of the population owns a fifth of the wealth and the top 10 percent nearly three-fifths. (But these figures differ little from those for the United States.)

Class differences are not so much a matter of wealth or income or employer as they are of customs and behavior, of contrasting ways of life. Whether one eats the main meal early or late in the day, drinks in one room or the other in a pub (bar), enjoys cricket or football, is paid in cash or by check—these are just a few of the myriad of differences between the middle class (including white-collar employees) and the working class (skilled or unskilled manual): the sharpest social divide in Britain.

The cumulative impact of these contrasts is great. Writing in the early 1980s about social class differences, William Rodgers noted not only that "Britain is still a society marked by self-conscious class differences and an instinct to preserve them," but also that "these are constricting to personal development and interfere with easy and fruitful relationships between individuals."[2] Some of those in the lower class may acquiesce in their status, may be willing to defer to their betters. Others resent the patronizing, condescending attitudes of those higher on the social scale. The British movie actor Michael Caine, from a working-class background himself, contrasted Britain and the United States by saying that in the latter when a worker sees someone in a fancy car he says, "One day I'm going to have a car just like that." In Britain the response would be, "One day we will get him out of that and destroy it." (That the achievement would be individual and the destruction collective should not be overlooked either.) Those with higher status, on the other hand, are antagonized when their social inferiors' presumptuous behavior suggests that they don't know their place in the social hierarchy. Those facing each other across this social divide bring with them so many preconceptions and prejudices that relating to each other as human beings, rather than stereotypes, is difficult.

To a considerable extent social class affects British society the way that race affects Americans. In each case those from one group regard members

2. William Rodgers, *The Politics of Change* (London: Secker & Warbury, 1982), p. 22.

Figure 2 ✦ 3 Modern council housing in London

of the other almost as aliens, whose normal activities simply are beyond comprehension. What makes this comparison especially apt is that in Britain appearance and speech make one's class standing as immediately obvious as skin color does one's race in the United States. Furthermore, housing has tended to be as socially segregated in Britain as it has been racially in the United States. The bulk of the British working class has lived on council estates, what would be called public housing in the United States. Most American public housing is so appalling that no one who had any alternative would choose to live there. Some housing built by British government is equally bad, but much of it is a good value for the rent charged. You can see the variety in council housing in Figures 2.3, 2.4, and 2.5. Under Prime Minister Thatcher residents of council houses were given the right to buy. Since this often meant little more than that what you had been paying each month as rent you now paid toward a mortgage, many tenants took advantage of the opportunity. Although these people now are becoming home owners, they continue to live in the same place and remain part of what is primarily a working-class enclave.

The British housing pattern probably has had greater impact on the working class than on the middle class. Perhaps low incomes meant that neighbors had to help each other to survive or that recreation had to be more social — going to the local (bar) to talk and drink rather than attending the opera — or

Figure 2 ✦ 4 Redbrick council housing in London

cheap, cramped housing meant that everyone could hear everyone else's business. Whatever the reasons, working-class communities developed. Personal relations within each community tended to be open and warm. Community provided not only a sense of belonging but a support group to help one survive in a society dominated by "them" of the higher classes. Such feelings produced considerable social solidarity within the working class. Just as is true for the Scots, a sense of distinctive group identity exists, although specifying the exact content of this subculture is difficult. Some anticipated that the development of a consumer society in Britain would produce a single lifestyle and obliterate class distinctions. While experts disagree on the details, most assert that acquiring a house, car, and income comparable to white-collar workers has not erased manual workers' feelings of separateness.

Beyond the impact of housing and community, a key element in producing and perpetuating social cleavage in Britain is the educational system. In the United States education and occupation tend to determine social status; in Britain social status tends to determine education and occupation. Although the government provides education up to age eighteen, only about a sixth of students stay beyond the compulsory schooling age of sixteen. Put bluntly, Britain is a nation of high school dropouts.

The government-supported schools used to be of two main types. The secondary modern schools provided a general education with some vocational

Figure 2 ✦ 5 High rise council housing in London
....

emphasis for the great bulk of the students, while grammar schools offered an academic, college preparatory education for the more able few. To bridge the gap between this elite education and the mediocre offerings of the secondary moderns, the comprehensive school was devised. Comprehensives were similar to American high schools in taking all types of students, but their curriculum distinguished between students planning to go to university and those who were not.

The Labour party, in keeping with its egalitarian principles, strongly favored such schools and passed legislation requiring all local school boards to "go comprehensive." (The fact that the national legislature could order this is a good example of how a unitary system differs from a federal one.) The Conservative party opposed this policy, arguing that abandoning the grammar schools would dilute the quality of education. When the Conservatives returned to power in 1979, one of their first actions was to repeal Labour's requirement for comprehensives.

Nonetheless, the great majority of British children attending government-supported schools (nine out of ten) goes to comprehensives, and fewer than one in twenty goes to grammar schools. The grammar school remains important, however, because it is a significant entry route to higher education. Most comprehensive students drop out at age sixteen; most grammar school students not only stay until they are eighteen, but then go on for higher education.

If you have been reading carefully, you may have wondered why I've been using the awkward term "government-supported schools." Why not just say "public schools"? Because, what the British call public schools are, in fact, private. British public schools are not owned and operated by the government. Although they may receive a financial grant, most of their money comes from sizable fees charged to their students. Unless you can win one of the few scholarships offered by such schools (remember, I'm talking about secondary schools, not universities), you can attend only if your parents can afford the fees. Room and board (public schools typically are boarding schools, although some take day pupils, who live at home) plus tuition at a top public school can run close to $20,000 a year and even at an average one would be more than $12,000. Parents wishing to educate a child privately from age five through eighteen must plan on a total cost of over a quarter of a million dollars. Most parents with children in public schools spend up to a quarter of their income on fees; nearly a fifth of parents spend up to 40 percent of their income for education.

Although only about 7 percent of the school-age population attends public schools, this alternative educational experience is immensely significant politically and socially. Attending the proper public school enhances (or perhaps I should say, attests to) your social status much more than does graduating from Oxford or Cambridge University (the British equivalent of the Ivy League). Controversy over the role and status of the public schools exceeds even that concerning the comprehensives and the grammars. The public schools are at the heart of class cleavage in Britain.

The most illustrious British public school is Eton, founded in 1441. Although it has a student body numbering little more than a thousand, Eton has produced eighteen Prime Ministers over the years. Nearly three-fifths of the Conservative Cabinet ministers in the first half of the twentieth century and about a quarter of Conservative Members of Parliament were Old Etonians.[3] The old school tie is the bond that men (few public schools are coeducational, and those that exist for women do not have the same prestige) who have attended the same public school, however many years apart, feel for each other. A significant factor in relations among the British political elite, this tie has almost no American parallel. Only a handful of prep schools exist in the United States (mostly in New England), and the link among fraternity brothers is a pale imitation of the British old school tie.

On the other hand, the "hazing" to which fraternities used to subject pledges continues to have its counterpart at public schools. Furthermore, the faculty of most public schools remains convinced that corporal punishment is an effective form of discipline. Noel Harrison, son of the actor Rex Harrison

---

3. W. P. Buck, *Amateurs and Professionals in British Politics* (Chicago: University of Chicago Press, 1963).

and himself an actor, reflected on his educational experience by labeling "the English boarding school the most evil institution still existing in the world. You are taught to accept authority and above all never to protest. You accept whatever suffering and brutality and injustice is meted out to you, but you say nothing, show nothing, tell nothing." Similarly, a Briton held captive in Iran for five years commented after his release, "I can say that anyone like me, who has been educated in an English public school and served in the ranks of the British Army, would be quite at home in a Third World prison."

Some members of the Labour party would like to abolish the public schools. However, the party usually has concentrated less on attacking the privileges of the elite and more on providing opportunities for those who merit it among the less well-off. Labour's view is that those who have demonstrated intelligence should not be prevented by financial constraints from realizing their potential. This means that even in the Labour party few people hold the American belief that almost everyone has a God-given right to attend a university. In Britain higher education is not mass education; only about 600,000 students attend colleges and universities full time. In the United States well over 50 percent of those aged twenty to twenty-four are in higher education; in Britain only about 5 percent are. Britain, in fact, has fewer people in higher education than does Spain.

Of those who are admitted to higher education in Britain, however, the overwhelming majority (about 90 percent) receives financial aid from the government. Tuition charges are low—lower than for public schools and even lower than the cost at a state university in the United States. The grants that students receive from the government vary according to the financial circumstances of their parents, who may be expected to contribute to their children's support. The idea that British university students might work at part-time jobs while going to school, however, is regarded with horror. Students may complain about trying to live on their grant and the money from parents, but they almost never get a job. Rather than spend their time in a way familiar to most American students, British students would prefer to lobby the government for larger grants.

Despite the government's generous (by American standards) financial assistance, British higher education is not egalitarian. Students from working-class families account for only about a fifth of those in higher education. Furthermore, those from working-class backgrounds aren't evenly distributed among all the student bodies. Very few working-class students attend Oxbridge (Oxford and Cambridge, the two ancient and most prestigious universities). Traditionally, they go instead to "redbrick" universities, such as Manchester. While instruction there is high quality, the degree lacks the social cachet of an Oxbridge one, thus helping to perpetuate class differences even among the highly educated. The universities opened in Britain since the end of World War II have tended to resemble American state universities in their curriculum and student body. While students from various social backgrounds may mingle at these universities, they do not recruit from the most prominent levels of society. At all levels, the British education system serves primarily to train a social elite and, in doing so, to perpetuate social divisions. Because of the divisive effect that education has on society, it will continue to be an important political issue.

At the heart of social divisions in Britain is the way in which people treat each other and how they feel about their place in society. As you have seen, Britons, much more than Americans, are aware of and feel separated by social divisions. Differences in lifestyle have segregated the manual workers from the rest of society and frequently given them an embattled sense of class solidarity — us against them. Class barriers will exist until people can relate comfortably to others from another class as fellow human beings. In Britain that time remains in the future. For now Britain is a country divided into two contrasting lifestyles, almost two subcultures: middle class and working class.

Such a statement might seem to overlook the aristocracy. Britain still has a system of hereditary titles, most carrying with them a good deal of social prestige. Many businesses are willing to pay a retainer to have Lord So-and-So's name on their letterhead. Titles do not, however, automatically confer wealth on their holders. Many aristocrats have had to turn their country estates into tourist attractions to pay the costs of continuing to own them. Furthermore, the political system is run by an upper-middle-class elite, not by aristocrats. Social prestige doesn't translate into political power.

On the other hand, the honours system does reinforce social cleavages. The monarch, usually on the recommendation of the Government, bestows a bewildering (to Americans) array of awards. Knighthoods (Sir What's His Name), Commanders of the British Empire (the letters *CBE* after your name), and the like are supposed to be given for various outstanding service and performance. Occasionally an honour will go to someone of a working-class background — the Beatles received one by generating so much foreign currency for Britain by the sale of their records abroad. But typically these go to the pillars of society. Of course, a nouveau riche businessman may be given something in recognition of huge contributions to the Conservative party, but that hardly is a blow for social equality. Retiring high-level civil servants will expect to get their "gong," but most of them will be from a middle-class background and will have gone to the right school. In short, the honours system tends to reinforce the belief that there are "them" and there are "us."

Summary

In matters of religious preference Britain is less diverse than is the United States. Religion has little impact on British life except in Northern Ireland. Only there does it divide society into antagonistic groups. Britain also is less racially diverse than is the United States. Nonetheless, race divides British society significantly and has considerable potential for becoming an even more important cleavage in the future. Despite Britain's small area, regional contrasts are as great as in the United States. Furthermore, separatist feeling — the sort of attitude not present in the United States since the Civil War — has some strength in Wales and Scotland. The paradox (or perhaps the cause) is that Britain grants less autonomy to subnational areas than does the United States. Finally, social class divisions are much more stark and deep in Britain than in the United States. Lifestyle, education, occupation, and housing combine to produce a major cleavage in British society.

Britain's divisions don't threaten to tear the country apart. Just as the *United* States is united despite its many internal contrasts, so also is the *United* Kingdom. But equally, just as the United States is a pluralistic society, so also is the United Kingdom. British society is not homogeneous. The priority of social contrasts in Britain differs from that of the United States, but those of greatest significance are cleavages just as much, if not more, than in the United States. Social stress matters as much for British politics as it does for American politics. The contrast between the countries is that Britain has not sought to accommodate divisions by fragmenting or devolving power. Despite possessing a pluralistic society, Britain, unlike the United States, has concentrated power. The pattern of power relations and the structure of society tend to coincide in the United States; in Britain they do not.

3
✦

Basic Values

Everyone knows that the U.S. Supreme Court can declare laws unconstitutional. You will search in vain, however, for any such grant of power to the Court in the explicit provisions of the U.S. Constitution. Everyone knows that the U.S. Constitution specifically forbids Congress from enacting any laws abridging freedom of speech. Many people are surprised to learn, however, that that provision permitted high school students to wear black arm bands protesting the Vietnam War contrary to the wishes of school authorities. Clearly, the meaning of written constitutions changes over time.

Historical evolution is likely to play an even greater role in Britain because the country is said to have an unwritten constitution. Britain's basic governmental structures have developed out of its extraordinarily lengthy history. To what extent has this process produced a form of constitutionalism unfamiliar to Americans? How has it contributed to concentrating power and to facilitating calling that power to account? What does such constitutionalism imply for protection of rights and liberties? How does such a system affect the fundamental political values of the people, and to what extent do they accord the system the legitimacy it requires to be effective?

Constitutional Elements and Values

Pick up any textbook on American government, turn to the back, and you'll find: the Constitution. Do the same with a text on British government and you will find: nothing. Britain never has had a constitutional convention; a group of illustrious political leaders never gathered to draw up a framework document that allocates powers and functions among the various organs of government, prescribes procedures for making decisions, and establishes limits on governmental action. Perhaps this is why an opinion poll in the spring of 1991 discovered that a tenth of Britons never had heard of such a thing as the British Constitution and two-thirds admitted that they knew little, if anything, about it. Although it sounds like an oxymoron, Britain is said to have an unwritten constitution. Nonetheless, Britain, like the United States, practices constitutionalism. To push the paradox a step farther, one could argue that although Britain never has had a constitutional convention, it has a perpetual one.

Clearly, some explanations are in order to sort this out and make it comprehensible. First, constitutionalism: Its essence is restraint, both substantive and procedural, of political power. That is, not only must the powers granted to the government be limited, but those that it is permitted to have must be exercised only in specified ways, not in any way the power-holder finds convenient. Don't confuse constitutionalism with democracy. A country can follow constitutionalism without being democratic; its government's powers and procedures may be limited, but the people may be given little voice in making policy decisions for the country or in selecting those who do make them. This, in fact, accurately summarizes the state of affairs in Britain until the latter part of the nineteenth century. You can see from the historical summary in Chapter 1 that various limitations on governmental power have existed in Britain for some time. Britain was not democratic, however, before 1867 because so few people had the right to vote and, in some sense, did not become fully democratic until 1929 (more about this in Chapter 7).

But how does a country practice constitutionalism with an unwritten constitution? Although that term has been used for many years in discussions of British government, it is misleading. It doesn't mean that governmental powers and procedures are unrestrained in Britain, and that no guidelines exist specifying who can make policy. All that is implied by *unwritten consti-tution* is that Britain doesn't have one, single document setting forth these rules. In fact, Britain's situation is not very different from the U.S. situation. The Constitution of the American political system is a great deal more than the words that the Founding Fathers wrote two centuries ago in Philadelphia. Were you to read only that document, your knowledge and understanding of American government would be distorted. Most of the elements of which the British Constitution is composed have their American analogues. The four basic elements in the British Constitution, only one of which is *not* written, are: historical documents, acts of Parliament, judicial decisions, and conventions of the Constitution.

Heading the list of historical documents is Magna Carta, or the Great Charter, which was not the result of a popular revolution (how un-English that would have been) and, frankly, contained little that was new at the time. In 1215 a handful of barons forced King John (the same one mentioned in Chapter 1 who first called representatives of the knights to the Great Council) to sign what they regarded as primarily a statement of existing feudal law in the hope that he would feel honor-bound to stop abusing their rights by autocratic rule. What importance does this little skirmish have centuries later? Magna Carta is a constitutional landmark. First, it contributed to the idea that the monarch was not above certain principles of law and, should he or she disregard them, the nation had the right to force the monarch to follow them. Second, although the chief motivation that produced the charter was to protect the barons' privileges, some of its provisions went further: Towns were guaranteed their ancient liberties (limits on arbitrary monarchial power) and a basic fairness was proclaimed ("to no one will we sell, to no one will we refuse or delay, right or justice"). Third, such provisions became ideals. Over the centuries whenever Britons felt that a monarch was exceeding royal authority, they invoked Magna Carta in protest. Totally apart from its original purpose or specific provisions, Magna Carta came to be regarded as the perfect embodiment of constitutionalism. Furthermore, its significance is enhanced by its great age. (Never forget the Importance of Being Ancient in British affairs.)

Another historical constitutional document is the Petition of Right, a seventeenth-century version of Magna Carta. Parliament petitioned the monarch, rather than passing a bill, because it knew that Charles I would be strongly opposed to redressing their complaints. Like Magna Carta, to which it specifically referred, the Petition was not a grand proclamation of fundamental rights but a practical listing of specific royal violations of basic liberties. The people should not be forced to pay taxes that had not been passed by Parliament, nor should they be "imprisoned without any cause showed." Although Charles I did very reluctantly accept the Petition, this didn't make it a statute and he failed to cease all the abuses of which it complained.

Later in the century following the Glorious Revolution of 1688, a Declaration of Rights was drawn up. William and Mary were required to accept its provision before they were declared the new rulers of Britain. Again a list of specific forbidden practices (such as cruel and unusual punishment) and constraints on royal behavior were enumerated. Most of these provisions were enacted the following year in a statute known as the Bill of Rights. Strictly speaking, the Bill of Rights belongs in the second category of constitutional elements, but given its great age and genesis it might be included among the historical documents as well.[1]

Turning to the second constitutional element, not every act of Parliament becomes part of the Constitution. Only statutes dealing with fundamental matters are included: the distribution of power among various governmental organs, the procedures for making authoritative decisions, the basic rights of the people. Among the acts of Parliament typically considered part of the Constitution are the Reform Acts, which extended voting rights during the nineteenth century, and the Parliament Acts of 1911 and 1949, which reduced the powers of the House of Lords. I say "typically considered part" because nothing explicitly distinguishes such constitutional legislation from other laws. Nothing in the statute itself says anything about amending the Constitution, and no special procedures like the extraordinary majorities required to amend the U.S. Constitution are involved. The fact that Parliament can alter the Constitution through its normal procedures is the reason for my earlier comment that Britain has a perpetual constitutional convention.

Judicial decisions, the third element, form part of the Constitution although no British court has the power of the U.S. Supreme Court to declare laws unconstitutional. Nonetheless, judges must interpret the law as they apply it to the cases that come before them. When these cases involve the fundamental matters noted in connection with constitutional statutes, the judges are modifying the Constitution. Their role can be significant because traditionally, in matters of basic liberties, they will interpret the law as narrowly as possible to preserve basic rights. Important as these judicial interpretations are, judicial decisions make an even greater contribution to the Constitution through the common law. One of the world's most influential law systems, the common law, is a body of legal rules and principles deriving from judicial decisions that developed apart from any action by Parliament.

Early in English history judges often had to rule on cases to which no statute enacted by the monarch and Parliament applied. Since these cases had to be decided to prevent people from taking justice into their own hands, judges looked for a fair solution that embodied the customs and values of the local community. (Centuries later the U.S. Supreme Court suggested that the same approach should be used in deciding what is pornography.) As you learned in Chapter 1, these judges were itinerant, sent by the king to travel throughout the country establishing law and order by deciding conflicts. From time to time these travelers would return to London and get together to discuss their interesting experiences. When, in their subsequent travels, they encountered a case similar to one they had heard about in those

---

1. Technically, even Magna Carta is an act of Parliament.

conversations, they were likely to settle it the same way another judge said that he had done. Thus, the elaborate body of legal rules that developed was common for two reasons: It was based on the practices of the commoners—the people—and became common—uniform—throughout the country.

The development of the common law was aided by the medieval notion that law was divinely ordained. Governments did not make law, but were to discover God's law and state it explicitly. Although common law sometimes is referred to as judge-made law (to distinguish it from the statutes passed by a legislature), the judges who developed the common law would have rejected any thought that they were making law.

Note that the common law was written down, just as were the other two elements of the British unwritten Constitution discussed so far: historical documents and fundamental statutes. The records of the various courts stated what judges had decided and why. What didn't exist was any coherent summary of the various cases in a topic-by-topic form. As you can guess, someone eventually got the bright idea that such a summary might be useful. Noted jurists, such as Glanville, Coke (pronounced "Cook"), and Blackstone, attempted to summarize all the decisions courts had made on a particular subject having a similar set of facts. These collections or commentaries served to codify, that is, to make uniform and systematic, much of the common law. It is in this body of legal practice and comment that most guarantees of British civil rights are rooted. The same can be said about American rights. The Fifth and Fourteenth Amendments to the U.S. Constitution say that you can't be put in jail without due process of law, but the required procedures stem from the British common law.

Conventions of the Constitution (the fourth element) are basic practices or traditions; in the United States these are known as custom and usage. Although most of these conventions are not written, this is not the key factor distinguishing them. The basic criterion is whether a particular practice is enforceable, whether it can be the basis for a legal judgment. If so, then the practice is common law rather than a convention. For example, the principle of *stare decisis*—courts will decide a current case according to the rulings made in previous similar cases—is common law. So also is the supremacy of Parliament: Any law passed by the legislature is valid and cannot be declared unconstitutional since the courts do enforce it. Practices that the courts do not enforce are conventions.

The fact that something has been done a certain way for some time does not by itself create a convention. Conventions are more than mere custom. The distinction I made above between fundamental and ordinary acts of Parliament applies here as well. Traditional practice is a convention (rather than a custom) when any change would alter basic arrangements of power and authority, thus transforming the way in which the country is governed. Beyond this, the practice also must have logical and normative support; that is, doing things this way makes sense and people feel bound to continue the

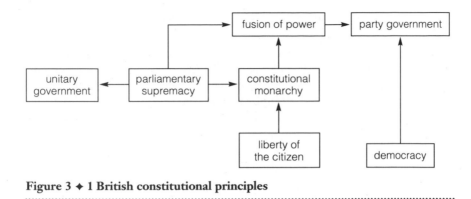

Figure 3 ✦ 1 British constitutional principles

practice. For example, if the monarch refused to accept as Prime Minister the person preferred by a majority of the House of Commons, the government could not function. No other person would have the support necessary to get any legislation approved by the Commons. Thus, it is sensible for the monarch to accept the Commons' preference. The Prime Minister must have a seat in the House of Commons not because the law requires it. Instead, the reason is that for him or her to be in the nonelective House of Lords seems inappropriate, undemocratic in the twentieth century. The prevailing democratic political values provide normative support for this practice and help to make it a convention.

Don't be too concerned if all this is puzzling to you; you're in good company. A recent opinion survey found that only a quarter of Britons claimed to know a fair amount or more about the British Constitution. A third admitted that they knew hardly anything about it, and a tenth confessed that they never had heard of the British Constitution.[2]

The elements of the British Constitution indicate the source of the provisions, but say nothing about the content. Fully understanding the structure requires examining the principles as well. Be aware that the list I'm about to present is unique; no two authors will agree exactly, given the rather ambiguous nature of the British Constitution. Figure 3.1 should help you visualize how some of these principles are based upon or logically implied by others.

- **Liberty of the Citizen** The rule of law is fundamental to the British system. This means, among other things, that the government is not above the law; it can't do whatever it pleases but must be able to cite legal authorization for its actions. All citizens are equal before the law. Convictions for breaking the law must conform with due process;

---

2. "The State of the Nation 1991," Market & Opinion Research International (MORI) for the Joseph Roundtree Reform Trust.

torture, for example, may not be used to secure confessions. The law must be publicly known in advance before it is enforced.

- **Democracy** Citizens have the opportunity to participate in authoritative decision making. The majority determines what the government does, not some elite. In Britain, as in most democracies, this means universal suffrage, buttressed by the right to form parties and pressure groups and to communicate with one's representatives. Perhaps a referendum system would enhance democracy, but that procedure is not essential for a country to be considered democratic.

- **Parliamentary Supremacy** The ultimate legal authority in Britain is Parliament. Since Parliament can alter the Constitution at will, its actions never can be declared unconstitutional by any court. In sharp contrast to the U.S. system, the judiciary *cannot* veto the actions of the legislature. The British judiciary may influence the legislature's action, but cannot ultimately check its power. British membership in the European Community raises some questions about this principle because, similarly to the supremacy clause in the U.S. Constitution, Community law is superior to national law. Thus, in some matters Parliament no longer is the final authority for public policy in Britain.

- **Constitutional Monarchy** Given liberty of the citizen and Parliamentary supremacy, Britain's monarchy must be constitutional and limited rather than absolute and autocratic. Although a hereditary monarch continues to reign over Britain, the occupant of this position does not rule, as I'll explain at the start of the next chapter. You could almost label the British system "a symbolic monarchy."

- **Unitary Government** Unlike the United States and Germany, Britain lacks division of powers. Its subnational units of government owe their power and existence to Parliament, which can alter or abolish them at will. As you learned in Chapter 2, that is exactly what was done in Northern Ireland a couple of decades ago. Subsequently, in the mid-1980s, the national government abolished the Greater London Council, turning the city's governmental functions over to various boards and subcity units of government. Similar action was taken against the metropolitan counties, the units of government for the country's major cities. In a unitary system, power is centralized in the national government; it is not divided between the national and the subnational units, as in a federal system. Perhaps the rise of nationalist feelings in Scotland and Wales will produce some change in this principle of the British Constitution.

- **Fusion of Power** Another contrast between Britain and the United States in relations between governmental institutions is that the British Constitution doesn't provide for separation of powers. As indicated by the above comments on Parliamentary supremacy, although the courts are separate organs, they are not intended to check Parliament. Britain goes beyond this, however, to fuse powers. The executive structures are not separated from the legislature but are intertwined with it in both their origin and maintenance. The Cabinet system is related as well to the principle of constitutional monarchy. Historically, the Cabinet developed to serve as a buffer or mediator between the ruler and those political leaders empowered to make authoritative policies for the country. In the twentieth century the Cabinet has become the most powerful structure in the British system. Chapter 5 will explain that although Parliament is legally supreme, in practice the Cabinet is.

- **Party Government** Parliamentary government is unlikely to produce stable Cabinets without well-organized, disciplined parties. The life of British Cabinets was much more tenuous when political groups coalesced around individuals, prior to the latter part of the nineteenth century, than it has been since then when loyalty to party principles has had priority over personal attachments. Furthermore, it is difficult to imagine a mass democratic (the second principle mentioned above) political process that didn't produce a fairly well-developed party system to channel and stimulate demands for governmental action. On the other hand, highly disciplined parties tend to produce monolithic voting blocs in Parliament, which undermines accountability. Increasingly after World War II a Cabinet with a working majority in Parliament could do almost anything it desired, knowing that its troops would loyally support it. Concentrated executive power was little constrained by formal responsibility to the legislature. Party government has tended to subvert Parliamentary supremacy.

British constitutional principles contain elements of both concentrated power and accountability. Furthermore, the tension between these two aspects of government set forth in Chapter 1 is again evident. The search for an acceptable balance has not ended. At one level this is a matter for constitutional lawyers, but at another it should be of fundamental concern to the people. What support does the Constitution have among the people? How much legitimacy do they accord to its particular mix of power and accountability?

Fundamental Political Values

Many aspects of the British Constitution will seem unfamiliar to Americans, but the absence of a Bill of Rights is the one that is likely to cause them the most disquiet. Yes, Britain has one, but, although a venerated document, it is simply a statute passed by Parliament three centuries ago and can be altered by the current Parliament whenever it chooses in the same way ordinary legislation is passed. This may not sound like much protection for basic liberties.

In recent years some Britons have become concerned about this situation. Talk about the need for some sort of written bill of rights that could not be altered by Parliament (an "entrenched" bill of rights) has become common. Nearly three-fourths of the British public wants a bill of rights to protect individual liberty; over half say that the government can change individual citizens' rights too easily.[3]

Proponents of civil liberties have cause to be anxious. In Britain the government has considerably greater control over the media than is true in the United States and recently has used it much more intrusively. Britain lacks a legal mechanism to obtain easy access to governmental information, such as the U.S. Freedom of Information Act. When early in 1992 (not for the first time) a Member of Parliament attempted to get such an act passed, the Government defeated the effort. At times British journalists have been forced to use the U.S. Freedom of Information Act to obtain information about Anglo-American relations and international activities that their government denied to them.

Nonetheless, too much information (in the government's view) has become public in recent years about the secret intelligence services: Spies, both retired and current, are writing memoirs and talking to journalists and Members of Parliament. Part of the difficulty is that the old D-notice system is no longer effective. In the past when the government thought that some journalist had gotten wind of something confidential, it would send a D (for defense) notice to newspaper editors telling them that it would be best if they didn't publish anything about the matter. The editors invariably responded, we wouldn't think of doing so. More recently some of them have decided that the public might be entitled to know some things.

Therefore, the government has gone beyond mere suasion to prosecution to block the publication and sale of some books and to censor various newspapers. The public's apparent concern to protect basic liberties, however, doesn't seem to extend to freedom of the press. Invasions of privacy and scandal mongering (which are even more prevalent in British papers than in American) have brought journalists into great disrepute and made the press

---

3. The information in this section comes in part from various surveys of British public opinion conducted by Social Surveys (Gallup) and by Market & Opinion Research International (MORI), especially "The State of the Nation 1991." I wish to thank Robert Wybrow of Gallup and Robert Worcester of MORI for making available these survey findings. Additional sources were Roger Jowell, Sharon Witherspoon, and Lindsay Brook, eds., *British Social Attitudes: the 1986 Report* (Aldershot, England: Gower, 1986) and *British Social Attitudes: the 1987 Report* (Aldershot, England: Gower, 1987).

vulnerable. Only a sixth of those surveyed by Gallup in March 1991 expressed a great deal or quite a lot of confidence in the press, the least support for any of the ten social institutions inquired about. Another poll found that two-fifths of the public would not protest action to restrict freedom of the press. Although television's reputation is less sullied, no great uproar occurred when, incredibly, early in 1987, the police ransacked the offices of the British Broadcasting Company (BBC) in Glasgow and carried away boxes of video-tapes, scripts, and journalists' notes to prevent the televising of a program about a spy satellite.

The basis for control of information in Britain is the Official Secrets Act, which has been law since around the time of World War I. Under the provisions of this Act, civil servants could be prosecuted (although they weren't) for revealing the brand of tea served in government cafeterias. The OSA was "reformed" in 1989. On the one hand, the definition of the information that could not be revealed was tightened considerably to eliminate the tea bag question. But the defenses available to those prosecuted under the law as amended were curtailed as well. Both current and former security and intelligence agents were denied any defense: Revealing secret information whatever the circumstances automatically entailed guilt. As for others, either civil servants or those to whom they might communicate secret information, the defense that revealing it was in the public interest was precluded as was the defense that someone else already had published the information. The government would have to prove, however, that publication did result in harm.

Additional evidence suggests that support for some other basic rights may be no more than lukewarm. The British have little sympathy for extreme political action. While about four-fifths of them believe that public meetings and pamphlets protesting the government should be allowed, less orthodox behavior is not as acceptable. Three-fifths think that protest marches and demonstrations are permissible, but many don't seem to regard these actions as basic rights. Nearly a third wouldn't protest if the right to demonstrate peacefully were withdrawn. As for occupying a government office and stopping work there for several days (behavior similar to what has occurred on many American college campuses), only a tenth would allow that. Almost no one (only 2 percent) would condone serious damage to government buildings.

Before you begin casting stones, however, you should be told that opinion surveys show that the British are no less tolerant than the Americans in extending political freedom to groups they strongly dislike. A bare majority in both countries would let such people make a public speech, but overwhelming majorities in both would bar them from teaching in state-supported schools and most would not permit them to hold a public rally. Furthermore, substantial majorities in both countries would prohibit people from groups they strongly dislike from running for office and would prefer to outlaw the groups entirely. One of the few rays of hope at the mass level for the civil libertarian is that Britons seem strongly committed to free speech (for themselves?). Half say they would sign a petition to protest any attempt to restrict free speech, a third would write to their legislator, and a quarter would attend a demonstration. Only a seventh say they would do nothing about it. Also encouraging is the fact that three-quarters of Britons (the same as the U.S. proportion) don't think that the police should be allowed to open the mail of a suspect, even one with a long criminal record.

In both countries defense of basic freedoms seems to depend more on the values of the political elite than those of the public.[4] National legislators in both the House of Representatives and the House of Commons are much more willing than are their fellow citizens to extend political rights to people from groups they strongly dislike. Interestingly, the American legislators are somewhat more tolerant than are their British counterparts. Whether this difference at the elite level has anything to do with the United States having an entrenched Bill of Rights and Britain lacking one, however, is unclear.

If what really matters in defending basic liberties is elite attitudes, then committing a catalogue of freedoms to writing in some sort of fundamental document might not add much of significance to British constitutionalism. After all, the former Soviet Union for years had an impressive list of freedoms in its Constitution, but this did not prevent its leaders from denying the people even the most basic rights. Conversely, even the U.S. Constitution could not prevent a powerful, ruthless group from establishing a dictatorship. Ultimately, written constitutions rest upon political, not legal, sanctions and supports — just as the unwritten British Constitution does. Limited government, fair play, and justice long have been part of British political culture, a culture into which the British political elite is fully socialized. In the past the British public has seemed content to leave protection of basic rights to the national legislators (much as Americans leave the matter to the Supreme Court). Whether the Britons will continue to do so has been called into question by two developments.

First, there is growing dissatisfaction with British government and its output. Early in the 1970s half the public thought that the system of governing Britain could be improved only in small ways, if at all — they felt it worked quite well as it was. By the start of the 1990s only a third held this view. Nearly a quarter of a century ago only a seventh of the public believed that the system needed a great deal of improvement; now a fourth thinks it does. Part of the problem may be that Britons expect more of their government. They tend to be more supportive of interventionist government; they show great enthusiasm for social welfare activities and are more likely to think

---

4. David Barnum and John Sullivan, "The Elusive Foundations of Political Freedom in Britain and the United States," *Journal of Politics*, No. 52 (August 1990), pp. 719–739.

that the government should do something to deal with social problems. Thus, when the quality of government-provided health care for everyone and of state-supported education seems to be declining, the public becomes discontent.

The malaise goes beyond this, extending to the way in which decisions are made — although here, also, the content of public policy is relevant. The majority of the public strongly favors restoring hanging for some crimes; the bulk of the political elite opposes the death penalty. The public wants tighter control of "coloured" immigration than the elite is willing to enact. And although public protest ultimately did succeed in getting the "community charge" (the flat-rate tax that everyone had to pay regardless of wealth or income) abolished, yet the elite was slow to respond to discontent and needed mass, violent demonstrations to be persuaded to act. Not surprisingly, then, Britons have a jaundiced view of representative government. They are less likely than Americans to feel that they can influence the government and get political leaders and representatives to respond to their views. Four-fifths of them feel that the public has little control over what politicians do in office, and three-fifths say that you get nowhere by talking to public officials (in the United States, little more than two-fifths say that).

The public, therefore, wants to take decision making more into its own hands. The British Constitution lacks the practice, common at the state and local level in the United States, of submitting some decisions to the electorate in the form of a referendum. (American national government doesn't use the referendum either, although the procedure for approving the Twenty-first Amendment to the Constitution — making the manufacture and sale of alcoholic beverages legal again — approximated a referendum.) Thus, the 1975 referendum on membership in the European Community was a major break with tradition. At the time this was said to be an exceptional situation and was not to be a precedent for future procedures. Nonetheless, four years later a referendum was held in Wales and Scotland on devolution. These two instances, one national and one regional, are Britain's only experience with referenda.

Whatever the political elite may wish, the public apparently does see these as precedents. Three-fourths want a referendum system so that the people can decide some important issues and not leave all of them up to Parliament. The same proportion wants to be able to force a referendum on a particular issue by means of a petition signed by a million or so electors. Had such a system existed, there can be little doubt that the British public would have voted against the community charge and for capital punishment. Three-fourths favored holding a referendum on abolishing the community charge and three-fifths wanted one on reintroducing the death penalty. Despite the public's enthusiasm for referenda, that change in the British Constitution has not been as widely discussed as has an entrenched bill of rights.

Another possible change that also has received more attention than referenda is a switch from the single-member, simple-plurality electoral system familiar to Americans to some form of proportional representation (PR). (I'll explain the political implications of such a change in Chapter 7.) Based on the two most canvased changes — a bill of rights and PR — two-thirds of the British public can be labeled "reformists." Two-fifths favor *both* changes and another one-fourth supports one change while not opposing the other. Additional evidence of interest in constitutional reform is the growth of interest groups (Charter '88, for example) organized for that purpose.

Changes in partisan politics also suggest that the British Constitution may be in flux. Although Labour instituted extensive reforms from 1945 to 1951, the Conservatives acquiesced to most of them and repealed few during their extended period in power from 1951 to 1964. As Chapter 1 explained this was a period of growing consensus in Britain in which party differences became as narrow as most Americans would perceive them to be between Democrats and Republicans. Having one major party ostensibly socialist and the other capitalist did not create a fundamental ideological cleavage in British politics. As explained earlier, however, during the 1980s Margaret Thatcher repudiated the post-World War II consensus. She was an apostle of traditional values, self-help, enterprise, discipline, and hard work. Coddling by the government was out. Although she brought to British government a much-needed purposeful decisiveness, she also projected an air of arrogant certainty that not only did she know everything, but she never was mistaken. The harsh dogmatism of her leadership created an image of a strict schoolmistress constantly rapping the knuckles of her unruly pupils with a ruler. Everyone was to behave and think as she did.

How much impact she had on the public's basic beliefs is unclear; reversing the values and expectations that have developed over the course of a third of a century is difficult even for someone as determined as Thatcher. Gallup opinion surveys for the BBC at the time of the 1983 and 1987 elections found that about half those interviewed believed that it was better to stick firmly to one's own beliefs rather than trying to meet political opponents halfway. On the other hand, two-fifths preferred the more accommodating approach. Interestingly, those who supported Thatcher's Conservative party were much more likely to favor sticking to one's own beliefs; nearly two-thirds of them preferred that to meeting opponents halfway. Just as their Leader had styled herself a "conviction politician," so they seemed to be conviction electors.

While the Conservative party was moving to the right, away from the postwar consensus, the Labour party was moving to the left. Marxist or Trotskyite groups gained control of local party organization in parts of Britain and were able to exert influence on the national party as well. As a result, the election of 1983 offered voters the most clear-cut choice in a generation in terms of political rhetoric. The drifting apart of the parties — what some might regard as the polarization of politics during the 1980s — stimulated interest in constitutional reform. In some instances, Colonel Blimps (the British term for right-wing, extremely stuffy traditionalists who believe that nothing should ever be done for the first time) became concerned that if the Labour party won an election, it might do fearsome things. A Labour Government could abolish the House of Lords and then there would be nothing to check a left-wing majority in the Commons. The more typical Briton in the center of the political spectrum was concerned that perhaps neither major party could be trusted not to go too far. In short, continuing to place your confidence in the political elite to preserve basic rights seemed a more tenuous guarantee than in the past.

By the start of the 1990s, however, this level of anxiety had declined. Labour, under Neil Kinnock, moved back toward the center, having expelled or marginalized many of its extremists. And the Conservative party decided that a decade of Thatcher was enough. Having deposed her late in 1990, they replaced her with John Major, about as unabrasive and easygoing a politician as one could hope to find. So unaggressive and undogmatic is he that many regard him as dull and colorless. Although he couldn't explicitly repudiate his predecessor's style and policies (in part because she favored him over the other two candidates to succeed her), his rhetoric was much more moderate and he sought to move the Conservatives back toward the center. Thus, the apparent urgency of placing explicit restraints upon the government no longer seemed as pressing. Little had been done, however, to remedy the public's dissatisfaction with representative government. What remained to be seen was whether that dissatisfaction could generate sufficient momentum to produce fundamental changes in the British Constitution.

Summary

Governmental institutions in Britain have evolved gradually over many centuries. Change has been incremental, almost imperceptible, and typically has been due more to altered practice than to formal, statutory reform. Given this tradition of organic growth, you should not be surprised that no one ever has written down all the rules in a formal constitution. (Cromwell's Commonwealth in the seventeenth century did have a written constitution, but that hardly is an inducement to the British to try again.) Despite the absence of a framework document, power is constrained in Britain. Although it does so in a way different from the United States, Britain, too, practices constitutionalism. Americans seek to constrain power through a written constitution prescribing a system of checks and balances among various branches and levels of the government. So suspicious of arbitrary government were the American Founding Fathers that they created a system of fractionalized powers intended to *impede* action.

The British weren't any less fearful of such government. They had had sufficient experience with it during centuries of autocratic monarchy. They were unwilling, however, to let their concern deny themselves the benefits that effective government can bring to the citizens. As we saw in this chapter, Britons are much more likely than Americans to prefer activist government. Thus, they were willing to *facilitate* action by concentrating power as long as those holding it could be called to account. At the heart of British government is the idea that power should be sufficiently concentrated and untrammeled that things can be done provided that those who are entrusted with power are required to justify their behavior. Such a constraint was deemed sufficient because it was coupled with the sanction that should power-holders abuse their trust or, even, simply fail to perform satisfactorily, they could be removed from office at *any* time, not just at periodic elections.

What is fascinating about current British political culture is that the public has concluded that accountability has become too attenuated. Britons' sense of political efficacy is lower than that of Americans; they are searching for some procedures that will strengthen this essential constraint on power in their system. Their unease has reached the point that they even are willing to adopt a portion of the American prescription for defense of liberties. While they are not yet willing to fractionalize power (although support for devolution does seem to be growing), they do favor the formal constraints of an entrenched bill of rights. The unwritten constitution of conventions, understandings, and ancient documents no longer seems adequate.

The constitutional elements and principles, along with the basic political beliefs of the people discussed in this chapter, should make it clear that Britain and the United States share many fundamental governmental values and goals; in that sense the two systems are the same. Specific practices, procedures, and institutions, however, often differ; in that sense the systems aren't the same. In the rest of this book you'll find some familiar ways of doing things, but many will seem rather curious. Britain's setting — the history, basic values, and characteristics discussed in these three opening chapters — has produced a distinctive pattern of institutions. Interesting as some specific contrasts between Britain and the United States are in themselves, more significant than any differences of detail are the British preference to facilitate, rather than impede, governmental action and the reliance upon accountability, rather than fractionalized power, to constrain government. Having examined this fundamental characteristic at length, I now can set forth in detail for you Britain's arrangement of governmental institutions. I begin with the executives because it is here that power is concentrated in the British system.

Part II

✦

Governmental
Institutions

Photo on previous page: Statue of Winston Churchill in Parliament Square at the foot of Whitehall.

4
—
✦

The Executives

The British system concentrates power. Of course, you may say, Britain has a monarch. That office, however, is not where power is concentrated. The location instead is the Prime Minister and the Cabinet. Surprisingly, in view of the system's requirement of accountability, the British chief executive is not directly elected. He or she is chosen by a process even less direct than is the American electoral college for selecting the U.S. President.

Although the American system separates governmental powers and allocates them among three distinct branches, the executive branch does culminate in a single official, a chief executive. In contrast, European countries tend to have bifurcated executives because most of them once were, or still are, monarchies. Britain is no exception. One of its dual executives is head of State and performs symbolic or ceremonial functions; the other is head of Government and formulates and coordinates public policy and supervises its implementation. So closely assisted by associates is the head of Government in performing these duties that the political executive in Britain comes much closer to being collective than in the United States. Besides the ceremonial executive (hereditary) and the partisan executive (elected indirectly), Britain has a merit executive (appointed) to implement policies and programs.

Relations between the ceremonial and partisan executives, a matter of great contention three centuries ago, no longer raise serious questions about the accountability of concentrated power. The locus of controversy now is relations between the partisan and merit executives. Many observers question whether the merit executives — who, as we'll see, go beyond simply implementing policy to play a significant role in formulating it as well — are accountable at all. Others are concerned that the power wielded by the partisan executive is not sufficiently accountable. In short, this chapter gets to some of the most fundamental problems of the British system.

Ceremonial

Despite living in a country that originated by rebelling against the English monarch, Americans seem to adore the British royal family. Queen Elizabeth ranks high on lists of women most admired by Americans, and supermarket tabloids regularly report on the latest doings of Di, Fergie, and the rest. You may think, therefore, that to the typical Briton the Royals are, both in formal language and slang, awesome. Generating awe *is* an important part of the ceremonial function. A leading British journalist, Walter Bagehot, in the latter part of the nineteenth century raised the issue in a less than respectful fashion. In a classic study of British government he observed (concerning Queen Victoria and her son), "it is nice to trace how the actions of a retired widow and an unemployed youth became of such importance."

Although he himself clearly was *not* awed, he attached great importance to this aspect of the monarchy. He asserted that the monarch was the dignified portion of the British executive and the Cabinet the efficient part. The dignified portion was to grab the people's attention through elaborate pageantry (rather the way a magician gets you to look somewhere other than where the trick is being done) while the efficient part got on with the business of governing unimpeded by popular input. Monarchical pomp was needed to awe the public into accepting laws and regulations; if the people discovered that the decisions were made by mere politicians, they would be less disposed to obey. Although the British public hardly can be said to be that credulous in the second half of the twentieth century, a public opinion poll in the 1960s suggested that the argument retained some validity. Asked whether the views of the Queen or of the Prime Minister *would* prevail in a conflict over policy and which *should* prevail, a substantial majority believed not only that the Queen's would, but that hers should.[1] The monarchy still helps legitimate action that might otherwise seem completely partisan.

---

1. *The Queen* (Harmondsworth, England: Penguin Books, 1977), p. 13.

The continued prominence of the monarchy makes symbol and power easy to confuse. Suppose that the British legislature were to pass a law that appalled Queen Elizabeth — perhaps that Buckingham Palace was being converted to a hospital and she would have to move out. She could refuse to sign the bill and, without her signature, it could not go into effect. (No big surprise here; the U.S. President can veto acts of Congress and he's no king.) Suppose that Queen Elizabeth decided that the French and Germans were trampling on British interests in the European Community. Without discussing the matter with anyone, she could announce that Britain was abrogating its treaty commitments and take the country out of the EC. Suppose she concluded that she could no longer abide whoever was Prime Minister. (Some claimed that that came close to being true the longer Margaret Thatcher remained in office.) She could remove that person and appoint someone else instead. Suppose she felt that Parliament simply wasted time in windy debates that accomplished nothing. She could send them all packing and not call them back into session. Although only a partial list of powers, it's impressive.

Now for the truth. A British monarch who took any of these actions would not violate any law — that is, any statute. Almost every constitutional expert would agree, however, that these actions would be unconstitutional. In short, the monarch could transgress The Law without breaking a law. So constrained is the British ruler that some have argued that had the Nazis conquered Britain in World War II, the monarch would have had to sign an order sending Jews to concentration camps for extermination. The British monarch has almost no discretion in matters of policy and governmental personnel.

Centuries ago the monarch exercised a wide range of powers. This was changed in typical British fashion. Instead of passing statutes to reallocate powers and functions from one organ of government to another, practices were altered gradually to form new customs. As you can tell from Chapter 3's discussion of the Constitution, no obstacles prevented such changes. For example, the last time a monarch killed legislation by refusing to sign a bill was in 1707 — hardly a current precedent. No formal constitution had to be amended to prevent this happening again; no law needed to be passed. The practice simply changed. Increasingly, people came to realize that if the monarch could prevail over the rest of the governmental system, then Britain was in danger of arbitrary, tyrannical government. Avoiding that required a limited, rather than an absolute, monarchy and that, in turn, meant denying the monarch a veto power. Thus, the power that Americans are willing for an elected President to exercise (albeit with the possibility of a legislative override) the British deny to a nonelected monarch.

As for the Prime Minister, the term "Her Majesty's Government" suggests that the Queen can select whomever she wants and, indeed, for much of British history monarchs did exactly that. Now, however, the Queen must put up with the leader of whatever party wins a general election, despite her personal preferences. Not doing so would make a farce of democracy. Why bother to have elections if the monarch could ignore the voters' preferences? The same argument applies, as well, concerning a veto. If a majority of the legislators chosen by the voters want a particular law, who is the monarch to say that it shall not go into effect? So, constitutional monarchy and democracy — two of the fundamental principles of the British Constitution set forth in Chapter 3 — deny Queen Elizabeth any significant power.

The obvious question, then, is: Why bother to have a monarch? Granted the British are traditionalists (remember that the decade during the seventeenth century when England didn't have a monarch was not exactly a happy time) and many of them feel sentimental about the royal family, but surely they must question whether it is worth the money. The cost of monarchy, however, is a rather murky question. The main item for monarchy in the national Budget is the Civil List. These funds are not intended to provide salaries for the members of the royal family, but to cover the expenses involved in carrying out their public duties. About three-fourths of the money goes to pay those people — cooks, chauffeurs, secretaries, and the like — who work for the royal family. Several expenses associated with the monarchy, however, aren't included in the Civil List. The cost of the royal yacht and of airplanes appears elsewhere in the Budget. The cost of maintaining royal residences is a separate item, since buildings like Buckingham Palace (Figure 4.1) and Windsor Castle belong to the state and must be cared for like any other public building.

For most of the twentieth century (since 1910) the monarch has been exempt from income tax. In 1991 a bill was introduced in the House of Commons to restore the earlier practice of requiring payment from the monarch. This received only preliminary consideration and failed to proceed further in the legislative process.

On the other side of the ledger, the monarchy brings money into the public coffers. The Queen owns much valuable property that she has inherited from her ancestors. The bulk of these properties forms what is known as the Crown Estates. In exchange for the funds given her in the Civil List, she permits the government to receive all the rents from these Estates. Typically, this income is greater than the expenditure for the Civil List. Beyond that, the money brought into the country by tourists who come to see such sights associated with the monarchy as the changing of the guard at Buckingham Palace and the Crown jewels at the Tower of London is incalculable. All in all, Britain may turn a tidy profit on the monarchy.

No one would suggest, however, that such commercial considerations are the main reason for maintaining the monarchy. What governmental function does the monarchy have? To say that Queen Elizabeth has no power is not to say that she lacks all influence. Official documents such as Cabinet papers and Foreign Office telegrams are sent to Buckingham Palace daily. The Prime

Figure 4 ✦ 1 Buckingham Palace

Minister meets with her each week to report on what the Cabinet is doing. The Queen has the right to ask for additional information; she also can call on a variety of experts and exchange views with foreign dignitaries. She has the facilities to be very well informed on any public issue that interests her. This is especially so due to her much greater longevity than the politicians with whom she deals. At the start of the 1990s Queen Elizabeth had had nine different Prime Ministers during her reign. None of those serving in the Cabinet had even won their first election when she became queen in 1952.

Any sensible Prime Minister would welcome nonpartisan opinions from someone with the long experience and detailed knowledge of Queen Elizabeth. Furthermore, given her status, her opinions can't be dismissed lightly. On the other hand, her influence shouldn't be exaggerated. No Cabinet will reverse a major policy just because the Queen would prefer that. Only to the extent that her well-taken points don't clash with the policies of the party in power can she influence her ministers.

The Queen's policy influence, however, is only a minor aspect of her role as head of State. She also relieves the partisan head of Government (the Prime Minister) and his or her colleagues from many time-consuming duties, such as meeting foreign dignitaries on arrival in Britain, dedicating important buildings or monuments, and other similar functions. Useful as these ceremonial activities are, the significance of the role goes well beyond this. The monarch provides an apolitical focus for national loyalty. Queen Elizabeth personifies the State; she is a *living symbol* of the nation and thus is able to stir patriotic feelings of national pride much more successfully than a flag or a song.

In the United States, where the President combines the roles of head of Government and head of State, it is difficult to criticize him in his partisan capacity without appearing to attack him in his symbolic status. The former behavior is legitimate; the latter is not. Thus, Americans are forced to make such comments as, "I respect the office, but not the man." British bifurcation of the executive avoids such problems.

Whatever the shifts in partisan control of the government, the monarchy offers Britons a symbolic focus for loyalty, a constant presence. By providing such a focus, the monarch also serves a lightning-rod function. Many people want some personal magnetism or charisma in their politics. If an unscrupulous politician with such an attribute were to gain power, he or she would pose a serious threat to democracy—Americans are not unfamiliar with the dangers of populist demagogues. Rather than try to banish charisma from politics, the British seek to channel it through the monarchy. Doing so presents no danger because the monarch's powers have been reduced to almost nothing. Thus, the monarchy can help to discharge popular passions that otherwise might jeopardize democracy. The role of the monarchy in system maintenance should not be overlooked.

One example of the monarchy's ability to influence behavior is especially instructive. When the Labour party first came to office in 1924, its leaders went to Buckingham Palace for the traditional meeting with the king, the equivalent of a swearing-in ceremony. They didn't wear their normal business suits, but were concerned to acquire the correct formal attire, including top hats. The leaders of this supposedly reformist party of the people wanted to be certain that they didn't violate protocol. Perhaps these leaders simply were less radical than their policy pronouncements had made them seem; certainly, the left wing of the Labour party regarded their behavior as a sellout. The effect of the ceremonial executive, however, should not be dismissed out of hand. That Britain was a monarchy and not a republic did matter. Furthermore, their behavior must have reassured those on the right of the political spectrum, who had feared that Labour, given the chance, would subvert the British political system.

Performing the ceremonial function effectively requires strict partisan neutrality: The monarch must be aloof from politics. Although an unbroken line of development can be traced for most British governmental institutions, this is not true for the contemporary role of the monarch. Before the twentieth century British monarchs often violated the neutrality prescription. Queen Victoria in the nineteenth century, for example, made little effort to hide her dislike of Mr. Gladstone and his Liberals. As a result, republican sentiment was not uncommon. Only when, after decades of rule, she became the country's grand old lady (again, the Importance of Being Ancient?) did she regain the popularity and affection that she had had when first ascending the throne as a young woman.

The monarchy's shrewd advisors recognized that it could survive in the twentieth century only with a new strategy. If the institution was to provide an element of stability and a brake on social transformation, it would need, paradoxically, to be widely recognized as politically neutral. Maintaining this stance has become the overriding concern of every British ruler. Monarchical partisan neutrality now is a convention of the Constitution. If Queen Elizabeth were to identify herself with any particular group of politicians or specific set of policies, she would herself become a politician, subject to criticism and attack like all other politicians. She could not appeal to the people against the Cabinet without expecting the Cabinet to appeal to the people against her.

Avoiding partisan politics is more difficult than you might think. In 1977 at the elaborate ceremony launching the Jubilee celebrations of her quarter of a century as monarch, Queen Elizabeth made a speech. Referring to discussions then underway about devolution to Wales and Scotland, she commented, "I number Kings and Queens of England and of Scotland, and Princes of Wales, among my ancestors and so I can readily understand these aspirations. But I cannot forget that I was crowned Queen of the United Kingdom of Great Britain and Northern Ireland. Perhaps this Jubilee is a time to remind ourselves of the benefits which union has conferred, at home and in our international dealings, on the inhabitants of all parts of this United Kingdom."

Hardly inflammatory sentiments, you might think. But those politicians who favored greater autonomy for Wales and Scotland were upset. They said she had made "ill-advised remarks," that her comments were "unprecedented," "unfortunate." One of the papers reporting these events said that "the Queen stepped into the controversy over devolution." Adding to the uproar was the fact that after the speech an official spokesperson made clear that this was an instance in which the monarch *had* exercised some discretion. Contrary to the typical situation, she had not merely read a speech written for her by politicians but had composed it herself. In the end, it all blew over and the monarchy did not fall into disrepute. Still, the incident shows that almost any expression of even the most bland opinion is likely to offend someone as partisan.

A similar controversy arose in the late spring of 1992. Queen Elizabeth addressed the European Parliament. This in itself, totally apart from anything she said, was an interesting event. During her years as Prime Minister, Margaret Thatcher had refused to permit the Queen to make such a speech, to show Thatcher's disdain for the legislative organ of the European Community. Queen Elizabeth was the only monarch of an EC country who had not spoken to the European Parliament. Her appearance, therefore, was a signal that the new Prime Minister, John Major, wished to take a more sympathetic stance toward the EC.

An advance press release summarizing her speech suggested that she would assert that Britain's unique parliamentary traditions were of less significance than the move toward European democracy and should not be permitted to impede the EC's efforts toward tighter integration. Some Conservative Members of Parliament went incendiary, criticizing the Queen (or her advisors) for selling out to European federalism and for failing to proclaim the superiority that history had conferred on the British system in contrast with unstable and ineffective Continental regimes. In fact, all that the Queen said was that the style of debate in the House of Commons differed from that of Continental legislatures and that this was insignificant compared to a shared commitment to democracy. The incident differed from the devolution one because the Queen was not speaking in a personal capacity but as the official voice of Britain. It illustrated as well, however, how even the mildest comments by the monarch can raise political hackles (or hacks — slang for British journalists).

Being monarch, then, is a tough job. Because Queen Elizabeth became sixty-five (often regarded as the age of retirement) in 1991 and had been doing the job for nearly forty years, why didn't she make way for Prince Charles? At forty-three he hardly was immature and unready to perform the role of monarch. His mother is in remarkably good health, and if she serves until she dies, he will be an old man before he becomes king. Queen Elizabeth remains monarch because she has a highly developed sense of duty. She didn't run for the office of monarch; heredity — destiny — imposed the task upon her and she intends to see it through to the end. More important, to make way for Charles would require her to abdicate and that would remind people of what her uncle, Edward VIII, did nearly two-thirds of a century ago. After only a short time on the throne, Edward abdicated so that he could marry an American divorcée with whom he had been having an affair. Given his indolence, lack of intellectual ability, general frivolousness, and Nazi sympathies, Britain was well rid of him. What the country got in his place — George VI, Elizabeth's father — was a more dedicated, diligent, and respectable ruler than Edward could ever have been. And in his wife (also named Elizabeth and known during Elizabeth II's reign as the Queen Mum) the country gained one of the warmest, most genuine, and hugely popular Royals in the entire history of the monarchy. Even to mention her in the same sentence as the woman that Edward VIII married is a sacrilege. Although the Abdication was a good thing for Britain, it was a political trauma, a constitutional crisis. Queen Elizabeth would not want to do anything that would recall that earlier instance when the monarch clearly failed to do his duty.

In addition to political neutrality, the ceremonial function requires popularity. Although the monarchy is based on heredity, discharging its central role requires courting public opinion almost as assiduously as if the office were elective. The contemporary popularity of the monarchy is due largely to the efforts of Queen Elizabeth's mother and father. The incident that best summarizes their behavior is their refusal to evacuate from Britain when the country was under air attack during World War II. Elizabeth (the Queen Mum) almost seemed to rejoice when bombs damaged Buckingham Palace.

Now, she said, when she toured those areas of London where people had been bombed out of their homes, she could look them in the face. Such sensitivity, combined with firm nonpartisanship, have made the monarchy unassailable. About five-sixths of the British believe that it is very important or quite important for Britain to be a monarchy. Only 3 percent want to abolish the monarchy.[2] And even if pollsters press the issue and inquire about the expense, nearly three-fourths say that the value of the royal family outweighs the cost. As explained, that value lies not in ruling the country but in performing the ceremonies that help to unify it, those that give the people a sense of common purpose above and beyond the divisions of social status and partisan conflict.

On the other hand, royal marital problems tend to weaken the status of the monarchy. Many people were bothered when the Queen's sister, Princess Margaret, divorced several years ago. That seemed an isolated instance until the Queen's children grew up and began to have similar difficulties. The separation of Sarah Ferguson and Prince Andrew early in 1992 involved some scandalous rumors. Some wondered whether Princess Diana and Prince Charles would be next, since they had come to live almost entirely separate lives and various publications began reporting severe marital problems. The future of the monarchy seemed to hang on whether Diana would press for separation or would be willing to keep up formal appearances. An opinion survey found that half the public felt that the Royals were failing to set a good example of family life. Thus, the monarchy does perform useful functions. The current queen works diligently and is popular and her mother is even more so. Whether Charles, when he comes to the throne, will be able to maintain the status and influence of the monarchy, however, is uncertain.

Efficient

The part of the executive branch that actually does the work of running the country can be divided into two segments: partisan and merit. The latter is those civil servants who, having demonstrated their abilities, are appointed to staff the various government departments and agencies. The task for most of them is to implement public policy, but a few of them help to make policy. The partisan portion is composed of politicians who obtain office not through competitive examinations but through the support of the voters. They formulate and coordinate public policy. Since Britain fuses the legislative and the executive branches, the electorate can't vote directly for any of the political executive. The largest party in the House of Commons gets all

---

2. Roger Jowell and Colin Airey, *British Social Attitudes: the 1984 report* (Aldershot, England: Gower, 1984), p. 30.

Figure 4 ✦ 2 No. 10 Downing Street

the offices in the political executive. The party leader becomes Prime Minister and he or she appoints his or her top colleagues to the Cabinet. Other less prominent associates are given junior positions in the executive. These people, from the Prime Minister through the juniors, are known collectively as the Government (the comparable American term is the *Administration*, as in the Bush Administration). And, with only rare exceptions, all the members of the Government, although serving in the executive branch, continue to hold seats in the legislature.

The Prime Minister's official residence is No. 10 Downing Street. As you can see from Figure 4.2, it appears much less impressive from the outside than does the White House of the American President. Like many wealthy London residences, however, No. 10 is much larger and more elegant inside than you would think judging by its facade. Until a few years ago anyone could stand as close to the entrance to No. 10 as where this picture was taken. Margaret Thatcher had huge wrought iron gates constructed across the entrance to Downing Street, however, and now people must stand on the sidewalk of Whitehall (see footnote 9 and Figure 4.7) to watch the limousines come and go.

Traditionally, the Prime Minister was said to be *primus inter pares* — "first among equals." Over the years a small group of assistants to the monarch had developed. They advised the monarch on what actions the legislature would accept and supervised the operation of government departments. The most efficient way for these "ministers" (as they were called, despite having nothing to do with the clergy) to convey their views to the monarch was through a

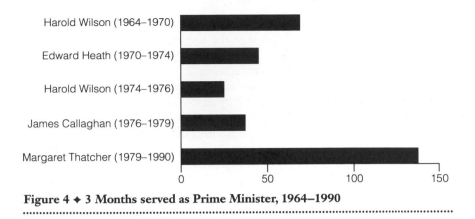

Figure 4 ✦ 3 Months served as Prime Minister, 1964–1990

leading advisor: a *prime* minister. This minister was intended to be little more than a presiding officer over a collective executive. In the second half of the twentieth century, however, the power of the Prime Minister has grown considerably; some people believe that British government has been "presidentialized." In short, the *primus* has come to be much more important for the efficient executive than is the *inter pares*. For this reason, I focus first on the Prime Minister and then on his or her colleagues.

Partisan: The Prime Minister

On November 4, 1990, Margaret Thatcher had been Prime Minister of Britain for exactly eleven and a half years, the longest period of service in that office since Lord Salisbury in 1902. How extraordinary her longevity was can be seen in Figure 4.3 by comparing her service with that of her immediate predecessors.[3] Almost everyone assumed that she would add to her record and, perhaps, eventually surpass Salisbury's nearly fourteen years as Prime Minister. Slightly over three weeks later she was simply one of 650 members of the House of Commons and had no executive power whatsoever. No general election had occurred, no scandal such as Watergate that had forced President Nixon to resign had been revealed; yet Thatcher had been replaced as chief executive. She was forced from office because she "lost" the support of her party's legislators, although a majority of them had backed her to remain as Prime Minister. Here was a graphic example of the fundamental

---

3. Note that Harold Wilson appears twice in Figure 4.3. Such repeat service as Prime Minister is not unusual in Britain. A person may lead a party for many years, during which time the party may swing between winning and losing elections, which would put the Leader in and out of the office of Prime Minster.

contrast between the U.S. Presidency and the British office of Prime Minister. The Presidency is firmly established in the Constitution and associated statutes; the office of Prime Minister has no comparable constitutional or statutory basis: Custom and practice is everything.

In 1975 the Conservative Members of the House of Commons had elected Thatcher to be their Leader. When the party won a majority of the seats in the Commons in the election of 1979, she automatically became Prime Minister. The electorate did not vote directly to install her in that office. Nearly 43 million people voted in 1980 for Ronald Reagan to be President; fewer than 21,000 voted for Thatcher in 1979 — only those who lived in the legislative constituency she represented. Again in 1983 and 1987, the Conservatives won most of the seats in the House of Commons and Thatcher, as Leader of the party, continued to serve as Prime Minister. Thus, changes of Prime Minister usually occur because an election has shifted control of the House of Commons from one party to another. Beyond that, a Prime Minister may decide, for reasons of ill health or age, to retire. His or her party picks a new Leader, who becomes Prime Minister. Thatcher did not want to retire, however; uniquely, she was deposed.

The Conservative party's rules provide for annual elections for Leader, should someone wish to run against the incumbent. Dissent within the party over Thatcher's policies and Leadership style led a former member of her Cabinet, Michael Heseltine, to challenge her. A majority (204) of the 372 Conservative legislators entitled to vote supported her. This clear victory was insufficient, however, because the rules also stipulated that the winner must lead by a margin of at least 15 percent of those eligible to vote. She had received fifty-two votes more than her challenger (sixteen people had abstained), four short of the fifty-six she needed. Although her combative nature caused her to declare immediately that she would fight on and contest the next ballot, colleagues convinced her that doing so might split the party and humiliate her, if some of her original supporters switched to another candidate. Therefore, she announced that she was withdrawing.

Two of her colleagues now joined her original challenger in running for the post of Leader. The winner was the candidate Thatcher most preferred, John Major. His victory was a further irony because he received only 185 votes, 19 fewer than she had on the first ballot. The rules for the second ballot drop the 15 percent requirement and specify only an absolute majority for success. Major was two votes short of this requirement, but so close that the other two candidates withdrew in his favor. So, Thatcher had a majority — but lost — and Major lacked a majority — but won. And since the Conservatives had changed Leaders, Britain had a new Prime Minister.

Although British parties had in the past voted their Leaders out, this was the first time in the twentieth century that a party had deposed a sitting Prime Minister. No one suggested that the action was unconstitutional and yet it clearly deviated from the way in which the British system was supposed to operate. Between elections, Prime Ministers are supposed to be accountable to, and subject to removal by, the House of Commons — not just a segment thereof, which is what Conservative legislators were. In Chapter 5 when I examine legislative–executive relations, I'll explain how the system of accountability is supposed to operate. Note also that had the Labour party, rather than the Conservatives, been in power, the procedures would have differed considerably. I discuss the way in which Labour changes Leaders in Chapter 8.

The procedures for the selection and removal of Prime Ministers are not the only curious aspects of the office. Statutes do not specify the powers and duties of the Prime Minister, nor the criteria for holding the office. None of the provisions that you can find in Article II of the U.S. Constitution exist in British law. The office was not even mentioned in a legal document until 1905, and not until 1937 was a statute passed to provide a salary for the post. Twentieth-century constitutional convention, however, requires the Prime Minister to have a seat in the House of Commons.[4] (This was not the convention in the nineteenth century; then the Prime Minister often was from the House of Lords.)

Given the divergent selection procedures, you won't be surprised to find that Presidents and Prime Ministers differ in the way they get to the top political office. In Britain the route is much more narrow. An ambitious British politician must work his or her way up in the party through service in the national legislature. Alternate routes — such as governor of a large state, war hero, or prominent businessperson, which often have been the means to a Presidential nomination — aren't available in Britain. This would appear to make an illustrious political career in Britain even more dependent on the favor of party leaders than is the case in the United States. Those who rebel against the leaders are unlikely to receive appointment to the subsidiary executive offices in which they can demonstrate that they have the abilities necessary for the top post; equally damaging to one's career is getting a reputation for being a troublemaker, for being "unsound." Nevertheless, four of the ten Prime Ministers since the end of World War II had been rebels at earlier stages in their careers. Despite stepping out of line, they were able, for a variety of reasons, to survive and advance.

The need for a legislative career, the product of British fusion of the executive and legislative branches, means that British Prime Ministers have

---

4. The only exception since 1902 came in 1963 when the Earl of Home became Prime Minister. He had agreed, however, to give up his title and won a by-election to enter the Commons. Thus, for only a few weeks, Britain had a Prime Minister not in the House of Commons.

considerable legislative experience before attaining that office. John Major's twelve years was the least prior service in Parliament of any of those who have become Prime Minister in this century; the average is twice as long. As for twentieth-century U.S. Presidents through George Bush, more than half (nine of sixteen) had not served in Congress at all. The seven that had been in Congress averaged under thirteen years of service—little more than the shortest period of prior legislative experience for Prime Ministers.

Fusion of powers means that British Prime Ministers will have had executive experience, as well as legislative, before attaining office. To focus only on the most preeminent executive positions, nine of the last twenty Prime Ministers had been Chancellor of the Exchequer, five had been Foreign Secretary, and three had served in both posts. During the last century no U.S. President has served as either Secretary of the Treasury or Secretary of State (the equivalent offices) before being elected. In addition, this lack of executive experience is not made up for by state politics, since only six of the last nineteen Presidents had been governor of a state.

Their long prior service in Parliament means that most Prime Ministers aren't especially young when they become chief executive. The average age on entering office in the twentieth century is nearly fifty-nine. John Major, not yet forty-eight, is the youngest person to become Prime Minister in this century. American twentieth-century Presidents through Bush average three years younger at inauguration than are Prime Ministers on assuming office. (Reagan, especially, and Bush—the two oldest at inauguration in this century—make the gap closer than it otherwise would be.)

Turning to the powers and duties of the office, the Prime Minister's authority and prestige since World War II have so outstripped that of the other members of the collective executive that he or she doesn't merely head the executive, but dominates it. This is not a matter of new laws or constitutional amendments, but simply of evolving practice. This trend has progressed so far that some observers argue that just as Parliamentary supremacy was in practice (although not in constitutional principle) superceded by Cabinet supremacy toward the close of the nineteenth century, so has Cabinet Government now been replaced by Prime Ministerial Government.[5] What had been a collective executive is said to have become a single executive. British government is supposed to have been "Presidentialized."

The theory of Prime Ministerial Government focuses on domination at three points in the political system: the Cabinet, the bureaucracy, and the party machine. The power to appoint and dismiss ministers from the Cabinet or shift them to less important departments enables a Prime Minister to

---

5. For a brief statement of these views see Richard Crossman, *The Myth of Cabinet Government* (Cambridge, Mass.: Harvard University Press, 1972), especially Lecture II.

dominate colleagues' careers. Control of the Cabinet's agenda permits the Prime Minister to determine what issues will be discussed and when, thus avoiding consideration of issues that he or she wishes to ignore. Since the Prime Minister formulates the Cabinet Conclusions (the official record of what the Cabinet decided), he or she can put the best face on the discussion. Although he always denied doing so, Prime Minister Wilson's fudging of the record to make it appear that his views enjoyed broad Cabinet support was a source of frequent complaint by members of his Government. The Prime Minister further controls the actions of the Cabinet through the power to create Cabinet committees and determine their scope of action and rules of procedure. These committees, which are used to shape issues so they can be dealt with promptly when they reach the Cabinet, exist only at the Prime Minister's discretion. Since the Prime Minister decides who will serve on them, he or she can stack the membership to get the type of recommendation desired. Finally, the power relation is one-sided because the Cabinet must support any new policy announced by the Prime Minister, despite whether they were consulted about it beforehand. In contrast, ministers are likely to get the sack (be removed from office) should they initiate a change in policy without the Prime Minister's approval.

Turning to the second element in Prime Ministerial Government, domination of the bureaucracy, by serving as both First Lord of the Treasury and Minister for the Civil Service, the Prime Minister is the ultimate authority for the entire civil service. The Prime Minister decides which civil servant will be the top bureaucrat (the permanent secretary) in each department. (I'll explain the importance of the permanent secretary in the last part of this chapter.) This power is of greatest significance in the case of the Treasury. So prestigious is this department and so great is its control over financial management that the Treasury is perceived as having virtual veto power over proposals for new policies anywhere within the Government. Finally, the Prime Minister appoints the civil servant who functions as Secretary of the Cabinet, a post that controls the flow of the documents essential to decision making. In addition, the Cabinet Secretary serves as the professional, or career, head of the civil service.

The final element—domination of the party machine, which has long been a characteristic of the Conservative party—recently has become true of Labour as well. Campaign literature (see Figures 4.4 and 4.5) emphasizing party Leaders has become common. In addition, television coverage of elections and nonelectoral politics has tended to focus on the Leaders. Increasingly, British elections have seemed to turn not so much on which party should control the government—as had been the basic choice for the electorate—as on who should be Prime Minister. Being an electoral asset strengthens a Prime Minister's position as party Leader. No sensible party would want to lose or weaken someone who can help it gain votes. Thus, a popular

Figure 4 ✦ 4 Conservative poster for the 1979 election campaign

Prime Minister is likely to have firm control of his or her party. Beyond this, the Conservatives long have organized their party to make the national head-quarters the personal machine of the Leader. Although Labour's organization continues to differ, during the 1980s Neil Kinnock, its Leader, was accorded

The majority of British people
don't want thirteen years of
Margaret Thatcher.
  They are certain of that.
  What the majority is less
certain of is how best to
achieve that result.
  You can object to Margaret
Thatcher by voting for just
about anyone.
  And if you vote Liberal or SDP
you may - you just may - hope to
dislodge a Tory MP.
  But there is a hard fact of
political arithmetic you should
always remember.
  The SDP and Liberals can never
gain enough seats to change the
government of this country.
  Only by voting Labour is it
possible to defeat the
Conservatives.
  The choice before the majority
is therefore:
  Do you vote with a protest?
  Or do you vote with a purpose?
  Only Labour can win.
  Together we will win.

**Together
we will
win**

Figure 4 ✦ 5 Labour leaflet for the 1987 election campaign

sufficient latitude in making the party electorally competitive again that his control over the party machine began to rival that of the Conservative Leader.

Strong as this evidence is supporting the theory of Prime Ministerial Government, a contrary case can be made. Power relations within the executive depend a great deal on the experience and style of the Prime Minister. During her early years as Prime Minister, Thatcher lost several battles in the Cabinet and had to alter her policies to satisfy her colleagues. A key event in giving her dominance was the success of her military response to Argentina's attempt to seize the Falkland Islands, which greatly enhanced her popularity with the public. Furthermore, as time passed she was able to eliminate, one by one, critics from the Cabinet to produce a group likely to agree with her views. Her style became increasingly imperious and is nicely summarized by the following widely told joke. Thatcher takes her Cabinet to dinner. After the waiter has her order for the main course, he inquires, "What about the vegetables?" She responds, "They'll have the same thing I'm having." What made this humorous was that such a comment from her seemed all too plausible. She dominated her colleagues to a greater extent than any other peacetime Prime Minister in the twentieth century. Uniquely among all Britain's Prime Ministers, she so shaped Government policy to her values and goals that her name became an "ism." The label "Thatcherism" was commonly used to refer to the Government's program during her period in office.

Despite her great power, however, she was vulnerable. One of the charges made by the former Cabinet member who challenged her for the Leadership was that she had destroyed all aspects of collective decision making. Furthermore, although being an electoral asset helps a Prime Minister to dominate the party machine, being an electoral liability undermines one's continuance in office. Thatcher was so closely identified with the hugely unpopular community charge that many Conservative legislators came to fear that they would lose their seats if she led the party into the next election. Fearful as they were of retribution for failing to support her in the Leadership election, they were even more concerned about being cast out of office by the voters. Her hold on the party machine proved insufficient to mobilize all the support she needed.

Her successor as Prime Minister, John Major, is said to have restored a considerable measure of Cabinet Government. The Prime Minister now listens to what other members of the Cabinet have to say and decisions are made on a more collective basis. No law had been altered; only the personality of the Prime Minister had changed. Thus, British Government can be Prime Ministerial, but it needn't be so.

Furthermore, the idea that Prime Ministerial Government is presidential should be questioned. A comparison of the two offices indicates the constraints on the British chief executive. The Prime Minister lacks the huge staff of the U.S. President. The total number of employees in the Prime Minister's private office — counting not only clerks and typists, but messengers and cleaners as well — is under a hundred. Including those who work in the political office, the policy unit, and the press office would add only a handful more. Nor is the Prime Minister serviced by anything equivalent to the Executive Office of the President. The National Security Council, for example, is part of the Executive Office of the President; the similar Defence Committee is under the Cabinet in Britain.

Perhaps the most fundamental contrast is that Presidents enjoy a fixed term and Prime Ministers do not. Prime Ministers, as Thatcher discovered, are always vulnerable. From Theodore Roosevelt through Ronald Reagan, Presidents served from two and a half to twelve years. The average was about five and three-quarters years. During that same period, although Prime

Ministers served as long as eleven and a half years, they also served as little as six months. For them the average was four years.[6]

Since they can be forced out of office at any time, Prime Ministers must work constantly to retain the support of colleagues and followers. Lacking a fixed term, they can't be certain of surviving the bad times that any but the most lucky chief executive's government will encounter. A President can ignore dissent within the Cabinet with relative impunity; a Prime Minister cannot. Should key members of the British Cabinet resign, the Government might fall. Thatcher had managed to weather several resignations during her years in office. In the end, however, the departure of one of the most senior members of her Cabinet, who proceeded to deliver a highly critical speech in the House of Commons, triggered the Leadership challenge that drove her from office. She had flaunted her power and exhibited her disdain for her colleagues once too often.

Thus, whatever the strengths of the Prime Minister and however much they may have grown in recent years, Prime Ministers still have a long way to go to dominate the executive to the extent that U.S. Presidents do. The power concentrated in the office of Prime Minister is more accountable to the rest of the executive than is the President's power to the executive branch in the United States. Paradoxically, however, the British executive as a whole occupies a stronger (that is, less accountable) position within the political system than does the U.S. executive branch. The absence in Britain of the U.S. separation-of-powers system with its checks and balances gives the executive a dominance over the legislature unknown in the United States. Fusion of powers in Britain was supposed to make the executive *more* accountable; in practice, in the second half of the twentieth century, it has made it *less* accountable. (Again, explaining why this is so must wait until the legislative–executive relations portion of Chapter 5.)

Partisan: The Cabinet

British law says little more about the Cabinet than it does about the Prime Minister. Its powers, functions, and membership are almost wholly a matter of custom (the unwritten constitution again). No statute lists the offices whose holders must be included in the Cabinet, nor is its size specified, both in contrast to the United States. Usually the Cabinet numbers about eighteen to twenty-four politicians. With only rare exceptions, all its members will have a seat in either the House of Commons or the House of Lords. Despite

---

6. Were it not for assassination and death in office of Presidents, neither of which has occurred in the twentieth century to Prime Ministers, the greater longevity of Presidents would be even more marked.

Britain's fusion-of-powers system, this practice is not required by statute but simply is a constitutional convention. Most Cabinet members also serve as the head of some executive department, but not every department head is sufficiently important to be in the Cabinet. Those appointed to certain key offices, like the Foreign Secretary (the equivalent of the American Secretary of State), invariably are included in the Cabinet (again, as a matter of custom, not of statute). Although who is included is entirely up to the Prime Minister, the choice will be circumscribed by political considerations. Several of the Prime Minister's party colleagues will have to be included because of their experience and popularity within the party, which means that some will be people that he or she would have preferred to leave out. Many of those chosen will have served in the "Shadow Cabinet," the term designating the Parliamentary leaders of a party when it is out of power.

Since the Cabinet is so seldom mentioned in statute, it possesses little formal legal power. But because it is composed of the leaders of the party controlling Parliament, the Cabinet is in fact the most powerful organ of government. It can get the bills it wants passed by Parliament and prevent those it opposes from being enacted. It instructs those having statutory authority, such as department heads, how to use their power. Since the Cabinet is mainly a meeting of department heads, the group, in effect, is telling the individual members what they are to do. The Cabinet, then, decides what policies shall be enacted, coordinates those decisions to prevent their being contradictory, and supervises their implementation.

Prior to World War I, the Cabinet operated very informally; there were no agendas, no minutes, no record of decisions other than a letter sent by the Prime Minister to the monarch reporting on the meetings. This produced frequent confusion, as you might expect. Such a system was tolerable in peacetime but not during a major war. So, in 1916 a Cabinet secretariat was created; it now is institutionalized as the Cabinet Office. The Cabinet Office issues notices for meetings of the Cabinet and of Cabinet committees, prepares the Cabinet agenda (under the Prime Minister's direction), circulates memoranda and documents relevant to items on the agenda, and takes minutes of Cabinet discussions and decisions. These minutes, called Cabinet Conclusions, outline the main points of the discussion (without attributing them to any particular member) and summarize what the Cabinet agreed on. All ministers (those holding executive positions), despite whether they are members of the Cabinet, receive copies of the Conclusions. This informs them of any action required by their departments. The Cabinet Office monitors action to verify that Cabinet decisions are implemented.

Normally, the Cabinet meets for two to three hours one morning each week. The Prime Minister can convene it at any time and additional meetings are not uncommon. Because the relevant ministers or Cabinet committees are expected to have discussed an issue in some detail before it comes to the

Cabinet, lengthy debates on a single topic are unusual. Thus, the Cabinet can cover several matters in a typical meeting.

The Cabinet does much of its work through a variety of committees — some composed of politicians only but others including civil servants as well. Technically, these committees were secret; not only was no list published of who served on each of them, the committees were not even acknowledged to exist. Nonetheless, journalists and scholars managed to obtain some information about them from time to time. A legislation committee, for example, was in charge of seeing that Government bills progressed through Parliament on schedule. Other committees deal with subjects like defense or education. In 1992 as a contribution to his goal of open government, Prime Minister Major released a list of some of these committees and their members.

Formal voting in the Cabinet is extremely rare. When the Prime Minister feels a subject has been discussed sufficiently, he or she will "collect the voices." Cabinet members in turn briefly state their views. The Prime Minister sums up with what seems to him or her to be the sense of the comments (not necessarily the same thing as just counting the number for and against) and that becomes Government policy.

No matter how much they may disagree behind the closed doors of the Cabinet room, all Cabinet members are obligated to tell the public the same story. Unless a member is so opposed to a decision as to be willing to resign from the Cabinet, he or she becomes as responsible for it as those who supported it. Even ministers outside the Cabinet, who have had no direct voice in making most of the Government's policies, must resign if they are not willing to defend all Cabinet decisions. No one remaining in the Government can later defend themselves from criticism by saying they had argued against the policy.

This united front, known as collective responsibility, is required not by any constitutional document or statute, but by convention; collective responsibility is an excellent example of this element of the unwritten constitution. A practical effect of collective responsibility is to transform any challenge to a minister in Parliament on his or her department's policies into an attack on the entire Government. To censure the minister would drive the Government (Prime Minister, Cabinet, and all) from office. The Government need not, however, defend a minister's errors of judgment or faulty administration. Collective responsibility is concerned only with matters of policy. If a minister resigns for failure to run his or her department properly, the Government does not fall because in that case only individual responsibility is involved. (I discuss individual responsibility later in this chapter.)

Although widely regarded as a constitutional principle, collective responsibility was flouted during the 1970s. Despite the Labour Government's support for continuing British membership in the EEC, many Labour supporters, including some Cabinet members, wanted Britain to withdraw. As the

1975 referendum on the issue approached, Labour's leaders decided to permit Cabinet ministers to oppose the Government's policy in speeches around the country and even to vote against it in the House of Commons. They were prohibited, however, from speaking against the Government's position in the Commons; thus, the fiction that the Government had a single official view was maintained. Clearly, collective responsibility was violated.[7] This departure from collective responsibility was defended on the grounds that the issue was unique and thus would create no precedent. But only two years later the same violation of collective responsibility was permitted on the issue of popular election of the EEC Parliament.

Controversy over the doctrine arose again in the mid-1980s during the Westland Affair. The Cabinet had decided that a British manufacturer of helicopters seeking a defense contract should be allowed to decide for itself whether to be linked with an American company or with a European group of companies — the latter option being strongly favored by the Defence Secretary, Michael Heseltine. Instead of demanding Heseltine's resignation, Prime Minister Thatcher colluded in an effort to discredit him. He then resigned, complaining that Cabinet meetings that were to have been held weren't and that no chance had been given to settle the matter on the basis of full information. Collective responsibility, Heseltine asserted, required collective decision making, not Prime Ministerial domination. (As you learned earlier in this chapter, a few years later he challenged her in the Leadership contest that drove her from office.) Thatcher responded that she was the true defender of collective responsibility. In her view the Defence Secretary was violating it by working for the European option when the Cabinet had taken a hands-off stance. Either the practitioners themselves don't know what collective responsibility involves or they regard the doctrine not so much as a constitutional principle but as a club to be used to beat up on one's political opponents.

The doctrine seems to have become a weapon for dealing with relatively manageable dissent within the Government. If the dissidents are few or insignificant, they are required to accept the majority view or resign. But collective responsibility no longer has much force when sharp cleavages divide the Government. Should the minority be sizable or include prominent party leaders, collective responsibility is modified or ignored to avoid splitting the party and driving the Government from office.

Furthermore, circumstances common in the United States, but previously unusual in Britain, are beginning to occur: People who did not resign from the Government later seek to divorce themselves from its shortcomings.

---

7. For the relevant documents see Harold Wilson, *The Governance of Britain* (New York: Harper & Row, 1976), pp. 191–197.

They suggest that they tried at the time to convince their colleagues that certain policies were undesirable and, when they couldn't do so, simply went along with them. They grant that they were part of the Government that took the unpopular action, but deny that they were to blame for it. Political expediency seems to have triumphed over collective responsibility; now, in practice, the United States and Britain do not differ greatly on this aspect of executive policy making.

The shifting meaning of collective responsibility in Britain — the change in required behavior — demonstrates how Britain's unwritten Constitution evolves over time. Practice alters, new precedents are created, a constitutional convention is modified. Note also that because collective responsibility is a convention (which, as I explained in Chapter 3, means a practice that can't be the basis for a legal judgment), no one could haul Prime Ministers Wilson or Thatcher into court on a charge of violating the Constitution because they had permitted departures from past practice.

Since the Cabinet is composed of the top executive leaders, most of its members will have the formal title Secretary of State for . . . , such as Secretary of State for Defence or Secretary of State for Health.[8] The Secretary, along with two to four associate colleagues, gives political direction to the department (see Figure 4.6). The Secretary serves at the pleasure of the Prime Minister, as do the associates, who are picked by the Prime Minister in consultation with the Secretary.

Policy and administration fuse at the Secretary's level. As Members of Parliament and of the Government, Secretaries are both policymakers and administrators. Clearly, they can devote only part time to the latter job, although they are responsible to the House of Commons for it. Secretaries must spend much time in the Commons for debates, keep in touch with their constituents, and be involved in party activities. In addition, a fair amount of time is consumed by meetings of the Cabinet and its committees.

Secretaries can delegate some of their tasks to their political assistants, variously titled Minister of State, Undersecretary of State, or Parliamentary Secretary. Holders of one or another of these positions usually are referred to as junior ministers to distinguish them from the full ministers, the Secretaries, who hold the top executive positions. Unlike the other assistants, Ministers of State have some discretionary powers. The Parliamentary Secretaries

---

8. The title used to be Minister of . . . or Minister for . . . hence the generic term *minister*, which I've been using to refer to a holder of executive office. Now the head of virtually every department is styled Secretary of State for . . . ; the main exception is the Chancellor of the Exchequer at the Treasury. In addition there are a few sinecures, offices without departmental duties, such as the Lord Privy Seal or the Lord President of the Council.

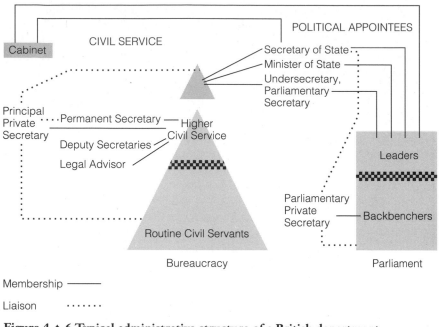

Figure 4 ✦ 6 Typical administrative structure of a British department

and the Undersecretaries, however, merely relieve their superiors of less important duties. By learning the business of a department, these assistants gain the experience that will help them qualify for eventual promotion to the rank of Secretary of State — should their careers prosper. But meanwhile they cannot decide policy on their own. They cannot even override the civil servants, but must refer any problems or questions to their Secretary of State. Nonetheless, junior ministers are members of the Government. Counting both ministers and junior ministers, a typical Government will number about a hundred people. Since the Prime Minister has the sole or major voice in appointing these, the breadth of his or her power is manifest.

Almost all ministers and junior ministers have seats in either the House of Commons or the House of Lords (remember the constitutional principle of fusion of powers). When a Secretary of State is in the Lords, his or her immediate assistant must be in the Commons, so that someone will be present to defend the department's policies in the legislative chamber that can censure the Government. Since all ministers of whatever rank must loyally support the Government, the Prime Minister can count on a disciplined voting bloc (well over a quarter of the controlling majority) to help get his or her legislation through the House of Commons. The crucial core of support is referred to somewhat derisively as the payroll vote.

Also assisting the Secretary is a Parliamentary Private Secretary (PPS), who *is* a Member of Parliament, but, strictly speaking, *not* part of the Government. He or she receives no pay in addition to a legislator's salary (unlike the others I've mentioned) for helping with executive activities. Since PPSs aren't members of the Government, they are allowed a bit more freedom in their legislative voting. Nonetheless, they "are expected to support the Government in all important divisions . . . no Parliamentary Private Secretary who votes against the Government may retain his or her position."[9]

Given their lack of prominence, PPSs can mingle freely with other ordinary legislators, who are likely to be less guarded in their comments than they would be if talking to someone in the Government. By conveying rank-and-file legislators' concerns, PPSs help their Secretaries avoid making proposals that would not be endorsed by those usually supporting them. They also can explain their Secretaries' views to ordinary legislators without seeming to threaten them, as similar information from one of those responsible for managing the Government's supporters might be perceived.

The Secretary alone is responsible to Parliament for a department's actions. Civil servants do not have to answer publicly for administrative errors or bad judgments. Those who make mistakes will be criticized and, perhaps, disciplined by their Secretaries, but in private. The British do not believe that civil servants should be dragged into the political arena; only politicians should face that occupational hazard. The Secretary, therefore, shields the civil servants from blame and, in return, expects to receive from them faithful service and absolute loyalty. A grave failure of administration by a civil servant may force a Secretary to resign as political head of a department and leave the Government. If he or she can assure the Commons, however, that it was impossible to know about the action before it occurred and that steps have been taken to ensure that this can't happen again, then a mere apology to Parliament may be sufficient to avoid resignation. These customary procedures are known as individual ministerial responsibility, which differs from the doctrine of collective responsibility I discussed earlier in this chapter. Individual responsibility focuses on shortcomings in administering the government; collective responsibility is concerned with the substance of policy.

Although the requirements of individual responsibility are well known to those to whom they apply, this convention, like that of collective responsibility, seems to have seriously eroded in recent years. In four and a half decades since the end of World War II only eighteen Secretaries have resigned on grounds of individual responsibility. Furthermore, recent cases have been more likely to involve personal scandals than bad administration. Even where administration was the issue, individual responsibility has received only ambiguous

---

9. Cabinet Office, "Questions of Procedure for Ministers," paragraph #47, published by HMSO, London, 1992.

support. In 1982 the Foreign Secretary and two of his associates resigned because they had failed to perceive the seriousness of the Argentine threat to the Falkland Islands (and thus had voiced no diplomatic warning that could have discouraged the invasion that occurred). Although they clearly were accepting blame for having run things badly, this hardly was a case of civil servant error for which supervising politicians had to pay the cost.

I've already mentioned the Westland Affair in the mid-1980s. The resignation of the Defence Secretary, Michael Heseltine, was an example of collective responsibility; he was unwilling to support the Prime Minister's position and objected to what he regarded as her high-handed manner of setting policy without adequate consultation of colleagues. Another minister, Leon Britton, who headed the department from which the information was leaked — information intended to undercut the Defence Secretary's position — resigned at the same time. This resignation appeared to be a clear case of individual responsibility. The minister endeavored, however, to escape blame for the leak by saying that it was the fault of his civil servants. Furthermore, contrary to traditional practice, the civil servants involved were publicly identified rather than being accorded the usual anonymity. When the minister resigned, he commented that he felt he had to do so because he no longer enjoyed adequate support among his party's legislators. He was well aware that many of them were disgusted with the devious way in which this affair was conducted and had sufficient admiration for the Defence Secretary that a sacrificial victim had to be found.

The practice of individual responsibility also has been made less compelling by instances in which a minister did not resign despite failures in administration. For example, in 1983, thirty-eight members of the terrorist Irish Republican Army, in jail for various criminal activities, escaped. Although the subsequent investigation cited a wide range of failures at the prison and recommended seventy-three improvements in security, the relevant minister declined to resign. Furthermore, in contrast to previous practice, he did not even argue that he was remaining in office because he had made changes that would ensure that such a thing couldn't happen again; he specifically said that he couldn't guarantee that it wouldn't. Another smaller such jail break occurred in 1991 involving a different minister; he also declined to resign.

These instances pose serious questions about whether individual responsibility remains a convention of the British Constitution. Cabinets now seem inclined either to treat a colleague's poor administrative performance as a matter of collective, rather than individual, responsibility or to overlook it entirely, thus sparing the minister the embarrassment of resigning. Individual responsibility tends to be enforced only for matters that *don't* raise fundamental issues. Late in the 1980s Britain had a brief scare when it appeared that due to inadequate inspection British eggs might be a source of salmonella. Although the furor was overblown, the Undersecretary of State for Health, Edwina Currie, appeared to dismiss the problem too lightly. The resultant

Figure 4 ✦ 7 Government Office buildings on Whitehall

public outcry forced her to resign from the Government. Apparently, only in such instances does having egg on your face cost you your job.

The decline of the convention of individual responsibility weakens the accountability of administrative power. If the minister is not, in practice, responsible and the civil servants continue to be insulated from public criticism to guard their efficiency, then *no one* is accountable. Abandoning the doctrine of individual ministerial responsibility destroys the effective solution that the British had devised to the basic problem of public administration: how to reconcile efficiency with accountability.

Merit

The job of the partisan executive is to make policy; the job of the merit executive is to implement it. In practice, however, the division of responsibility is not quite that neat. A small portion of the merit executive is involved in making policy, which raises important questions of accountability. British bureaucracy often is referred to as Whitehall, the name of the London street on which many head administrative offices are located (see Figure 4.7).[10]

As Figure 4.6 shows, immediately below the handful of politicians at the top of a department is a career civil servant, known as a permanent secretary, who is the actual administrative chief of the department. He or she is responsible for the organization and efficiency of the department and for the advice

---

10. The picture at the start of Part Two is taken from the foot of Whitehall, where it joins Parliament Square. The Palace of Westminster (where Parliament meets) is just out of the picture to the right.

given to the Secretary of State by the career staff. Subordinate civil servants may not deal directly with the Secretary of State without the knowledge and approval of the permanent secretary. Since the permanent secretary will, in most cases, have been at the top of the department much longer than the Secretary of State, the former is excellently placed to influence policy. The British elite believes that truly capable people can't be recruited into public service and be motivated to make it a career unless they see some prospect of eventually reaching a position of influence. The structure of the British civil service facilitates doing so because, in contrast to the structure of the American executive branch, top positions (often referred to as the higher civil service) are much nearer to the locus of policy making.

The officials working most closely with a minister are the permanent secretary and the principal private secretary.[11] The latter is a promising young civil servant (a "high flyer") whom the minister has designated as a special assistant. The principal private secretary shields the minister from unnecessary engagements and needless paperwork. He or she also has the delicate task of maintaining good relations with both the permanent secretary and the medium-level civil servants in the department. In attempting to make the department seem completely in agreement on a particular policy or to make decisions easier by limiting the range of options, the permanent secretary may not wish to report conflicting views. On the other hand, the private secretary must be certain that contrasting views and doubts are *not* filtered out but reach the minister. Medium-level civil servants may speak more freely to the private secretary because he or she, unlike the permanent secretary, is not their superior in the chain of command and has no direct control over their career prospects. In short, the role of the principal private secretary on the administrative side is quite similar to that of the PPS on the legislative side.

Although the position is a coveted appointment, a private secretary must endure the tension of divided loyalties. The role requires being the minister's personal assistant, but that minister soon will move on to another position. The permanent secretary, however, will continue to serve as part of the network of elite civil servants. If a high flyer has been so assiduous in reporting activities within the department to the minister that he or she has crossed the permanent secretary, a crash is entirely likely and a promising career may never again take wing. Those who can serve two masters without irritating either deserve any subsequent promotion they receive.

A department's legal advisor and its few deputy secretaries also will have some contact with the minister. All the civil servants mentioned are expected

---

11. Despite the similarity of initials, do not confuse the principal private secretary with the previously mentioned Parliamentary Private Secretary.

to serve each succeeding minister loyally, whatever their political views.[12] Only by keeping out of the political arena and performing as faceless mandarins can they play this role. British practice contrasts sharply with the practice in both the United States and France. In the United States turnover in top posts within a department is high from one Administration to another because most of the jobs are political and are not career positions; in France a political executive brings along to a department a personal group of trusted advisors, many of whom are career civil servants. Thus, in both France and the United States, the political head of a department has his or her trusted colleagues to run things. In Britain, the politician (the Secretary of State heading the department) must make do with assistants already in place; they owe little to him or her for having advanced to where they are, and they can expect little help from him or her in furthering their careers in the future. Thus the tradition of loyal service to all masters is all that the British minister can count on in trying to direct the department in implementing his or her party's program.

Trust between politician and civil servant has been more of a problem for the Labour party than for the Conservatives, due to the social background of the typical civil servant. This problem may be a result of the alleged bias in the recruitment procedures. Both written examinations and oral interviews are used to recruit for higher-level positions in the civil service. The written exam tests general knowledge, proficiency in English, and command of two or three academic subjects that the applicant selects from among many options. The British recruit civil servants on the basis of general ability rather than on the basis of technical expertise and training for a specific position. Conventional wisdom holds that top minds can quickly learn the specific requirements of a position after being appointed to it. Much of the British elite remains convinced that a knowledge of classical Greek excellently prepares one for life and is admirable training for being in charge of public affairs. This bias in recruiting is the reason for the most frequently heard criticism of the British civil service: It is obsessed with the cult of the amateur. The subject-matter expert, it is charged, too often is relegated merely to supplying technical information to the amateur or generalist, who is the one empowered to make the decisions that shape policy.

The other bias in recruiting is related more directly to the question of trust and loyalty. A disproportionately low number of people from working-class backgrounds is recruited into the higher civil service. The typical civil

---

12. When Bernard, the private secretary on the British TV comedy series "Yes, Minister" (which has been aired on U.S. TV) worried about whether he was becoming a moral vacuum, Sir Humphrey, the permanent secretary, responded, "Oh, I hope so, Bernard, I hope so."

servant at the level to influence policy has gone from a public school to Oxford or Cambridge. Many people, particularly those supporting Labour, feel that the oral interviews are the culprit. They believe that the interviewers are easily impressed by applicants with the proper social background. Even lack of knowledge and shallow thinking are excused if an interviewee, because of the right background, is thought to be suitable for the civil service. Similar shortcomings in a person from the working class would be treated as grounds for rejection, and an able person with that background may be passed over because he or she lacks some of the social graces. A TV documentary on the work of interview committees provided evidence that these practices are not just some class conspiracy theory, but the reality.

Few would deny that the top British civil servants are highly intelligent and extremely able. The concern is whether their academic preparation provides them with too little knowledge of science and technology and of management techniques. To the extent that this is true, efficiency is undermined. And to the extent that the class base of the civil service is narrow, accountability is jeopardized. Calling any bureaucracy to account without harming efficiency and introducing undesirable partisanship is difficult. In Britain the problem is compounded further: how can a civil service — composed of people who have had little direct experience with the lives of average citizens — adequately consider the people's needs and concerns? Is not such a bureaucracy more likely to require accountability than one rather more representative of the population?

In addition to the impact that social class background may have on their political views, top civil servants may be cautious and suspicious of innovation for another reason. Almost invariably the top civil servants, as career merit personnel, will have been with a particular department considerably longer than the Secretary of State, whose service depends upon shifting electoral fortunes and changing power relations within a party. Thus, the civil servants may know more about a topic than does the minister; they certainly are likely to think that they understand the practical complexities better. Furthermore, since ministers come and go, the civil servants feel they are the ones who will have to clean up any mess resulting from a mistake in policy.[13] If the British are a people who believe that nothing should ever be done for the first time, this attitude reaches its apotheosis among the higher civil service. The problem is particularly acute for a reform party, like Labour. The difficulty is not so much that civil servants are Conservative partisans, as that they resist change simply because it is inconvenient. Change disrupts the comfortable

---

13. "Yes, Minister" was not just humorous, but highly accurate as well. If you have seen even one or two episodes, you will have a good idea of the way in which British civil servants are likely to regard politicians.

existing pattern of activities. Thus, top civil servants are likely to respond to any new proposal with reasons why it shouldn't be implemented rather than trying to figure out how it can be implemented. Only a determined minister can avoid having reforms shunted onto a side track. For probity, loyalty, discretion, and intelligence the British civil service probably is unsurpassed. Whether it provides the ideal instrument for reform — of whatever type — is another question.

Summary

Britain has a dual executive: the monarch serves as head of State and the Prime Minister as head of Government. The monarch's duties are ceremonial; he or she reigns, but does not rule. Despite lacking any significant power, the monarch performs an important function in legitimating and maintaining the governmental system.

The partisan portion of the executive in Britain had developed as a collective entity, a *group* of advisors to the monarch. Eventually, however, a *prime* minister emerged and, increasingly in the latter part of the twentieth century, became preeminent. Nonetheless, to say that the British executive has been "Presidentialized," is an overstatement. The story that after everyone but he in his Cabinet had voted nay, President Lincoln declared, "The ayes have it," may be apocryphal, but nicely captures the essence of power relations in American government. A British Prime Minister could not defy his or her Cabinet that way. Furthermore, although the Prime Minister's staff surpasses that available to the Cabinet, it fails to rival the size and complexity of that supporting the U.S. President. The President dominates the executive branch of American government to a much greater extent than the Prime Minister dominates the British executive. Even under Margaret Thatcher, who probably was unique, the British executive was more collective than the American. Thus, although some observers have worried about whether the Prime Minister remains responsible, this is *not* the point in British government at which to worry about whether accountability still is able to constrain concentrated power.

A cause for greater concern is whether the merit executive is accountable to the partisan executive. The British executive differs from the American in the structure of the government departments and the influence over policy that this gives to top-level civil servants. Permanent secretaries and their immediate associates shape government's action to a greater extent than do the highest civil servants in the United States. One might think that this would give Britain more expert government than the United States, but the cult of the amateur in the British civil service makes that questionable. The failure to capitalize fully on a potential asset is not nearly as important, however, as is the potential liability of undermining democratic accountability. The attenuation of individual ministerial responsibility makes the structure of British administration more of a flaw than an advantage.

Accountability concerns are not limited to relations between various segments of the executive. Also at issue is whether the Cabinet — both as a group and as individual members — is accountable. In theory, Parliament constrains the power concentrated in the British executive by keeping its activities under surveillance and calling it to account. Why, as Sherlock Holmes might put it, has this watchdog failed to bark? As this chapter explained, both collective and individual responsibility have weakened in recent years. Their decline has hampered Parliament's ability to call the executive to account.

Chapter 5 will show that the problem is even more serious. Defects in Parliament's powers and procedures also impede effective performance of its key role in the British system of monitoring the executive. So, we need to turn to examining how Parliament operates and considering whether the steps that Britain is taking to remedy its flaws are sufficient. Given the extent to which this chapter has shown that power is concentrated in Britain, the status of Parliament clearly is a crucial issue.

5

✦

The Legislature

The American Founding Fathers separated powers among three branches of government so that no single one would predominate. Thus, at times the United States has had strong Presidents and at other times Congress has been the focal point for making public policy. The British system is fundamentally different. As I explained in Chapter 3, one of its basic constitutional principles is Parliamentary supremacy. In its early years the Cabinet was to be a buffer between the monarch and the Parliament. As the monarch came merely to reign and no longer rule, however, that Cabinet function atrophied. That left the Cabinet with the job of coordinating public policy and organizing the work of Parliament so that two chambers, each with hundreds of members, could function efficiently. The executive was to be something of a business manager for the legislature.

Performing this function implies some element of leadership. Nonetheless, the Cabinet was not intended to have an independent life; fusion of powers meant that the executive was to be a creature of the legislature. The Cabinet was *not* to dominate the legislature at any time. Parliament was willing for the Cabinet to exercise some power because the executive was on a leash. Whenever it wished,

Parliament could rein in an executive that had gotten too big for itself. The executive was accountable to the legislature.

To a considerable extent this is the way in which the system functioned for two centuries following the Glorious Revolution in 1688. Parliamentary supremacy (in practice, as distinct from constitutional theory) reached full fruition in the middle of the nineteenth century, a time often referred to now as the Golden Age of Parliament. In the twentieth century this evolution has been reversed. Parliamentary supremacy has given way to Cabinet Government, which in turn may have been replaced by Prime Ministerial Government. Chapter 4 examined these developments on the executive side; this chapter discusses the associated, perhaps, enabling developments on the legislative side. The central issue is the extent to which the executive has come to dominate the legislature (contrary to the traditional structure of the system) and what that implies for constraining concentrated power through accountability.

As in the American legislature, the British legislature has two chambers. The so-called upper house — the House of Lords with its hereditary earls, viscounts, and barons — is the more showy, apparently prestigious, part of the legislature. Just as the more glamorous part of the executive is the least powerful, however, the same is true of the legislature. The Lords has lost the great bulk of its power to the plebeian House of Commons. Nonetheless, like the monarch, the Lords serves a function. Therefore, although the heart of this chapter concerns the House of Commons and its relations with the efficient executive, an initial focus on the House of Lords is worthwhile.

The House of Lords

A prominent Labour politician who served in the Cabinet from 1945 to 1951 and later was a member of the House of Lords wrote a text on British government after he retired from politics. He observed that the "fact that the House of Lords has many irrational features is not in itself fatal in British eyes, for we have a considerable capacity for making the irrational work; and if a thing works we tend rather to like it, or at any rate to put up with it."[1] A more quintessentially British comment would be hard to find.

Perhaps the first irrationality is the Lords' size: a formal membership of around 1,200, so huge as to be completely unwieldy. A member of the Lords once commented that "this is undoubtedly the only institution in the world which is kept efficient by the persistent absenteeism of the great majority of its members." Indeed, most of those eligible to attend never show up. The

---

1. Lord Morrison of Lambeth, *Government and Parliament*, 3d ed. (London: Oxford University Press, 1964), p. 205.

largest vote occurred in 1971, when 509 lords voted on the question of British membership in the EEC. The issue of the poll tax produced nearly as large a vote in 1988. The typical working size of the Lords, the number of active members, is around 300 — much more manageable.

A second apparent irrationality is the requirement for membership. That a leading Western democracy could, at the close of the twentieth century, still fill a governmental structure on the basis of heredity boggles the mind. This explains why most of the members never attend: They did not seek membership; their fathers (most titles descend through males) died and left them a title — formally, known as a peerage — and that in itself makes them members of the Lords. What saves the Lords from being a complete anachronism is appointive, as well as hereditary, membership. Since (as you learned in Chapter 2) Britain has an established religion, the twenty-six men (women aren't permitted to hold these positions) appointed archbishops and bishops of the Church of England automatically become members of the Lords. Eleven distinguished jurists are appointed as lords of appeal in ordinary to serve as the country's highest judges (more about the judicial functions of the House of Lords in Chapter 6).

The main source of appointive members, however, is the Life Peerages Act of 1958, which permits appointing people to the Lords for their lifetime only; their title and membership do *not* pass to their descendants. Prior to that Act, able people who objected in principle to hereditary aristocracy would refuse a title and, thus, could not be appointed to the Lords. Perhaps equally important, this Act brought women into the Lords for the first time. Another irrational arrangement held that even the few women who had inherited a title were barred from the Lords. Life peerages, however, could be awarded to women as well as men. Life peers (a peer is someone holding a peerage) now account for about a third of the Lords' total membership and are an even larger proportion of its active members.

Even in the latter part of the nineteenth century when the Lords possessed some power, it was an object of ridicule. The well-known musical comedy team of Gilbert and Sullivan wrote a song whose lyrics proclaimed that "the House of Peers, throughout the war, did nothing in particular, and did it very well." Few laughed, however, when early in the twentieth century the Lords created a constitutional crisis by vetoing the Government's Budget because their lordships felt that the tax increases needed for new social programs were too radical. This conflict led to passage of the Parliament Act of 1911, which curtailed the Lords' power and clearly made the Commons the dominant house.

The Lords' powers became controversial again following World War II when it appeared that the upper house might try to block the Labour Government's program of taking many privately owned enterprises into government ownership, in particular, the iron and steel industry. Again a statute was passed (the Parliament Act of 1949) further curtailing the Lords' power. As noted in Chapter 3, since both statutes altered the power of a governmental organ, they usually are considered part of the British Constitution. Yet neither required extraordinary majorities for passage, nor approval by a referendum or subnational units of government.

The arrangement following these two Acts is that both Houses must pass a bill for it to become law (just as is true in the United States). When they disagree, however, no joint conference committee of members from both Houses (such as is used in the U.S. Congress) is set up to work out a compromise. Instead, the bill is shuttled back and forth in an attempt to revise it sufficiently to be acceptable to both Houses. Should these attempts fail, the bill cannot be enacted unless the Commons wishes to override the Lords. To do so, the bill must be reintroduced in exactly the same form the following year and passed again by the Commons. Thus, the Lords can delay, but not block, the will of the popularly elected House. This power of delay can be especially important near the end of a Government's term. Should the Government lose the election and be turned out of office, it will have no opportunity to reintroduce the bill; the Lords' suspensive, delaying veto will be transformed into a permanent one. For financial bills the Lords' powers are much more curtailed. Such bills become law thirty days after passage by the Commons despite any opposition from the Lords.

Usually these limits on the Lords do not come into play. Should the Commons insist on a bill and refuse to accept the changes the Lords favors, then the Lords gives in and doesn't block passage. Although Government defeats in the Lords have become more prevalent recently, a total of about 100 instances for the decade of the 1980s hardly makes them an everyday event. Slightly more than half the time, the Government accepts the Lords' wishes and does not use the Commons to override the upper house.

Some examples will help to clarify the Lords' typical effect on policy. When the Conservative Government was abolishing local governmental organs in the metropolitan areas, many people in the left wing of the Labour party were surprised to find themselves applauding the Lords — hardly their favorite organ of government. One of the Lords' concerns was that the proposed transitional arrangements would undercut accountability to the voters. The compromise that the Lords managed to wring out of the Government was to extend the life of the existing metropolitan councils for an additional year. Thus, the Lords could not prevent the Government from implementing its changes but was able to modify the process to help maintain a measure of popular control over local government. The House of Lords is not accountable, but that doesn't mean it is not unresponsive. Certainly some left-leaning local governments thought it worth the effort to produce ads and banners urging their Lordships on. The offices of London's local government were right across the river from the Houses of Parliament and anything displayed there was easily visible to legislators. Figure 5-1 shows the Palace of

Figure 5 ✦ 1 Palace of Westminster viewed from the south

Westminster (where Parliament meets) from the south. This end of the building is where the Lords meets (although their chamber can't be seen) and the River Thames is just to the right.

In another instance the Government planned to require local government to sell public housing accommodations to elderly tenants. Although this might seem like a reasonable idea, interest groups working for adequate housing for the elderly were concerned that such action would result in a shortage of low-rent housing for retirees who couldn't afford to buy. Here again a popular movement made common cause with the hereditary chamber. Because the relevant legislation contained other provisions that the Government was anxious to have enacted without delay, it gave way to the Lords' opposition and didn't try to restore the right-to-buy provision that the Lords had cut from the bill.

Such interest group activity in the Lords is common. A survey of interest groups of all types found that 70 percent of them had contacts with peers, nearly as many as had contacts with Members of the House of Commons.[2] The overwhelming majority (five-sixths) of the groups said that in recent years their organization had been concerned about one or another bill that

2. Michael Rush, ed., *Parliament and Pressure Politics* (Oxford, England: Clarendon Press, 1990) is an outstanding study of interest groups in the British legislative process. The Study of Parliament Group surveyed more than 250 groups of all types. An appendix (pp. 280–296) to the report provides the full distribution of responses to the questionnaire used.

Parliament was considering. When they were asked what they did about it, the *most* prevalent action (taken by more than three-fourths) was to contact a peer! Although one-fourth of the groups having contacts with peers thought dealing with the House of Commons was more useful in seeking to influence policy, nearly as many regarded the Lords as the more useful connection; nearly half felt that one chamber was no more useful than the other.

When asked why he robbed banks, the famous American criminal Willie Sutton replied, "That's where the money is." Similarly, interest groups in any country seek to focus their efforts where the power is. A leading authority on the Lords has offered a surprising view of that location: "By 1987 the impact of the Upper House in amending the actual content of bills was widely recognized to be greater than that of the House of Commons."[3] Some would question this assessment, while others would suggest that it says as much about the declining power of the Commons as it does about the importance of the Lords. British interest groups may labor under some misconceptions about their country's governmental system. Nonetheless, their interactions with the House of Lords caution against dismissing the upper house as irrelevant to the policy process.

Regardless of the Lords' importance in the policy process, a strong argument can be made to support its continued existence. The Lords' diverse membership enables it to hold informative debates by nonpartisan experts on topics of public interest. More important, the Lords performs significant tasks for which an overloaded Commons lacks time. The Lords can more fully debate bills that received only perfunctory discussion in the Commons, focusing in particular on amendments that the Commons added with little or no debate. Such supplementary activity also helps to prevent possible abuses and arbitrary action in the case of delegated legislation, provisional orders, and other such executive decrees. Much contemporary legislation in any democracy only sets forth general provisions and procedures and leaves the details of implementation to the bureaucracy. The framework law authorizes the executive branch to issue detailed regulations to achieve the goals set by the legislature. The power to issue such rules, typically called statutory instruments in Britain, must be controlled to ensure that the executive does not become a law unto itself. Parliament must be certain that the executive does not abuse this grant of power.

The Commons lacks the time, however, to discuss more than a handful of the approximately 1,000 statutory instruments issued each year. The Joint Committee on Statutory Instruments (composed of seven Members from each House) and the Commons' Standing Committee on Statutory Instruments do manage to examine many of them, but most receive little scrutiny by Parliament before going into effect. The House of Lords' consideration

---

3. Donald Shell, *The House of Lords* (Totowa, N.J.: Barnes and Noble, 1988), p. 151.

of some of them helps make this situation more tolerable. The Lords has more free time than does the Commons; it has people with legal training, and, since its members need not be concerned with attracting attention to help them get reelected, its people are willing to work on matters generally regarded as dull. Power is more accountable in Britain than it would be were the Lords to be abolished.

In summary, then, the verdict on the Lords is rather similar to that on the monarch: little power, some influence, and serving a useful purpose. This is not to say that one couldn't dream up another body that could perform the Lords' functions equally well. But, as Lord Morrison in effect said (in the quotation on page 94), if what you have already works, why bother?

The House of Commons

Peers luxuriate in a chamber of bright red leather-covered benches; the chamber is decorated with elaborately painted heraldic designs and coats of arms along with intricately carved woodwork and extensive gilt trim. The Members of the House of Commons make do with a chamber of subdued green leather-covered benches with little ornamentation. In fact, suggesting that all the irrationalities aren't concentrated in the House of Lords, the chamber for the House of Commons is too small to provide seats for all its Members. This arrangement is not as ridiculous as it might seem, however, and was done deliberately. When the chamber was rebuilt, after having been destroyed by a Nazi air raid during World War II, the original plan was basically replicated. (You can see the detailed arrangements in Figure 5.2, which presents an aerial view of the main floor of the Commons and its balcony as though you were looking straight down from the roof.) A small chamber was retained to preserve the conversational style of speaking that had characterized Commons' debates for centuries. A larger chamber, it was feared, would encourage bombastic rhetoric rather than reasoned discussion. Furthermore, if the chamber had seats for every Member, debates would seem poorly attended even if a majority of the Members was present. (First-time visitors to the U.S. House of Representatives are shocked to see what appears to be an almost empty chamber.)

The traditional floor plan of benches facing each other also wasn't altered because this arrangement was believed to reinforce a system of only two, clearly distinct parties. Crossing the floor (that is, switching parties) would require a more decisive move than in a semicircular seating arrangement, where one party's seats would shade into another's.[4] This argument seems

---

4. The prominent twentieth-century politician Winston Churchill was a Conservative, a Liberal, and a Conservative during the course of his lengthy career. Once when being wooed by the Liberals to return to them he commented, "You can rat and you can rerat, but you can't re-rerat."

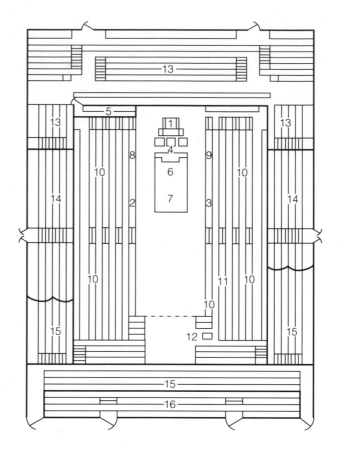

1. The Speaker
2. Prime Minister or Government spokesperson
3. Leader of the Opposition or Opposition spokesperson
4. Clerks at the table
5. Civil servants in attendance
6. The table
7. The mace
8. Government front bench, occupied by ministers
9. Opposition front bench
10. Back benches
11. Other opposition parties
12. Serjeant-at-arms
13. Hansard and press gallery
14. Members' side galleries
15. Special galleries, including peers', "distinguished strangers," diplomatic, and Commonwealth galleries
16. The public gallery

Figure 5 ✦ 2 Arrangement of seating in the House of Commons

curious to Americans, since both houses of the U.S. Congress and most state legislatures seat their members in a semicircle and still maintain a two-party system, with only a rare legislator, like Strom Thurmond, switching parties. However, Continental systems, where semicircular seating is associated with multiparty systems, are what the British had in mind.

At the head of the chamber sits a large, canopied chair, the seat of the presiding officer of the Commons: the Speaker; the Speaker wears the traditional garb of knee breeches, wig, and long black gown.[5] Contrary to the practice of the U.S. House of Representatives, the Speaker doesn't lead the majority party. Although when the position is vacant the majority party in the Commons usually determines who will become Speaker, it usually chooses a rather obscure, not leading, legislator who has been a Member of the Commons sufficiently long to demonstrate dedication to Parliament and knowledge of its procedures. Immediately upon election as Speaker, he or she severs all ties with his or her former party to perform the duties in a strictly nonpartisan fashion. Besides maintaining order in the Commons, the Speaker must ensure that all Members are treated fairly. The position is one of great authority and is widely respected.

In the United States explaining the powers of Congress requires examining not only Article I of the Constitution but also the myriad of Supreme Court cases interpreting its provisions. The British provision is much simpler. Recall that one of the constitutional principles is Parliamentary supremacy. This means Parliament can do whatever it wants; no limits whatsoever exist. Parliament may legislate on any subject it chooses and may require whatever action it prefers. The laws it enacts always are valid; no court may void them in whole or in part.

Bills go through three Readings in the House of Commons, just as in the U.S. Congress. A significant difference in procedure, however, is that committee stage comes *after* Second Reading, not *before*. This helps explain why committees are organized and operate much differently in the British legislature. Members of Congress introduce hundreds of bills each year. After a formal First Reading, which involves no discussion, they are sent to the relevant subject-matter committee. Part of the committees' function is to kill most of the bills they receive and only to report back for Second Reading a handful of bills to make Congress' workload manageable. In Britain few legislators propose bills because they know that almost no bill opposed by the Government has any prospect of passage. Furthermore, the Government so controls the Commons' agenda that little time is available to debate and vote

---

5. The British TV series (which has been shown on U.S. television) "Rumpole of the Bailey" provides a better description of procedures but isn't entirely realistic even though the writer, John Mortimer, was a barrister for years.

on bills introduced by individual Members. Thus, Commons committees, unlike Congressional ones, do not have to weed out bills. They do not need to guess which ones the full chamber wants to have reported out of committee for further consideration because the House already has made that clear. The legislative stage after the formal First Reading in the Commons is Second Reading. Then a bill's general purpose is discussed and only if this wins approval can the bill go on to committee. Such support means that the committee is not supposed to kill the bill but make those detailed changes that the Second Reading debate indicated the House desired.

The Commons' committees, in contrast to Congress, aren't organized by subject matter and, despite being called standing committees, don't have permanent membership (with the exception of committees dealing with legislation for Scotland and Wales). Committees are designated by a letter of the alphabet, not by a subject-matter title. When a bill passes Second Reading and is sent to a committee, the Committee on Selection appoints sixteen to thirty Members of the Commons to consider that bill only. The Committee on Selection tries to appoint Members particularly interested in or knowledgeable about the subject of the bill but isn't especially influenced by length of service in the Commons; nothing like the seniority system of the U.S. Congress exists. Nor does seniority determine the chair of the committee. The Speaker of the House appoints a Member who he or she feels can be just as impartial as is the Speaker. Therefore, the Speaker need not confine the choice to the party supporting the Government, but may select a Member from an opposition party. Once the committee has finished its detailed consideration of the bill and reported it back to the Commons, all the Members who served on it are discharged. Should that committee's letter of the alphabet be used again later in the session when another bill is sent to committee, the members would be selected afresh.

Clearly, the Commons' standing committees and, especially, their chairs are not significant foci of power, as in the Congress. Committee work is drudgery with few rewards. Rather than competing for appointment, the trick is to find enough legislators willing to be saddled with the task. Detailed revision of bills is all that standing committees do. Unlike Congressional committees, Commons standing committees do not gather information; they don't hold public hearings. This doesn't mean that their meetings are secret. The committee rooms have a few seats where the public may listen to the discussion, although few people bother to attend.

The limited function of British standing committees significantly affects the activity of interest groups. British committees don't call a long list of expert witnesses to speak for or against a bill. Anyone having relevant knowledge can do no more than contact one of the Members and hope that he or she will convey the information during the committee's work. The survey of interest groups mentioned above found that about half the groups sent material to standing committee members when a bill of concern to the group was being considered. To give such input its maximum effect, a British interest group might want to have a Member linked to the group serve on a committee considering a relevant bill. But, equally, the primary purpose of such a link might be to ensure that the group was fully informed about the details of the new legislation.

Bills of the greatest importance aren't sent to standing committee; instead they receive detailed consideration in the full chamber. This procedure is known as Committee of the Whole. The detailed changes made by committees of either type are discussed by the Commons during Report Stage. This is the last opportunity to consider substantive amendments. About half the interest groups expressing concern about particular bills say that they attempt to get them amended during either Committee or Report Stages.

Following Report Stage, a bill goes to Third Reading. The question now is whether the bill in its revised form is acceptable. Some Members who had questions about a bill may have voted for it on Second Reading because the executive promised that the bill would be revised in committee to meet their concerns. If this has not been done, these Members may be unwilling to vote for the bill on Third Reading; their previous support was conditional upon the detailed provisions of the bill being improved during the legislative process.

When a bill passes on Third Reading, it goes to the Lords. (Bills can begin in the upper house, but most start in the Commons.) I've already discussed what happens should the two Houses disagree. When they agree, the bill goes to the monarch for, as explained in Chapter 4, an automatic signature.

About three-fourths of the interest groups surveyed in a recent study reported having frequent contacts with Members of Parliament and, of those who did, half had a particular Member who looked out for their concerns. This may suggest more interest group involvement in the legislative process than actually is the case. Little more than a third of the groups had an employee responsible for keeping track of what was going on in Parliament and not all of these employees worked full time. Nonetheless, somewhat more than half the groups concerned about particular bills being considered by Parliament felt that their attempts to influence the legislation had been very or quite successful.

Although not a typical case, the conflict over the Shops Bill offers some insight into the role of groups in the legislative process.[6] The Government had introduced a bill that would permit stores to remain open longer hours—

---

6. Francis Brown, "The Defeat of the Shops Bill, 1986," in Michael Rush, ed., *Parliament and Pressure Politics* (Oxford, England: Clarendon Press, 1990), pp. 213–233.

especially, to do business on Sundays. Churches and various religious groups strongly opposed this change and launched an elaborate campaign to defeat the bill. Surprisingly (as you'll see later in this chapter the Government almost always gets what it wants from Parliament), the bill failed to pass the House of Commons. Was this due to the effectiveness of the interest group campaign? Not according to Members of Parliament. Among those Members of the governing party who broke with their leaders to vote against the bill, about twice as many reported that the views of their constituents, as opposed to the churches, had had the greatest impact on their vote. On the other hand, one could argue that the interest group campaign must have played a major role in alerting their constituents to the bill and galvanizing them into communicating their views to their Member. This case demonstrates that although the opportunities for interest groups to influence legislation are more circumscribed in Britain than in the United States, at times groups can make a difference.

Turning from the stages of legislation to the cycle of activities, each fall Parliament begins a new session (unless a general election has occurred at such a time that the usual schedule has to be altered) with the Speech from the Throne.[7] The monarch delivers this speech while sitting on a throne in the House of Lords, with the Lords seated as usual and Members of the Commons standing crowded together at the foot of the chamber. The monarch has no say about the content of the speech; the Cabinet has decided what will be in it. The speech outlines the Government's legislative plans for the new Parliamentary session. Thus, the Speech from the Throne is the equivalent (although much shorter) of the President's State of the Union Address in the United States.

For the following week the Commons discusses the contents of the Speech; the Government's supporters proclaim the virtues of its legislative program, while Members of opposition parties denounce these plans and bemoan the absence of the reforms they would prefer to see. Then the Commons gets down to business and starts considering the specific bills that the Speech from the Throne indicated the Government would introduce. With occasional recesses (Christmas, for example) a session continues until the following autumn. Usually the Commons will return from its summer holiday (as the British call vacations) for about a week of wrapping up loose ends. Again the monarch delivers a speech in the House of Lords, but this time summarizing the accomplishments of the session (again, the Cabinet's assessment, not the monarch's). The session formally closes, and all bills and

---

7. The luxurious, horse-drawn coach carrying the Queen and Prince Philip is drawn through the arch appearing in Figure 5.3. This arch is located at the base of the tower seen to the left in Figure 5.1.

Figure 5 ✦ 3 Sovereign's entrance to Victoria Tower

motions still on the books that weren't acted upon die. A few days thereafter a new session of Parliament is opened, and the cycle begins again.

Daily meetings of the Commons, known as sittings, begin at 2:30 in the afternoon Monday through Thursday and usually end at 10:30 P.M. Longer sittings are possible, however, and sometimes the Commons does not adjourn until the wee hours of the morning. In fact, a sitting can even last for more than 24 hours, thus running over into the next day's business and forcing it to be rescheduled. On Fridays the Commons meets from 9:30 A.M. to 3:00 in the afternoon to enable Members of Parliament (MPs) to leave London early enough for weekend visits to their constituencies.

As already noted in connection with rebuilding of the Commons' chamber, the ideal procedure is reasoned debate. To this end several customs have evolved concerning such matters as how Members refer to each other. They aren't permitted to address each other by name and instead use phrases like "the learned lady" to refer to a female Member with a university degree or "my gallant friend" to indicate a member of their party with a distinguished military record. In addition, a Member may not refer to another—even one from the opposing party—as a swine, jackass, stool pigeon, or guttersnipe, among other names on a truly impressive list of vituperative expressions.

After an experimental trial period in 1975, the House of Commons began regular radio broadcasting of its debates in 1978. Much of the public was appalled by what it heard. Heckling—shouting smart comments from the floor at the speaker on the platform—is a common practice in Britain; Members of the Commons saw no reason to forgo this behavior just because they were serving in the nation's legislature. Although the public, obviously, was familiar with such action, still the general hubbub and boorishness of shouting from one side of the chamber at the Member speaking on the other side didn't seem like the rational consideration of public policy that one would expect from an institution known as the mother of Parliaments.

When a few years later the question of television arose, some Members were concerned that their colleagues (not them, of course) would play to the cameras and prefer rhetorical declamations to the traditional "cut-and-thrust" of debate. Even in Britain things eventually do change, however, and at the start of the new session in 1989 television entered the Commons. This was not gavel-to-gavel coverage as on C-SPAN in the United States, but it did provide material that could be aired in newscasts; some major events, such as the Speech from the Throne, were broadcast live. Seeing, as well as hearing, the rowdy boys and girls doesn't seem to have had any further adverse effect on the public's perceptions of its representatives. More recently, early in 1992 a Parliamentary Channel was launched on cable television to provide continuous coverage. Now more than 200,000 homes in Britain can watch the House of Commons whenever it is in session.

You may know that the U.S. House of Representatives curtails the debate time of its members more severely than does the Senate. To a considerable extent this difference is a function of size; a body of 100 members can be less stringent than one of over 400 without losing too much efficiency. Since the House of Commons has 650 Members, you can expect it to limit speaking time. To be allowed to address the House, a Member must catch the Speaker's eye. Leaders of the Government party and of the main opposition party have little difficulty doing so. The Speaker also gives preference to Privy Councilors, a largely honorific title given to many of those who have served in a Government or are senior Parliamentarians. The average Member, known as a backbencher (for obvious reasons if you consult Figure 5.2), may sit through hours of speeches, popping up after each in hope of being recognized, without being any more visible to the Speaker than a ghost would be. Should a backbencher be given the chance to speak, he or she is expected to take no more than ten minutes and, unless the House is in Committee of the Whole, may not speak a second time on any motion. The Member's comments must be relevant to the motion or the Speaker will order him or her to stop. Since Members aren't permitted to read speeches that they have written in advance but can only use notes, being relevant may be difficult for some.

Once debate on a motion concludes and the House is ready for a formal vote, the Members do a strange thing: They all leave the chamber, disgorging through one of the six doors into the hallways that surround it. Doors in these halls are locked to produce two L-shaped lobbies. These doors then are reopened, and as Members file through, they call out their names to clerks, who record them as having voted aye or nay, depending on whichever lobby the Members were in. Once everyone has left these lobbies, the Members serving as tellers march back into the chamber, approach the Speaker's chair, bow, and report the result of the voting. The apparent absurdity of this procedure lends itself to ridicule. Members are called lobby fodder — recalling the infantry that went over the top of trenches unquestioningly in World War I only to be slaughtered by machine guns — or are likened to flocks of sheep being herded down the lobbies by the whips, Members who organize their party's voting.

Why not use a roll call or electronic voting? Think how long a roll call of 650 Members would take. And since each Member doesn't have an assigned desk, how would electronic voting terminals be installed? The traditional method of voting — a division of the House — requires only about twelve to fifteen minutes; this is less than the time consumed by a roll call vote in the U.S. House of Representatives, although it has only two-thirds as many members as the Commons. Not unlike the House of Lords, this irrationality serves a purpose.

Legislative–Executive Relations

The Government determines the Commons' agenda and grants the great portion of the time to its own legislative program. The Speaker selects the topic for a few of the brief debates at the end of a day's sitting. The parties not supporting the Government are granted twenty Opposition Days each year in which they can decide what will be discussed. The opposition parties don't introduce bills, however, because attempting to pass them in the face of the Government's domination of the legislative process would be futile. And twelve Fridays are reserved for bills introduced by individual Members. So inadequate is this for a house with hundreds of members that backbenchers actually hold a lottery to determine which of them will be able to use some of the allotted time. Even should a backbencher win a time slot, private members' bills (as they are known) can be impeded so easily that his or her bill has no hope of passing unless the Government decides to assist it. (The bill mentioned in Chapter 4 to require that the monarch pay income tax was a private member's bill, which explains why it didn't get beyond First Reading.) These instances don't add up to a great deal; all the rest of the time is the Government's. As stressed in Chapter 3, the fundamental idea of British government is to facilitate action.

Efficient progress toward passage of the Government's legislative program is further aided by two procedural devices: the guillotine and closure. The guillotine, known more formally as an allocation of time order, is used when the Government expects a bill to arouse lengthy and fierce opposition. The guillotine sets time limits for each stage (committee, Third Reading, and the like) of the bill's passage through the Commons. It also makes dilatory motions out of order and removes possible impediments to speedy action (such as time regularly set aside for dealing with recurring subjects). To prevent guillotine motions themselves from being obstructed by delaying tactics, debate on whether to adopt the schedule can't go on for more than three hours.

Closure, the procedure for ending a debate and taking a vote, requires only a simple majority vote in the Commons, provided that at least 100 Members vote in favor. If some significant views have yet to be heard, the Speaker may refuse to accept a motion for closure. Thus, the Speaker's impartiality, mentioned previously, is an essential check on possible abuse of the rights of the minority as the Government seeks prompt enactment of its proposals. Nonetheless, the filibustering that can kill bills in the U.S. Senate rarely impedes the Government's bills.

Helping to protect the Government's legislative program from distortion or mutilation are limits on introduction of motions. In contrast to Congressional practice, only the Government can propose measures to spend or raise money. Thus, a bill authorizing expenditure, even if it doesn't appropriate money, requires the Government's approval. Furthermore, backbenchers may not move to amend Government bills to increase proposed spending or to cut proposed taxes.

Thus, the Government's domination of the legislative process is complete. This seems to be the public's view. A poll at the start of the 1990s found that half those questioned either agreed strongly or tended to agree that Parliament lacked sufficient power over what the Government does, while less than a quarter disagreed strongly or tended to do so.[8] Policy making has passed to the Cabinet; the Commons does little more than ratify. Surprisingly, the main function of the British legislature is not to legislate. Exclusive of the time spent discussing financial matters, the Commons devotes only about a third of its activity to debating and voting on bills. The Commons' most significant task is to call the Government to account. It provides an arena where the merits of the Government's policy program are debated and grievances produced by its management of the country are ventilated. Here, more so than in the media, the Government must defend and justify its actions.

Given this essential function, the Commons' lack of American-style permanent subject-matter committees is curious. Remember that the Commons' standing committees are reconstituted for each separate bill they consider and serve only to revise a bill's detailed provisions. This means that Britain lacks the constant surveillance of executive actions and proposals by small groups of expert legislators provided by the U.S. Congress. The situation is worsened by the meager support available to backbenchers. They can claim reimbursement for only about £40,000 (about $62,800 at the November 1992

---

8. "The State of the Nation 1991," Market & Opinion Research International (MORI) for the Joseph Roundtree Reform Trust.

Figure 5 ✦ 4 The north end (where the Commons meets) of the Palace of Westminster viewed from the west. Some of the Members' offices are in reconverted buildings (one of which used to house Scotland Yard, the famous police headquarters) across the road just off the left edge of the picture.

exchange rate of 1.57) spent on staff salaries. Members can't afford a sizable personal research staff; many of them share secretarial assistance to stay within the financial limit. Doing so is "facilitated" by the shortage of office space. Many Members do not have a room of their own, but must share with one or more other backbenchers. Both individually and collectively the Commons finds it difficult to be well informed on the subjects it must consider. This hampers it in effectively challenging the Government's proposals, which appear to be justified by superior knowledge, based as they are on the expertise of the civil service.

British scholars and practitioners concerned about the decline of Parliament's power have worried about how to remedy this deficiency. Following years of academic discussion, the Commons began experimenting in the late 1960s with specialist select committees. In contrast to the Commons' standing committees, the select committees can call expert witnesses and hold public hearings. Such power does not make them the equivalent of Congressional committees. Information gathering is their sole function; no bills are sent to them. In effect, the British have divided the functions of Congressional committees in two: One set of committees works on the detailed content of bills, and another set gathers information on which to base a report to expand the legislature's expertise.

The current set of specialist select committees is a bit over a decade old. Sixteen committees, each with eleven members, were established with subject matters corresponding to particular executive departments (therefore, they sometimes are referred to as departmental select committees). Each committee is permitted to hire a few people, typically only three or four, to serve as expert advisors—again, nothing like the extensive staff support enjoyed by Congressional committees.

The select committees' effectiveness has suffered for several reasons. Although the committees can summon Government ministers and civil servants to testify, they lack any statutory power to compel testimony. The head of the civil service instructed civil servants testifying before select committees that they should not reveal anything about the advice they have given to their department's Secretary of State. The official note of guidance on duties and responsibilities issued to civil servants provides, "Ultimately the responsibility lies with ministers, and not with civil servants, to decide what information should be made available, and how and when it should be released, whether it is to Parliament, to select committees, to the media or to individuals."

Although a select committee was not directly involved, the Government's obsession with secrecy and its desire to keep the Commons from finding out much of anything about the way the country is run was made clear by the Belgrano Affair. Parliament was investigating whether the Argentine ship, the *Belgrano*, had been sunk unnecessarily—for political, rather than military, reasons—during the conflict between Britain and Argentina over the Falkland Islands. A civil servant gave some relevant confidential documents to a backbencher who had charged that Prime Minister Thatcher had authorized attacking the ship primarily to gain political capital from a dramatic success. The civil servant's action could be regarded simply as helping the legislature in an investigation. Unwilling to participate in what he regarded as a cover-up, he gave the information not to a journalist but to a legislator, who would seem to have a right to know. Nonetheless, the government prosecuted him under the Official Secrets Act. (I examined the "reform" of the OSA in Chapter 3.) Although the jury acquitted him, other civil servants who have divulged information to journalists have been convicted and sent to jail.

The point is that even select committees are going to be hard-pressed to get information out of any part of the executive. Matters came to a head in the aftermath of the Westland Affair, that I've mentioned a couple of times previously. When select committees tried to find out what had happened in the Cabinet to produce the Defence Secretary's resignation—surely the business of the House of Commons—they encountered a catch-22 situation. The minister who had headed the department that leaked information detrimental to the Defence Secretary refused to answer key questions on the grounds that he no longer was in office and thus wasn't responsible and, in any event, it was civil servants who had misbehaved in leaking the information. When committees then sought to question the civil servants involved, they were barred from doing so because civil servants are answerable to their ministers, not to the House of Commons. As the head of one of the committees observed, this logic created an accountability gap.

A lengthy debate ensued that led to a good bit of hairsplitting. The Government acknowledged that select committees had a right to question civil servants about their "actions" (that is, behavior consistent with ministers' desires) but not about their "conduct" (that is, misbehavior). Civil servants were instructed that they should refuse to answer if a select committee questioned them about their conduct or that of any other civil servant. The Commons' Liaison Committee (composed of the chairs of the various select committees) maintained that such instructions violated the rights of the select committees, but the Government refused to concede the point. Whatever the Iran–Contra hearings may have indicated about the ability of the U.S. Congress to get to the bottom of devious, illegal behavior in the American executive branch, the fact is that Congressional committees have stronger weapons to compel testimony than do the Commons' select committees.

Although the executive (which obviously doesn't want to give up any of its power and, therefore, opposes any change making it more subject to legislative control) is the principal culprit in thwarting the select committees from achieving their purpose of a better-informed legislature, the Commons itself must accept some blame. It has failed to devise a means of using the committees effectively. No procedure has been established to ensure regular discussion by the full House of the reports that the committees make. Thus, a committee's investigation makes most of its dozen Members more knowledgeable, but the Commons at large doesn't derive much benefit.

Two other select committees — one in the Commons and the other in the Lords — deserve mention, although they are not part of the set of departmental select committees. Chapter 3 noted the significant implications for the constitutional principle of parliamentary supremacy in light of the growing integration of the European Community. To the extent that matters that used to require Parliament's approval now are being decided by one of the EC's institutions, the ability of Parliament to call power to account is hampered. Because the British system is so slow to change, little has been done to maintain the check of accountability.

The House of Lords has a Select Committee on the European Communities. It is very elaborately organized with six specialized subcommittees. These groups devote much time to examining many EC matters and issue a variety of detailed reports. The Lords itself debates many of these at length. Furthermore, the debates typically occur at what could be called prime parliamentary time. The work of the Lords on EC matters is a fine example of the useful role that the upper chamber can play. The nature of the Lords — being an appointive and hereditary body — however, precludes the house from having much influence. Only a popularly elected house could hope to win much attention for its concerns.

Unfortunately, the corresponding committee in the Commons plays a much more diminished role. Its Select Committee on European Legislation lacks the breadth of the Lords' Committee. The Commons' Committee reviews only a fraction of EC legislation, and its only purpose is to identify the specific items that appear to need some discussion; it doesn't prepare elaborate reports as does the Lords' Committee. Some items that the Commons' Committee recommends for debate are discussed only in committee; only a few are considered in the Commons itself. The debates that the Commons does hold on EC matters tend to be shorter than those in the Lords and usually occur at the end of the day (around 10 P.M.) when most Members have gone home. Furthermore, some of these debates occur after the fact; the rules in question already have been approved to go into effect. Thus, some power that had been concentrated in the British executive has shifted to the EC, and the crucial link of responsibility to the Commons has been further attenuated.

Another major area of tenuous accountability is Britain's publicly owned industries. When these enterprises were nationalized (taken over by the government), they were organized as public corporations to retain the operational flexibility and efficient management of commercial concerns. Although each corporation fell in the jurisdiction of some Secretary of State, its day-to-day chief manager was empowered to make many decisions without reference to this superior. Parliament could question the relevant secretary about a corporation's broad policy but couldn't hold a secretary responsible for every detailed action. Creating the public corporation altered significantly the traditional convention (individual ministerial responsibility) that secretaries are accountable for every act in their departments. Only if their consent was required (for example, for borrowing) or if they could have voided a decision were they held accountable.

Secretaries were empowered to issue general instructions or policy directives to the boards of corporations but, typically, have preferred to express their wishes informally. When no directive is issued, Parliament can't question the secretary about the action and no report need be made disclosing why the decision was taken. Each year the secretaries supervising corporations submit to Parliament the enterprises' annual report and financial accounts. Here the problem resembles that already noted for the select committees. The Commons' Public Accounts Committee examines the finances of public corporations but, because it is responsible for scrutinizing the full range of government spending, devotes little time to the public corporations. A Select Committee on Nationalized Industries (a forerunner of the departmental select committees) had existed, but it disappeared without a trace when the current set of departmental select committees was launched. The Commons debates the annual reports of public corporations but manages to deal with only about two or three a year. Given the number of nationalized industries, several years usually pass between debates on any particular corporation. Whatever the problems of determining responsibility, the Commons simply has failed to do all that it could to be informed about the operation of public corporations.

Perhaps, therefore, even those on the left of the political spectrum should welcome the process begun under Margaret Thatcher of privatizing — that is, selling — government-owned enterprises back to the public. Now that they are in private hands, these industries may be as accountable to the public as they were as government property. Sales of gas, banking, telecommunications, and even water enterprises transformed the pattern of private investment in Britain. In only four years during the mid-1980s the proportion of the population owning shares more than tripled, going from about 6 percent to more than 20 percent. Nonetheless, several enterprises, such as the railroads and the coal mines, remain in government ownership and for them the problem of accountability continues.

American admirers of British government may protest that the picture I've painted for you is too negative, that the Commons possesses several devices for calling the Government to account, and that, indeed, American government would be enhanced by grafting some of these onto the U.S. political system. A careful look at these procedures, however, suggests that they are overrated. One of the best-known means of calling the Government to account is question time. Four days a week (no questions on Friday) one of the first activities of each sitting is replies by Cabinet ministers to questions that have been submitted at least two days in advance by backbenchers. However, questions that are handed in that late are unlikely to be reached in the time available so Members actually need to compose them about ten days beforehand. The result is that most questions covered during the proceedings are not very current. Each Member may submit two questions, directed to those ministers in whose sphere of responsibility the matter falls. The Prime Minister replies to questions twice each week. (You can watch these exchanges on C-SPAN on Sunday evenings.) Questions may be designed to embarrass a minister, call attention to minor injustices in bureaucratic action, or obtain information.

Ministers can refuse to answer a question if doing so would injure the national interest, but they try to avoid that response since it might suggest they are hiding something. Civil servants in each department prepare the answers the ministers give. After each question is answered, the Speaker will call on Members for related supplementary questions. Now the minister is on his or her own, and, if inadequately informed or unable to think on his or her feet, can prove to be a liability to the Government. The supplementaries are likely to be up-to-the-minute inquiries and may catch a minister completely off guard. Careers may be jeopardized and reputations broken by consistently poor performances during question time. In the hands of skilled Members question time often has been a potent weapon.

Whether that remains true, however, is dubious. About half the questions come from supporters of the Government. They tend to make silly inquiries like whether the Minister will agree that the Opposition is a bunch of dolts, which the Minister is only too happy to do. The Opposition Members, for the most part, are equally interested in superficial partisan accusations. In short, if a Member really is seeking some information, he or she will submit a question for written reply. Those who submit them for oral reply simply want to participate in what is largely a partisan mock battle. If ever the famous quote "full of sound and fury and signifying nothing" was applicable to an event, question time is it. Even the questions for written reply are of limited utility. Ministers and their civil servants, as you've seen, are skilled in not telling the Commons anything that they do not wish Members to know.

Despite their ineffectiveness, questions remain a popular tactic for interest groups seeking to influence the policy process. For those interest groups having frequent contact with Members, getting them to ask a question (done by five-sixths of the groups) was the action most frequently requested.

Recently, administrative restructuring has further weakened the ability of questions to call the executive to account. Several governmental units are being "hived off" to create largely autonomous, self-contained agencies. This procedure should not be confused with privatization, which involves selling enterprises back to the public. The hived-off agencies remain part of the government, but are moved outside the regular departmental administrative hierarchy. (An example is the agency that licenses autos.) Given the freedom that these agencies' chief executives have in directing their *operations*, as distinguished from setting their guiding *policies*, secretaries now can claim that they aren't responsible for the agencies' day-to-day actions. They refuse to answer any questions about these matters in the Commons, passing them on instead to the relevant chief executives. Some executives respond promptly, some are slow to do so or provide only partial information, and some try to avoid replying at all. Any replies that are given aren't published in the public record of Parliamentary activity (as is true for secretaries' replies to oral or written questions) but usually go to the Commons' Library, to which the public has no access. Since some executives say that they have given an answer in confidence and that it shouldn't become a public document, the extent to which Members can legally divulge the information to the public is unclear. Beyond that, only the Member who originally asked the question is likely to know that a reply has been received. Only after two years of agitation by Members did the executive agree to publish these replies in the public record of Commons' business.

The essence of the fusion of the legislative and executive branches is the power of the former to remove the latter from office whenever it chooses. American admirers of the British system think that Congress would be enhanced if the British vote of confidence procedure were imported into the United States. Surely this power gives Britain the edge in calling the executive to account? Not really, because again the reality fails to measure up to the potential. Only four votes of confidence have been carried against the Government during the past century. The most recent instance—March 1979, when a Labour Government was defeated by a single vote — occurred at a time of minority Government, that is, no party controlled a majority of seats in the House of Commons, so, naturally, the Government's position was precarious. In the half century since the end of World War II, however, Britain has had a minority Government for only a couple of years, so that instance tells us little about how the system typically operates. Prior to 1979 a Government had not been defeated on a vote of confidence since 1924 — again, at a time of minority Government.

Admittedly, a Government doesn't have to lose a vote to be driven from office. In 1940 early in World War II, the Government won a key division in the Commons by 81 votes but resigned nonetheless because its potential majority was around 200. So many of those who previously had supported the Government had abstained or even voted against it that Prime Minister Neville Chamberlain felt that he no longer had the confidence of the Commons. Therefore, he resigned and Winston Churchill became Prime Minister. Such displays of the Commons' power are so dramatic that they are long remembered. Nonetheless, they are extremely rare, not typical of the day-to-day relation between the legislature and the executive.

You would have to go back to the mid-nineteenth century to find a time when the vote of confidence procedure truly enabled the Commons to call the Government to account. The reason this once-feared muscle atrophied is the growth of party discipline. Americans are used to low party cohesion: some Democrats and some Republicans voting on one side of an issue in Congress and other Democrats with other Republicans voting on the other. Only rarely does a strict party-line vote occur in which Democrats are on one side and Republicans are on the other. In Britain, however, the party-line vote is the norm.

This dramatic contrast in legislative voting behavior between two countries having many political values and traditions in common is due to differences in party organization and fundamental structures. Each Thursday when the Commons is in session the Leader of the House (the majority party's business manager) announces the agenda for the coming week. The next day each party distributes to all its Members in the Commons a document called the whip. (Although not the correct term, I'll refer to this as the documentary whip to avoid any confusion with the organizers of each party's voting, who also are called whips, as I noted earlier in the chapter.) This document includes the schedule announced by the Leader of the House, indicates some principal speakers for important debates, and, most significant, designates the relative importance the party assigns to each item on the agenda. A matter of limited concern will be underlined once. Fairly important matters are underlined twice. A three-line documentary whip means that the party expects (read *requires*) a Member to be present, unless ill or unavoidably detained, to vote the party line. Sometimes even those two excuses are insufficient.

Members have been brought from hospital beds on stretchers to the precincts of the House of Commons so that their votes could be counted in crucial debates (it was the failure to do this in 1979 that cost the Labour Government a defeat on the motion of confidence mentioned above), and ministers have had to break off negotiations in foreign countries to fly to London for a key division. Votes on motions of censure always are designated as three-line documentary whips, as are the principal items in the Government's legislative program.

Strictly speaking, the documentary whip only tells Members when they should be certain to attend the Commons. Of course, their party is not just interested in the pleasure of their company but intends for them to vote as the party instructs them to do. Members are to vote the party line, despite their personal views, despite how persuasive the arguments may have been that were made during the debate by speakers from other parties. Abstaining is about as far as a Member can go in refusing to support the party line and even that can get him or her in trouble. On some issues involving morals or conscience (such as the death penalty) parties usually permit a free vote; that is, they do not take a position and let Members vote as they wish. On most issues, however, the parties do take stands and Members must fall in line or suffer the consequences.

A Member who rebels on a crucial vote or persistently deviates on matters of lesser importance is likely to have the documentary whip withdrawn. The Conservative party vests this power in the Leader; in the Labour party a majority vote of the Parliamentary Labour Party is required. Withdrawal of the documentary whip expels the rebel from the party in Parliament. In the Labour party the withdrawal is reported to the National Executive Committee of the mass membership arm of the party, which can expel the offender from party membership. Neither the Conservative nor the Labour party would permit one of their constituency parties to adopt an expellee as a candidate. Therefore, rebels risk ending their political careers.

The people who serve as party whips—the Members who organize their party's voting—don't need to do much to a rebellious Member; his or her constituency party is likely to warn that, unless this behavior ceases, it will find another candidate for the next election. This is a credible threat because most Members recognize that in Britain the typical Member has been elected not because of personal abilities or magnetism but largely because of the party label. The electorate votes to give a party enough seats in Parliament to carry out its policies; the individual candidate is to a great extent incidental to the process. Usually a local party is willing to tolerate dissent only when a Member is moving toward the fringe of the political spectrum, away from the party's opponents. Local activists tend to be farther from the center of the spectrum than are the party's national leaders. A Member who voted against the party's policy because it was too moderate might well survive (although he or she could not expect executive office), but one who refused to support the policy because it was too extreme would be likely to be disciplined by the local constituency party.

Thus British parties, both the one controlling the Government and those in Opposition, are organized, both in the Parliament and throughout the country, to produce disciplined voting blocs in the Commons. Similarly, American Congressional parties are organized along party lines, and this affects such important matters as allocation of committee positions. But these parties are not cohesive in legislative voting because party organization outside Congress is so decentralized. American legislators tend to be independent political entrepreneurs; each has his or her own local machine. Within either the Democratic or Republican parties these machines are linked only loosely. In Britain the local parties are fully integrated into the national party and the legislator is merely a creature of the party. I'll develop this point more fully in Chapter 8. The point here simply is that legislative party organization is much more effective in the House of Commons than in Congress because of the differences in party organization in the two countries and the nature of the relation between that organization and the individual legislator.

Highly developed party cohesion in Britain is not based simply on dragooning backbenchers. The whips don't just transmit the leaders' orders to their followers; they also communicate the backbenchers' complaints and misgivings to the leaders. Being thus kept in tune with the mood of the backbenchers helps leaders avoid proposing policies that are unacceptable to many. Each party's extensive backbench committee system also helps achieve this. Members belonging to the party in power, for example, often have the opportunity to express their views on possible legislation before the Cabinet introduces it in the Commons. Additionally, the executive often consults closely with relevant interest groups when considering new legislation or drafting bills. By the time it is introduced in Parliament, a bill is likely to be an elaborately developed set of compromises; major changes are highly unlikely at that stage, since they would tend to unravel the entire package. No one can be expert on more than a few matters, so, on any given issue, most Members will be uninformed. Why—when they typically know nothing about purpose or desirability of a bill—should Members do other than vote as the whips tell them? Why jeopardize one's career by being a troublemaker simply on the say-so of some ineffective Member well known to be part of the "awkward squad"?

The argument thus far has focused only on the first point—contrasts in party organization between Britain and the United States. Also crucial in explaining legislative voting behavior is the basic structural arrangement of British government and its contrast with the American system. Low party cohesion in Britain incurs a much greater cost than it does in the United

States. Although strictly speaking the Prime Minister and the Cabinet aren't required to resign unless defeated on a motion of confidence, no Government would be willing to remain in office if many of its key legislative proposals were defeated in Parliament. Despite the formal constitutional rule, the Government clearly would have lost the confidence of the Commons.

Thus legislators in Britain who fail to vote regularly as their party leaders instruct them to do risk driving their party from power. This, in turn, would bring an opposition party into office. Such an event has to be undesirable: If you preferred for that party to control the executive, you would belong to it rather than your current party. Whatever the shortcomings of your party's leaders, they must be better in your judgment than the Opposition leaders. So you can complain about what your leaders are doing, but when it comes time to vote you aren't going to support your opponents and help them get into power. Members of Congress aren't constrained in their voting by such thoughts since the President remains in power regardless of whether his legislative proposals are enacted. A Democratic Senator, for example, could vote against a Democratic President's bill without fearing that this might immediately turn the White House over to the Republicans.

Party organization and governmental structure combine in Britain to produce extremely high party cohesion, that is, disciplined voting in the same way by Members in the same party. Winning a working majority of seats in the Commons in a general election guarantees a party getting its legislative program through Parliament. Its proposals do not have to hurdle many obstacles or fear ambush by a hostile committee chairperson. The Government knows that it has the votes to pass the bills. Such a situation has a good deal to be said for it. Responsibility, as well as power, is concentrated. A British Government can never argue that its program was thwarted by the perversity of a handful of strategically placed legislators. In the British system not only does the same party control both executive and legislative branches, but the same section of the party controls both. In the United States, there are Congressional Democrats and Presidential Democrats responsible to contrasting constituencies and thus perpetually at odds with each other despite nominally belonging to the same party. This is not true in Britain. Thus, in Britain when things do not get done or when what does get done is objectionable, the voters know whom to blame. And at the next election they can remove them from power and give their opponents a chance.

The cost of such a system, however, is that the legislature is reduced to doing little more than rubber-stamping the Government's decisions. The typical Member of the Commons has little freedom in deciding how to vote, little chance to introduce legislation, and little opportunity to speak in the debates. Most backbenchers find themselves engaged in activities something like social work rather than helping to resolve the great public issues of the day. During the 1970s and the 1980s backbenchers evidenced some frustration with their increasingly inconsequential status. Many Members occasionally voted against their party; party cohesion did decline a bit. Nonetheless, only in the most exceptional instances did a threatened rebellion in the Commons induce the Government to alter its proposals. The clock had not been turned back to the mid-nineteenth century, when, before the development of well-organized parties, Parliament operated differently from the way it does today.

A paradox exists at the heart of the British system. Without disciplined, cohesive two-party competition, the executive is unlikely to enjoy a reliable majority in the Commons. Responsibility for failures would become ambiguous, and calling power-wielders to account would be impeded. But if parties are so disciplined that their members automatically toe the party line and unthinkingly vote as opposing blocs whatever the issue, then the executive can do as it pleases, secure in wielding power. Clearly that severs the accountability link as well.

What can be said more positively, however, is that calling the Government to account doesn't require defeating the Government to be effective. The main purpose of debate in the Commons is to force the Government to justify its actions. A Government unable to make a convincing case for its policies is likely to be considered incompetent or callous. Since Members don't enjoy appearing to be blind loyalists, support for such a Government can soon deteriorate. Nor is the public likely to view such a Government favorably. Thus, how the Government fares in the Commons' debates can be a means of calling it to account and the chamber's rules facilitate such procedures.

After question time each day, any Member may move that the Commons adjourn on "a specific and important matter that should have urgent consideration." If the Speaker agrees that the subject meets these criteria and the request (if opposed) is supported by forty Members, a special three-hour debate is scheduled for the following day immediately after questions. Alternatively, if the Speaker feels it necessary, the debate can be scheduled for 7 P.M. on the day of the request. When the debate occurs, the House does not argue the merits of whether it should go home but discusses the urgent topic that the Member raised. Although this procedure allows for debates of great topicality, it's employed only sparingly — one to four times each year.

More commonly, immediately after questions the Government itself may move that the House adjourn. This isn't because the Cabinet ministers are unprepared and want a day off. Under the Commons' rules of procedure almost any topic is relevant on a motion to adjourn. Such a motion, therefore, permits a wide-ranging debate on some topic of current interest without the Speaker having to exclude some Member because the relevance of his or her comments is not immediately apparent. The Government consults with the Opposition in arranging such debates, giving the latter some influence over the topics that are discussed.

The most frequent adjournment debates, however, are those occurring at the end of each sitting. At 10 P.M. the Commons' regular business is halted. (If a sitting is to continue beyond the usual 10:30 closing, then the adjournment debate does not occur until just before the end of the sitting.) During the next half hour before the House adjourns automatically, backbenchers can discuss a particular grievance or aspect of Government policy. At times a Member dissatisfied with a minister's reply during question time will be able to pursue the matter further during an adjournment debate.

Taken together, these three types of adjournment debates provide extensive opportunity to make the Government account for the full range of its actions — from matters of detail that seem trivial to all but the specific citizens involved to instances of the broadest matters of urgent public policy. British procedures, much more so than American, facilitate public, face-to-face discussions by leading politicians of current issues precisely at the time those subjects are of greatest importance. By criticizing the Government's policies in the Commons, the Opposition publicizes policy alternatives during the period between elections and does not have to rely on election campaigns alone to present its distinctive appeal to the electorate. (This may well be why British election campaigns, as you'll see in Chapter 7, can be much briefer than American campaigns.) In having to explain and defend its actions, the Government has a chance to clarify its program for the public. Thus, each side has an opportunity to work out a coherent set of policies and to stimulate some public response to them.

The result of any division of the House taken after an adjournment debate rarely will be in doubt (although it was a vote on such a motion that caused the fall of the Chamberlain Government in 1940). The aim is not to defeat the Government — the Opposition doesn't imagine that the force of its argument will win over wavering Members on the Government side — but to examine its actions. The accountability lies in the discussion itself, in recognizing that the executive can be required to justify its running of the country. Of course, after a debate Members supporting the Government may find themselves forced to concede that their leaders did not perform very well. Should this be repeated, rumbles of discontent will be heard within the Government party. Such dissent among "its own" Members will be taken much more seriously by the Government than are the attacks of the Opposition. As Margaret Thatcher learned, the vote of confidence that matters is not the one on the floor of the House of Commons but the one by your party's legislators in a Commons' meeting room.

Summary

The basic purpose of Britain's Parliament differs fundamentally from that of the U.S. Congress. Individual Members of Parliament are *not* supposed to have any good ideas for new programs that they try to get most of their colleagues to endorse. Their job is primarily to react to and to comment on the Government's policies and proposals for action. The Commons, in particular, is to call the Government to account.

An individual Member acting alone hardly could be expected to discharge that function effectively. Therefore, to make the challenge to concentrated power more influential, the Commons formally recognizes an Opposition. Parliamentary procedures are arranged so as to facilitate the Opposition's efforts to force the Government to justify its actions. The Opposition is not to *thwart* the Government's actions, however. The Opposition's function is *not* to shape policy; that is the role of Her Majesty's Government. The Government's job is to govern the country: to devise the policies needed to meet the country's needs and to see that these are implemented fairly and effectively. To be certain that the Government is accomplishing that and that it is not abusing its powers, it must report to Parliament. Furthermore, it must daily retain Parliament's confidence in the way it is discharging its functions.

But does the requirement of retaining Parliament's confidence mean anything in the last decade of the twentieth century? Beginning in the latter part of the nineteenth century, the rise of well-organized parties has brought to the House of Commons a strict party discipline that enables the British executive to dominate the legislature. The balance of power relations between these two branches is tilted much farther toward the executive than is typical of the balance between the U.S. President and Congress. Cohesive party-line voting, a modest and only occasional phenomenon in Congress, is so prevalent in the House of Commons as to turn it into the Prime Minister's poodle.[9] The Opposition may rail, but the outcome is a foregone conclusion; the Commons will rubber-stamp whatever the Cabinet wants. Even worse, because so many Members are careerists who wish to obtain executive positions, they will not even raise questions that might embarrass the executive when their party is in power. Finally, even were they disposed to do so the challenge would probably be ineffective because, as this chapter has shown, the Commons lacks the organization and staff support that enables the U.S. Congress to mount serious attacks on executive action.

I started this summary by asserting the Congress and Parliament differ fundamentally in purpose. In the respect that I've been discussing, that's true. In another regard, however, they share a fundamental function. Both are

---

9. When the powers of the House of Lords were in controversy early in the twentieth century, one Conservative politician praised the Lords as the watchdog of the Constitution. A leading Liberal retorted that the Lords was the Leader of the Conservative party's poodle.

entrusted with the task of mobilizing consent, of conferring sufficient legitimacy on most governmental policies so that the great majority of the people will obey them, even when they dislike them, without having to be coerced. Accountability is not only a check on concentrated power. Because accountability forces the British executive to justify its policies regularly in a public forum, it helps to legitimate those actions. People are more willing to accept losing, more willing to tolerate laws they opposed, if they feel that their views received an adequate hearing. You can't win them all, but at least we had our day in court.

However, if strict party discipline makes the Commons sittings just a charade, and if Parliament is merely yea–boo partisan games, then consent is not mobilized. The concern is not that the Commons doesn't influence policy—it hasn't done that for a century and a half. The danger is that it is failing to legitimate governmental output.

How critical this development has become is unclear. Various groups on the Labour party's left wing want to ignore Parliament and fight for their favorite causes on street-corner soap boxes. Even the Leader of the Liberal Democrats, Paddy Ashdown, has indicated at times that he is frustrated by how little Parliament's activity matters, and he questions whether many of its elaborate procedures are a waste of time. Nor does the public at large seem greatly impressed. A poll at the start of the 1990s found that three-fifths thought Parliament works very or fairly well, but a sixth believed that it works very or fairly badly.[10] That isn't exactly a repudiation, but it's hardly a ringing endorsement either.[11] The value of that assessment is questionable because nearly two-thirds admitted they knew little, if anything, about the way that Parliament works. That finding may be an even greater condemnation of Parliament than is the assessment. How can Parliament mobilize consent, how can it legitimate governmental output, when most of the population are ignorant of its workings? Whatever else may need reforming about Parliament, it seems essential to better educate the public about its activities.

Perhaps the departmental select committees and similar reforms will eventually provide a basis for Parliament to revitalize its ability to call the executive to account. Structural reforms are not unimportant, but the key to a puissant Parliament is Members' behavior. In the 1970s and 1980s party cohesion in the Commons declined somewhat, without approaching the

---

10. "The State of the Nation 1991," Market & Opinion Research International (MORI) for the Joseph Roundtree Reform Trust.

11. In 1960 I interviewed a woman who had run for the House of Commons as a Liberal. "I'd die to get into Parliament," she told me. True, that was only one person, but somehow I can't conceive of any candidate saying that to me now.

much lower Congressional levels. Some students of Parliament have argued that this shift in behavior has halted Parliament's long decline. They assert that the Commons is a much more vital institution near the end of the century than it had been at the midpoint. Whether concentrated power truly is becoming more accountable remains unclear, however; as always in Britain, change takes a long time to manifest itself.

6

✦

The Judiciary

The expression "fusion of powers" usually refers to relations between the executive and the legislature: Members of the executive are chosen from those holding seats in the legislature and the legislature can remove the executive from office at any time. In Britain fusion of powers extends to relations between the legislature and the judiciary, as well: Members of the highest court in the country have seats in the House of Lords and the head of the judicial hierarchy presides over the House of Lords. Since he or she also typically is in the Cabinet, all three branches are fused in this one person.

You learned in Chapter 3 that Britain practices constitutionalism without a written constitution. How do such departures from American practices affect the judiciary? In the United States the segment of fractionalized power given to the judiciary is substantial; thus it can help to prevent abuse of power. Does the British judiciary function similarly in a fusion-of-powers system? This chapter begins by examining the role played by British judges in making law. Following that, I sketch the organization of British courts.

The last part of the chapter focuses on law enforcement with a conclusion that assesses the quality of British justice.

As in previous chapters, we'll encounter serious questions about the British system. Criminal defendants are much better protected (coddled?) in the United States. British judges are widely thought to be biased and out of touch with everyday life. Public confidence in the judicial system is much lower than you might have anticipated. Even the police, once thought to be paragons by Britons, have received a good bit of bad press recently. Police abuse of basic rights may be as widespread in Britain as in the United States. Is all this due to the absence of a written constitution? And, if so, is the remedy enacting a bill of rights?

Judge-Made Law

The fact that the British judicial branch lacks the ultimate power of its American counterpart shouldn't cause you to conclude that British judges are of little consequence and have no influence in delineating and maintaining basic rights. Just as in the United States, judges in Britain make laws. In Chapter 1 I mentioned the early development of the English judicial system and the evolution of the common law. The constitutional foundations section of Chapter 3 also had to include comments about the common law. In neither section, however, was a focus on the common law itself appropriate. That leaves to this chapter the detailed attention that is due the common law as one of the two most extensively copied and influential legal systems (the other is the Roman or code law system). The common law system spread from Britain through most of the areas that it controlled, including, of course, the United States. The Roman law system is preferred on the European continent and in Japan and Turkey. Interestingly, Scottish law is in the Roman tradition; the centuries of separate development by Scotland before being amalgamated with England and Wales at the start of the eighteenth century made a considerable difference in this regard, as in many others. Therefore, Scotland's judicial system and procedures differ from those of England and Wales.[1]

You will recall that the common law is based on judicial decisions; Roman law is founded on legal codes. Of course, legislatures pass laws in common law systems and judges decide cases in Roman law systems. Statutes tend to be more elaborate and detailed in the latter, and judges expect to find in the statutes the rules to cover the cases they hear. In the common law system judges seek the correct decision for a current case by examining the decisions of judges in similar cases in the past.

---

1. Lack of space prevents discussing these differences so a single example will have to suffice: In Scottish courts a third verdict — not proven — is available in addition to the two familiar ones of guilty or not guilty.

Centuries ago royal courts were only one of several courts. Various feudal lords operated their system of courts distinct from those of the state. (This was a form of privatization not advocated even by Margaret Thatcher.) The royal courts were more popular (because they tended to be more just) and eventually superseded the others. By the end of the fourteenth century, the royal courts were staffed by professional judges appointed by the monarch from among the practicing lawyers. These courts sought to mete out justice in the cases brought to them. Strictly speaking, a decision applied only to the case at hand; the judges did not attempt to elaborate extensive rules to cover the subject generally. The common law said little or nothing about topics concerning which few cases had been brought to the courts for decision. The law developed fortuitously rather than systematically, although it grew most rapidly in the areas of greatest concern to the people, since these generated the most cases.

To make this haphazard accumulation of decisions more orderly, leading legal scholars such as Coke (pronounced "Cook") and Blackstone grouped together the decisions in similar cases and indicated what the typical ruling was. These commentaries revealed obvious defects in the law. In some instances cases that were only slightly similar were not adequately differentiated in existing common law rules; in other instances cases that were almost indistinguishable were covered by conflicting rulings. Furthermore, centuries of following the doctrine of *stare decisis* ("let the decision stand," — that is, the holding in a previous similar case should determine the decision in subsequent cases despite whether that produced a just result) had cost the common law its flexibility. Excessive devotion to precedent was becoming a cause of injustice.

For example, under the common law, contracts were invalid if they were agreed to because of threat to life and limb, but contracts were valid even though they were arranged under improper influences (such as getting a man or a woman drunk before hoodwinking him or her). The chief remedy available under the common law was to seek damages. Money, however, cannot restore circumstances to what they were. What was needed was a legal procedure that could stop an action *before* it did damage.

How could the law be kept sufficiently flexible to provide justice while not becoming so variable as to be arbitrary and capricious? The Lord Chancellor was charged with functioning as the monarch's conscience to prevent any miscarriages of justice resulting from rigid devotion to precedent. An entire system of legal rules gradually developed out of the Lord Chancellor's decisions in cases in which people had appealed to the monarch for relief from injustices of the common law. By the early part of the nineteenth century equity (also known as chancery) had taken its place alongside the common law as a humanizing element. Equity dealt with civil controversies (that is, conflict between private individuals), not criminal cases (conflict between the individual and the government). It established the practice of granting an injunction (an order prohibiting certain action) to prevent possible injury or nuisance before it occurred.

Note that equity, like common law, is judge-made. All British courts apply both equity and common law. Where the two sets of rules conflict, equity takes precedence. Any applicable statutes, however, supersede both common law and equity. The legislature, not the judiciary, has the final word—a considerable contrast with the United States. Increasingly, Parliament *has* legislated in areas previously covered only by common law or equity. Parliament has not so much wished to reverse judicial precedents as it has been concerned to provide comprehensive rules to cover the expanded scope of governmental programs and services. Despite the growth of statute law, judge-made law remains fundamental in most areas of British jurisprudence. Even in a fusion-of-powers system, the judiciary remains an influential branch of government. British judges have the power, should they choose to use it, to constrain power.

The Structure of the Court System

Like many other institutions in Britain, the court system has grown out of centuries of usage. Itinerant royal commissioners, who were originally concerned mainly with looking after William the Conqueror's financial affairs, were transformed into itinerant judges by Henry II in the middle of the twelfth century. They visited each county three or four times a year to determine whether charges of serious crimes were accurate (lesser offenses were left to sheriffs and justices of the peace). Thus, the practice of trying almost all criminal cases in the county where the crime was committed became well established.

In major civil cases, however, proceedings were held at Westminster (the seat of government in London), which forced the litigants, witnesses, and others involved in the case to travel to London for the trial. In those days travel not only was time-consuming and wearing but could be positively dangerous. So, Justices of the Assize Courts were sent to the counties to hear cases. The points of law continued to be argued mainly at Westminster, however, and formal judgment was rendered there.

Despite these and other measures that have decentralized the courts over the centuries, the British legal system remains unified into a national system both in structure and appointment procedures. As a federal system, the United States has two distinct court systems: the state courts and the federal or national courts. For purposes of jurisdiction and appeal these two systems are not entirely separate, but are intertwined very complexly. With respect to appointments, however, they are completely separate. To this extent, the British court system is more unified.

On the other hand, Britain divides its courts differently from the United States, providing separate hierarchies for civil and for criminal cases. Criminal cases are those trying behavior deemed to offend against society, regardless of whether the actual victim is an individual; kidnapping is an example. In such cases the government prosecutes, bringing the charges against the accused, so that it is one of the parties in the case. In civil cases the government is not directly involved; it merely provides an arena in which two or more private parties can obtain a fair resolution of the controversy concerning which they are in conflict. No one is prosecuted in such cases.

Figure 6.1 outlines the structure of the court system; referring to it while reading the following description should help to clarify the arrangements. In the courts trying charges of criminal behavior, virtually all (95 percent) of the cases begin in magistrates' courts. Summary offenses (minor violations not requiring an indictment or trial by jury and having a maximum sentence of six months in prison or a fine of £2,000 — $3,140 at the November 1992 exchange rate of 1.57) are tried here. Criminal cases account for most of the work load of magistrates' courts, but they also can hear some civil cases, primarily matters of family law. Magistrates' courts also function as do grand juries in the United States: They decide whether sufficient evidence exists for an indictment (a formal accusation that must be defended in court) to be issued for serious crimes.

The approximately 700 magistrates' courts are staffed by about 28,000 magistrates (judges), mostly unpaid laypeople appointed by the Lord Chancellor, national head of the legal system. Three magistrates hear each case; they are advised on points of law by a legally trained clerk (pronounced "clark"). In large urban areas, however, magistrates tend to be full-time, legally trained judges, who sit alone in hearing cases. Appeals from the magistrates' courts in civil cases go to the Family Division of the High Court of Justice. Appeals in criminal cases go to the High Court only when a point of law is involved. If the question is whether the verdict was correct or the sentence too severe, the appeal is to the Crown Court.

Besides hearing appeals from the magistrates' courts, the Crown Court serves as the original (the case starts there) court for serious crimes. For the most important of these cases, such as murder, a judge from the High Court of Justice sits alone. In other cases, such as assault or forgery, a circuit judge, or even a part-time recorder, presides and is assisted by two or four magistrates. In either instance a jury is used. Crown Court sessions are held in about ninety locations around the country. Those in the largest cities are designated as the first tier. This tier has some limited civil jurisdiction in addition to its main responsibilities for criminal cases. The second tier is located in smaller cities and the third tier, comprising about half the total

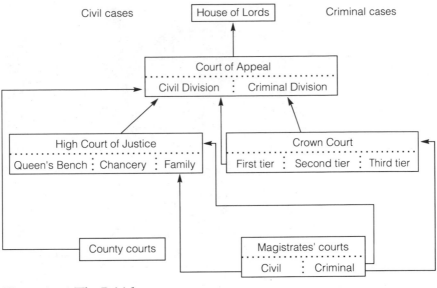

Figure 6 ✦ 1 The British court system

number of courts, in towns. Courts in these two tiers try serious crimes of lesser importance, such as assault with intent to rob or wound. Appeals are taken to the Court of Appeal, Criminal Division except for civil cases heard by first tier Crown Courts.

At the Court of Appeal the civil/criminal bifurcation ends. Before discussing that court, I need to shift focus to the civil law to consider the courts of that type below the point at which the criminal and civil systems are joined. The lowest civil court is the county court, of which there are about 300. County courts had been restricted to cases in which the claim involved did not exceed about £5,000 ($7,850 at the November 1992 exchange rate of 1.57), but this limit was dropped in 1991. The Lord Chancellor assigns circuit judges to these courts. No juries are used, and judges typically preside alone. Appeals go to the Court of Appeal, Civil Division.

Although after the recent changes county courts can try about any case that the High Court of Justice can, the more serious civil cases — ones involving large sums of money — probably will continue to originate in the High Court, as was true in the past. The High Court, which holds sessions in London and a couple of dozen other cities, has three divisions: Queen's Bench, for commercial law; Chancery, for wills and estates; and Family, for divorce and guardians of minors. One of the eighty judges presides alone when a case is being heard for the first time, but judges sit in twos and threes for appeals from lower courts. Appeals from the High Court go to the Court of Appeal.

Figure 6 ✦ 2 The griffin on the site of Temple Bar. In the eighteenth century the heads of criminals were displayed here. The buildings contain the Royal Courts of Justice: Queen's Bench and the like.

Although the two separate judicial hierarchies are joined at the level of the Court of Appeal, two distinct divisions are maintained, one for each type of law. The Court of Appeal has twenty-two judges. The name of the court is accurate; it only hears appeals from lower courts and has no original jurisdiction — that is, cases never begin here.

You probably will be surprised to see in Figure 6.1 that the court of last resort in Britain — the one to which any appeals from the Court of Appeal go — is the House of Lords. Although, technically, all peers are empowered to hear cases, by custom the Lords' judicial function is performed by only eleven of its members. As vacancies among this group occur, people who have demonstrated outstanding legal ability are designated by the Prime Minister to receive a life peerage. These lords of appeal in ordinary (or law lords, for short) try the cases heard by the House of Lords. Should the work load of cases be too heavy for these eleven to handle promptly, the Lord Chancellor, retired law lords, or peers having held high judicial positions can also be assigned to try cases. Law lords are appointed for life.[2] As they grow older, however, they may wish to be free from the duty of regularly hearing cases

---

2. The same is true for all British judges. A judge can be removed only by a vote of both Houses of Parliament. The last time this occurred was in 1830 when a judge was found to have misappropriated funds. Thus, despite this Parliamentary check, Britain has an independent judiciary.

and can retire. Since they remain members of the Lords, they are available for occasional judicial duties.[3]

This fusion of the legislative and judicial branches creates a bit of a problem. Since, formally, the entire House of Lords serves as the court, the law lords can't be permitted to hear cases when the Lords is in session as a legislature. The time that the Lords isn't in session is insufficient to try all the cases; thus, appellate committees were created. Cases are actually heard by only three or five of the law lords. Whatever such a committee decides is accepted by the other law lords as though all eleven of them had sat on the case, just as the Lords treats the law lords' decisions as though made by the entire House. The appellate committees decide cases by majority vote. As is the practice of the U.S. Supreme Court, concurring and dissenting opinions — in addition to the main opinion explaining the reasons for the decision — are permitted.

The Lords doesn't automatically hear all appeals; at whatever level a case began, at least one retrial would have occurred before an appeal to the Lords, so an opportunity would have been granted to correct any errors. The Lords hears cases, therefore, only when the Court of Appeal chooses to refer them for a definitive ruling or when the Appeals Committee of the Lords requests them. Trials heard by the Lords deal only with questions of law, never with matters of fact. The lower courts are responsible for clarifying what actually happened in a case. The Lords, then, can consider how to interpret the law and apply it to the facts that prior judicial proceedings have established.[4]

Although the House of Lords is the final authority for legal interpretation, remember that Chapter 5 explained that Parliament is supreme. All laws passed by Parliament are valid; not even the law lords can declare them unconstitutional. Furthermore, the law lords' interpretation of the law is not final; Parliament can reverse any of their decisions simply by passing a new law. Contrary to the situation in the United States, an elaborate process of constitutional amendment is unnecessary when the highest court interprets basic governmental powers and duties in a way that many people dislike.

On the other hand, British judges aren't able to protect people from arbitrary government to the same extent that American judges can. Until a

---

3. This contrasts with the procedure for archbishops and bishops of the Church of England. When they retire from their ecclesiastical posts, they cease to be members of the Lords. The religious members belong to the Lords ex officio, but the judicial members have life peerages.

4. The Scottish legal system differs from that of England and Wales. Only civil cases can be appealed from Scottish courts to the House of Lords. In criminal cases the High Court of Justiciary (located in Scotland) is the court of last resort. This is another indication of the importance of region in Britain.

law is amended, its provisions are what the British judges say they are. But a majority of Parliament (which typically enacts what the Cabinet wants) can alter the law. As Chapter 3 explained, this ultimate subservience of the judicial branch to the legislative one has made some Britons concerned about the adequacy of protection for basic freedoms. In one sense, the House of Lords is Britain's supreme court: No higher court of appeal exists in the country; but in another, the Lords aren't supreme. Britain's highest court doesn't wield the extensive power of the U.S. Supreme Court. Britain has Parliamentary supremacy, the United States has judicial supremacy (the more familiar way of expressing this would be constitutional supremacy).

Law Enforcement and the Quality of Justice

In most countries average people rarely, if ever, set foot inside a courtroom. More likely, they may need to seek legal assistance from a lawyer or may have to deal with a police officer. These are the circumstances in which the law enters one's life as a practical matter. What are these contacts like for a Briton?

The legal profession in Britain is divided into two types of lawyers: solicitors and barristers. When you need help on a legal problem (civil or criminal), you contact a solicitor, who will advise you about the relevant law and, should a trial be necessary, will prepare the necessary documents and related material. Frequently, especially in the most important cases tried in the higher courts, your solicitor will not present your case at the trial. He or she will select a barrister to actually argue the case in court. Barristers are courtroom lawyers only. They are likely to possess considerable rhetorical skills; they know how to present the material that the solicitor has compiled in such a way as to be most persuasive to the judge and/or jury. One can't, at the same point in his or her career, be both a solicitor and a barrister, nor can lawyers of the two types be partners in a law firm. Changes in the law in recent years have tended to erode the sharp distinction between solicitors and barristers, but the two separate groups still exist with the barristers being the more prestigious.

The Inns of Court, barristers' professional society, maintains professional standards, specifies the course of legal training, and sets the examinations that determine who shall be called to the bar, that is, entitled to practice as a barrister. Several barristers may agree to associate and share facilities and staff. The resultant "chambers" is much more loosely organized than the comparable U.S. law firm. Fledgling lawyers seeking to become barristers serve what is in effect an internship with a chamber to prepare for the bar exam.

Although barristers are articulate, rhetorically skilled advocates, they seldom engage in blustering or hectoring in court. The Perry Mason stereotype,

Figure 6 ✦ 3 Entrance to Middle Temple, one of the four Inns of Court

which has little validity in the United States, is even less accurate in Britain.[5] The atmosphere of British courts tends to be more formal and sedate than often is true in the United States. Not only are judges attired in robes and wigs to lend dignity to the proceedings, but so are the lawyers.[6]

Attitudes in Britain differ considerably from those in the United States concerning contacts with the police. A poll found that three-fourths of those who sought aid from the police felt they were very or fairly helpful. Even among those whom the police questioned about a possible offense, two-thirds regarded them as very or fairly polite. Three-fourths of those surveyed told

5. The British TV series (which has been shown on U.S. television) "Rumpole of the Bailey" provides a better description of procedures but isn't entirely realistic even though the writer, John Mortimer, was a barrister for years.

6. In the spring of 1992 the commercial court judges considered a proposal from the Commercial Bar Association that lawyers and judges in those courts should stop wearing wigs. Barristers have complained that wigs are uncomfortable, old-fashioned, and intimidating to the public. Perhaps three centuries of tradition is about to come to an end in Britain.

Figure 6 ✦ 4 The entrance to chambers for a group of barristers located in the Inner Temple, another of the four Inns of Court

Gallup in March 1991 they had a great deal or quite a lot of confidence in the police; the army was the only social institution receiving greater support. Parliament and major companies were tied for a distant third at 47 percent. When in another poll Britons were asked to assess the honesty and ethical standards of those in various occupations, they rated the police second only to doctors, with half believing police standards were high. In contrast, less than a fifth thought the same of business executives.

Finally—and this was a truly practical and demanding inquiry—nearly two-thirds would be pleased if their son became a policeman. You might say that's well enough for the parents, but what about the young people, the ones more likely to actually have to deal with the police. Surprisingly, Britons of your age (those fifteen to twenty-four) also had a positive view of the police. When asked which two or three of a list of occupations they most respected, over half mentioned the police—again, second only to doctors. Only a quarter of the young people surveyed had most respect for teachers. In another survey over half those eighteen to twenty-four said that the last time they had talked with a policeman, he was friendly. The bottom line is that regardless of age, two-thirds or more of Britons agree or agree strongly that the British police are the best in the world.

Unfortunately, although Britons' evaluations of the police are positive, they aren't as favorable as they once were. Those who feel that the police have mistreated them can file a grievance with the Police Complaints Authority. The PCA received a record number of complaints in 1991. More than 8,000, an increase of 10 percent over the previous year, were lodged.

Some increased dissatisfaction with the police is attributable to partisan politics. The police were an important factor in helping Margaret Thatcher win her confrontation with the coal miners in the mid-1980s. Not only did the police ensure that nonstriking miners were not prevented from working, but they constrained the movements of "flying pickets," miners from other areas seeking to demonstrate at mines where a strike had been called. This was not just a matter of maintaining law and order at the mine itself, but of preventing the pickets even from entering that section of the country. This curtailment of citizens' basic right of free movement reinforced the belief of many people on the left-wing of the Labour party that the police were an instrument of state oppression.[7]

However, the decline in esteem for the police is not just partisan politics. Britons had thought that the police were absolutely incorruptible, but recently cases have come to light of police dishonesty and abuse of authority. The problem goes well beyond venality, beyond merely accepting bribes to ignore criminal behavior. Cases of beating confessions out of prisoners, of planting evidence, and of denying defendants basic rights have become public. Charges of police racism, of being abusive toward black Britons (a category that includes Indians and Pakistanis), have become common.

Despite a reputation for fairness, British judicial procedures have had some flaws that permit, if not abet, abuse by the police. Although the police have no legal power to hold a person for questioning, they frequently do so. People taken into custody for this purpose are said, in a classic British phrase, to be "helping the police with their inquiries." As Michael Zander, professor of law at the London School of Economics, has commented, this really means "being held illegally by the police while they decide whether there is enough evidence to charge [them] with some offence."[8] The police need not make clear to such detainees that their presence is entirely voluntary and that they have the right to leave at any time.

Those who are formally arrested have no choice about "helping the police with their inquiries." Being arrested, however, is not the same as being charged with an offense. The key question concerns how long the police may

---

7. For a fully committed statement of this view see Edgar Wilson, *A Very British Miracle: The Failure of Thatcherism* (London: Pluto Press, 1992), pp. 114–119. For a less partisan but nonetheless hard-hitting and legally knowledgeable summary of police action during the miners' strike see K. D. Ewing and C. A. Gearty, *Freedom Under Thatcher: Civil Liberties in Modern Britain* (Oxford: Clarendon Press, 1990), pp. 103–112.

8. *The Guardian*, 16 December 1977, p. 5.

detain and question a suspect without making a charge. Under the Police and Criminal Evidence Act, the limit is twenty-four hours, except that those suspected of a serious offense may be held without charge for thirty-six hours. The police can obtain an additional thirty-six hours if a magistrate approves (in a full hearing with the detainee present and legally represented). And after seventy-two hours, a further extension of twenty-four hours is possible, again after a full hearing. About three-quarters of all suspects are charged within six hours, and virtually all (around 95 percent) within twenty-four hours. Nonetheless, a suspect could be held for as long as four days without ever having been charged with committing any crime.

Obviously, this is a time, if ever there were one, when a person needs a lawyer. The British police were not very good about protecting the right to counsel. Suspects often were held incommunicado. Even if a friend or relative knew one had been arrested and sent a lawyer to the police station, the police did not have to tell the suspect that legal help had arrived. Since the reforms of the mid-1980s, however, the law requires that police must tell those who are arrested that they have a right to a lawyer. Suspects may call their lawyer or may obtain one free of charge from the pool of those on call at the police station. The right to counsel is not absolute, however. For serious crimes the police need not inform the suspect of this right if they believe that doing so would have injurious effects (for example, if allowing a suspect to call a lawyer would alert confederates in the crime to the fact that the police were on to them). The police cannot delay permitting a suspect to contact a lawyer for more than thirty-six hours, since the suspect must have legal assistance at the hearing to determine whether he or she can continue to be held without charge.

As I mentioned earlier in this chapter, a magistrates' court decides whether the evidence against a person accused of a serious crime is sufficient to justify a trial. A lay magistrate, assisted by a legally trained clerk, presides over the hearing. If the defense argues that too little evidence exists for a trial, weeks or even months will go by before the issue is settled. The defendant must spend this time in jail unless he or she is granted bail. Given most magistrates' limited legal knowledge, they tend to commit people for trial almost automatically; only about 2 percent of those brought before them are discharged from further proceedings. Close to half the cases tried in the Crown Court, however, result in acquittals. Apparently, magistrates fail to review the evidence properly and impose the cost and stigma of a trial on many people who should not have to endure them. Even worse, the magistrates' behavior tends to encourage slipshod police work; police are not deterred from seeking committals despite a lack of sufficient evidence to obtain a conviction.

The British police used to have the primary responsibility of deciding whether to prosecute someone; no official comparable to the District Attorney in the United States existed in Britain. In the late 1980s, however, a national Crown Prosecution Service (CPS) was established to perform this function. The Director of Public Prosecutions (DPP), appointed by the Attorney General (a national politician, although, in contrast to American practice, usually not in the Cabinet), heads the CPS. The DPP decides whether or not to prosecute a few of the most difficult and serious cases, but the majority of the decisions is made by Crown prosecutors at the local level. The new system is intended to provide greater consistency in deciding which cases to prosecute, without losing sight of local circumstances that may counsel some variation in the pattern of enforcement from one area to another. In addition, the new system is intended to weed out the weak cases with which the police often proceeded when they were in charge of prosecutions.

The CPS has had several problems establishing itself. Inadequate funding has left it woefully understaffed and unable to discharge its responsibilities effectively. Not surprisingly, given what I've said in the two previous paragraphs, conflicts with the police have been common. The police complain that the CPS frequently fails to prosecute the cases they submit to it. As a result, they allege, those the police accuse of crimes go free, and law enforcement efforts are discouraged. For its part the CPS complains about lack of cooperation from the police and their failure at times to appear in court when they are scheduled to give evidence. In the long run these jealousies and suspicions probably will disappear, but they have made the early years of the CPS difficult. Shifting to a prosecution structure more akin to the American one has not been a smooth process.

The cost of defending against a serious criminal charge is so great that virtually all defendants in the Crown Court qualify for legal aid.[9] The government finances this program, which is administered by the legal profession. A person committed for trial may have to wait some time before the case can be heard. The number of prisoners awaiting trial doubled between 1979 and the mid-1980s. Delays of over a year were not unknown.

Once a case gets to trial, the accused may be disadvantaged by the rules of evidence. Search warrants authorize looking in specific places for specific types of evidence. Although the police may fail to turn up any of the specified evidence in searching someone's home, they may find evidence of a totally unrelated crime and decide to seize it. Even more of a problem is the fact that many searches are conducted without a warrant, although the law requires obtaining one. At times the police simply don't bother to get a warrant

---

9. Unfortunately, the same cannot be said for civil cases. In 1950 the great majority of the population qualified for civil legal aid, but now only a minority are within the disposable income and capital limits. Many middle-class and skilled working-class people must bear legal costs unassisted and find they simply can't afford to go to court no matter how strong their case is.

because the law permits them to search the home of someone arrested and any premises that he or she occupied immediately before arrest. In such warrantless searches the police can seize any evidence possibly related to any crime (not just to the one related to the arrest) they happen to come across while ransacking the premises. Thus, it is not uncommon for the police to have evidence obtained by questionable means.

Can such tainted evidence be used against the accused? In the United States an absolute exclusionary rule applies in federal cases: Illegally obtained evidence will not be admitted because the Fourth Amendment to the U.S. Constitution prohibits "unreasonable searches and seizures." But the British, you recall, have no bill of rights so they must rely on the concept of fairness embedded in the common law. As a result, in Britain the exclusionary rule is discretionary, not absolute. British judges can exclude any evidence that they feel is unfair—involuntary confessions, for example. This means, however, that the defendant's fate turns on views of the particular judge who happens to hear the case.

In sum, the rights of defendants and suspects clearly are better protected under the American legal system than under the British system. Some would argue that this means criminals are coddled in the United States; others would say that in Britain people are less protected from arbitrary police action. This lack of protection is of some importance because many people in Britain feel that judges are biased. The Prime Minister and the Lord Chancellor (both politicians) select the judges, and since judicial appointments do not require legislative approval, they have a relatively free hand in their choices. As far as the higher judges are concerned, however, professional competence matters more than partisan activities. At the intermediate level of circuit court judges, those chosen are more likely to be drawn from the ranks of barristers than from among solicitors. But the justices in the magistrates' courts are unlikely to have been either solicitors or barristers, since legal training is not required for appointment. Recalling that 95 percent of all criminal cases start in magistrates' courts will help you understand that the views held by most of those who have had trouble with the law are likely to have been shaped by the treatment they received from a magistrate. Since the legal knowledge of these justices is uncertain at best, they may be swayed in deciding cases by factors that are extraneous to proper judicial procedures.

Just as is true of the civil servants, the justices are unrepresentative of the public. Even if they do not consciously favor one segment of society over another, their background may dispose them to believe those with similar status and to look askance at those unfamiliar with the social graces. Three-fifths of those surveyed by Market & Opinion Research International in March 1991 favored a change to allowing the people to elect the magistrates in their local area. Especially interesting were the contrasts in response of various subgroups. Less than half of those in professional and managerial occupations wanted to change the procedure, compared to nearly two-thirds of those in skilled manual jobs. Only slightly over half of those who supported the Conservative party favored elections, while nearly three-fourths of Labour party adherents did. Clearly, certain segments of society believed that a fairer group of magistrates could be obtained if the people had a voice in their selection.

The bias perceived is not so much a matter of partisan politics as it is a question of that divisive factor I discussed in Chapter 2: social class. Only a quarter of those questioned by Gallup in the spring of 1990 thought that the courts were impartial, and more than three-fifths believed they favored the rich. Although the higher judges, in contrast to the magistrates, are legal experts, they are no more (perhaps less) representative of the population. Beyond any blatant social class bias, they are likely to be socially conservative, that is, to favor the status quo and to defend existing authority.

Such an outlook is related to their inclination to give the police a good deal of latitude in their law enforcement activities and to be unduly trusting of police testimony. I mentioned earlier the recent cases in which the police eventually were discovered to have fabricated evidence against the accused. When these defendants attempted to establish this fact in their trials, judges were dismissive of any evidence that would have discredited the police. Innocent people have spent years in prison on the basis of trumped-up charges. One prominent British judge rejected any concern about these matters with the comment that there wouldn't have been "all these campaigns to get the Birmingham Six [a group of defendants eventually shown to have been imprisoned through a miscarriage of justice] released if they'd been hanged. They'd have been forgotten, and the whole community would be satisfied."[10] A quality newspaper said of another such case that it "was a test of the capacity of English justice to admit that it could make serious mistakes. Once again, ... the Court of Appeal has failed the test."[11] A public inquiry had found that the defendants were improperly convicted and had spent a decade and a half in prison unjustly. (One of them had died while in prison.) Although the Court of Appeal overturned their convictions (thus finally releasing them from prison), it did so on such narrow grounds that questions about their guilt weren't repudiated. The complete vindication that the public inquiry gave them and that led to the reopening of the case was denied to them by the Court of Appeal.

In Britain the attitudes of judges are more important than they are in the United States. Although in both countries the burden of proof is on the

---

10. Quoted in *The Independent*, 27 June 1991, p. 24.
11. *The Independent*, 27 June 1991, p. 24.

prosecution, British judges, unlike American ones, don't simply serve as referees, requiring contending parties to play by the rules. Instead, they take an active part in the trial, commenting on the evidence as it is presented; for example, they might choose to note a failure by the defendant to testify, should that occur. British judges' instructions to the jury—the summary of the questions to be decided that is given to the jury just before it begins deliberation—leave little doubt about how the judges think the case should be decided. Given such judicial attitudes and procedures, a poll's finding that less than a third of Britons thought the system of law and justice was fair to everyone is understandable. Such feelings no doubt contributed to an additional finding that only two-fifths professed a great deal or quite a lot of confidence in the legal system. The legal system tied for fifth place (with the civil service) on a list of ten social institutions in terms of the public's support. These two essential elements of government received less than half as much support as the most favored social institution—the armed forces—in which 91 percent had a great deal or quite a lot of confidence.

Lack of confidence in the legal system and feelings that judges are biased affect the debate over a written constitution with a bill of rights. You might think that the prevalence of such views would be a strong argument for formally specifying the basic rules, rather than leaving them to tradition. The matter is more complex, however. A written constitution would end Parliament's supremacy; it would confine the legislature to certain specified powers and prohibit it from acting in certain matters. Something like a supreme court would have to be established to decide whether Parliament had abided by these constraints. Although such questions would arise in the form of judicial proceedings (as in the United States), one person's legal/constitutional question is another's political issue. British judges would gain significant political power—and, were the American system followed, not just a few top judges. Although the Supreme Court is the final authority on the meaning of the U.S. Constitution, even lower courts can refuse to enforce a law because they hold it to be unconstitutional. If circuit judges in Britain were able to make such rulings, concern about bias probably would become even more widespread. Reform may be needed, but it is not clear how best to accomplish it.

Enforcement of the law is not just a matter of police, courts, and judges. Also involved is the action of administrators in making regulations to flesh out the skeletal statutes passed by Parliament and their procedures in applying these to particular individuals. Two major concerns exist: (1) how to ensure that administrators exercise rule-making authority in conformity with the relevant statute's basic intention, and (2) how to protect citizens' rights from abuse by administrative boards and tribunals, especially when their action can't be challenged in the courts.

Laws that attempt to provide for every conceivable case would be too rigid; some flexibility to deal with changing circumstances and human variability is desirable. Administrators must be permitted some leeway to make rules adapting the general principles of the law to the practical circumstances of everyday life. On the other hand, their discretion can't be unlimited. They aren't elected; the people have no means of replacing them should they abuse their power or make unreasonable rules. The problem is more acute in Britain than in the United States because no written constitution limits the British legislature and the role of the courts is far more modest than in the United States. British courts cannot inquire whether Parliament has the right to legislate, and, consequently, to bestow rule-making power. They can only decide whether or not the rule-making agency is acting in accordance with the procedural framework prescribed by law.

The British have attempted to deal with the problem by establishing certain safeguards. First, administrators are able to make rules and regulations that have the effect of law only when authorized to do so by statute. Second, all rules made in a department must be confirmed by its Secretary of State. Third, an increasing number of statutes requires the department to consult advisory committees before issuing regulations. All departments in the economic and social sphere use advisory committees. Their effectiveness depends, however, on how willing the Secretary is to consult and also on how representative of the relevant interests the advisory groups are.

Some departments have established administrative tribunals to resolve conflicts with citizens who allege that their rights have been violated. These are staffed by experts with experience or training in the relevant field. Because procedures are less formal in tribunals than in courts, the former tend to be cheaper and quicker. Tribunals have been criticized, however, precisely because they do not follow all the procedures that courts do. For example, the lack of any right to cross-examine those who testify at a tribunal may make refuting them difficult. Furthermore, since the Secretary of State for a department appoints the members of the tribunal that deals with controversies caused by that department's actions, the department (and the Secretary, who is held accountable by individual ministerial responsibility) appears to be a judge in its own case.

The courts can scrutinize any points of law involved in tribunals' findings. And a special council reviews and reports on the workings of many tribunals. Nonetheless, it was thought necessary in 1967 to add a further safeguard similar to one pioneered by Scandinavia and New Zealand: establishment of an ombudsman, formally known as the Parliamentary Commissioner for Administration. Since, as you by now know, the British never want to move too far too fast, the Commissioner was granted powers more limited than those of the typical ombudsman in other countries. The Commissioner is an officer of Parliament and is permitted to consider only those complaints channeled through its Members. Any complaints sent directly to the Commissioner are culled to ascertain those that appear to be the most worthwhile, which are then passed on to Members with a request that they consider referring the matter back for action.[12]

The Commissioner can investigate cases where administrative action is so "thoroughly bad in quality" that it suggests bias or perversity. Should considerable hardship or injustice have been caused, the Commissioner can examine the case, even if the rules have been applied correctly, to ascertain whether the department concerned had adequately reviewed the applicable rule with the aim of making changes to prevent such results in the future.

Unfortunately, most of the complaints referred to the Commissioner have to be rejected because they fall outside the post's authority. The Commissioner can't, for example, deal with complaints about general policy, and certain subjects, such as nationalized industry and foreign policy, are ruled out entirely. An even greater limitation is that the Commissioner can only investigate and then report to Parliament, that is, can only recommend redress, not order it.

Nonetheless, the Commissioner has enjoyed some success. In some instances departments respond to the Commissioner's investigation by making the necessary corrections. In other cases Parliament has passed special legislation to compensate those who were improperly treated. And in many cases — the majority, in fact — the Commissioner finds that there really was no justification for a complaint. Although some individuals who receive such a finding may feel shortchanged, others may be satisfied that their complaint was investigated thoroughly or that misunderstandings were cleared up. The Commissioner provides a useful supplementary safeguard, but not a complete solution, to the problem of abuse of administrative power.

Summary

Although both Britain and the United States are common law systems, the judicial structures of the two countries differ in many ways. Perhaps the most fundamental contrast is that British judges lack ultimate authority to define the limits and procedures of government. Whereas the American system might be termed one of judicial supremacy, the British system remains one of Parliamentary supremacy. Nonetheless, the British judicial branch is not without significant influence. This makes the frequently expressed lack of

---

12. The one exception to this procedure is for the National Health Service. Complaints about its operation can be made directly to the ombudsman.

confidence in the judicial system and charges of bias matters of concern. Basic rights in Britain are not as thoroughly protected as in the United States. Whether this defect could be remedied by establishing a written constitution with a bill of rights, however, is open to question, since this could simply mean enhancing the power of judges at Parliament's expense.

Perhaps the British tradition of relying on elected officials, rather than judges, to protect rights is superior to the American one of relying more on the Supreme Court than on Congress. As the conservative justices appointed by Presidents Reagan and Bush have turned the Court in a new direction, many civil libertarian and social reform groups have begun to seek redress of their grievances more through legislative action than through judicial proceedings. Such a shift in focus could be regarded as a welcome development. In a democracy shouldn't political conflict be fought in the legislature more than in the courts?

However limited the actions of the British judiciary may be in constraining governmental power (and regardless of whether it differs fundamentally from American courts in this respect), Britons do have a safeguard against arbitrary administrative action that Americans lack: an ombudsman. This quasi-judicial institution has in some instances provided redress from improper government action and in other instances may have deterred wrongdoing by its existence alone. Administrators know that the ombudsman, in combination with Parliament, can require them to account for their actions.

Thus, although the mix of rights and protections differs between Britain and the United States, Britons don't lack for defenses against concentrated power. Some of these defenses are embedded in judicial structures. In the past these structures may have played a greater role in these matters in the United States; currently the contrast may be diminishing.

Part III

✦

Political Structures

*Photo on previous page: Entrance
to a polling station.*

7
✦
Elections

As previous chapters have emphasized, accountability comes to a focus in Parliament. If that were the end of the chain, however, Britain would have elite government. Democracy requires adding the link of responsibility to the people. Periodically, Members of the House of Commons must submit themselves to the judgment of the electorate. The Members must be accountable for the way in which they have discharged their primary function of monitoring and calling to account the other institutions and officials of government.

The right to vote is the most basic factor in enabling elections to call public officials to account. In the United States the right to vote was not fully established until the civil rights movement of the 1960s, despite a constitutional guarantee of the right a century earlier. (Perhaps written constitutions aren't all that more effective than unwritten ones?) In Britain, too, the struggle for the right to vote dragged out for a century, although there the battle had been won by the end of World War I and the conflict did not involve the same issues as in the United States. I begin this chapter by chronicling the growth of the franchise in Britain, emphasizing how the process incorporated social groups into the political system and transformed the party system.

During any given six-year period, an American can vote for a representative three times, for a senator once or twice, and for President and Vice-President once or twice. An American will have had five to seven opportunities to call national political officials to account. A Briton will have had considerably fewer opportunities — only one or two in a typical six-year period — despite the greater emphasis on accountability in the British system. Elections are not nearly as prevalent in Britain as in the United States.

The goal of accountability does, however, shape the *format* of British elections. Much more so than in the United States the focus is on calling the Government to account, rather than on selecting representatives for subnational areas. In practice, however, the votes of most Britons matter very little. For all but a handful, the sanction of accountability is considerably attenuated. This is one of the reasons why interest in electoral reform continues to flourish in Britain, in contrast to the United States, although both countries use basically the same system.

In the second section of this chapter I discuss the British electoral system and examine the prospects for reform. Then I conclude with a section devoted to the system in operation, describing campaign procedures and regulations. Here you'll learn how a candidate "stands" for election; in Britain it would be unseemly to "run" for office.

The Growth of the Franchise

The election of 1828 was a watershed in American politics. Power shifted from the Eastern Brahmins of Massachusetts and the patricians of Virginia to the self-made men of the frontier. The patronage of the spoils system brought the common man into government. The Age of Jackson was an age of mass democracy.[1] What was the contemporary political situation in that model of liberal democracy, Britain?

Only about 10 percent of the British men (were women considered as well, then only 5 percent of the adult population) could vote. In 1828 the population of the United States was under 13 million; more than a million voted in that year's Presidential election. Britain's population then was 24 million; fewer than a half million could vote. The rules conferring the right to vote were confused and chaotic in early nineteenth-century Britain. In some towns many adult males could vote; in others not even 1 percent could do so. In some places a man had to own property of a certain value to be entitled to vote; in others, the right was obtained through membership in the municipal corporation — membership that could be bought or acquired by marriage or

1. This was true only for white men. The political situation of African Americans and women was in no way democratic.

heredity. The model democracy of Britain lagged well behind American mass democracy. In some ways Britain resembled the classical democracies of ancient Greece in which denial of rights to women and slaves meant that only a fraction of the population had a role in politics.

Adequate representation of the people was further undermined by malapportionment of the House of Commons' seats, which were not allocated according to the population. Each county and each borough (town or city), regardless of size, had two Members in the Commons. Barely tolerable in an agrarian society, this distribution became farcical due to the Industrial Revolution. New factory towns, such as Manchester and Birmingham, grew rapidly in population, but, not having been boroughs when legislative seats were allocated, were unrepresented in Parliament. Many previously thriving rural market towns that became almost deserted, however, retained their traditional representation. Despite having slid into the sea, Dunwich still had two Members in the Commons; so did Old Sarum, although it had become merely a pasture for sheep. The fish of Dunwich and the sheep of Old Sarum were better represented than the people of Manchester.

The representatives from these "rotten boroughs" often were selected by just a handful of "freemen" (usually nonresidents) who owned a few dilapidated buildings there. Membership in the House of Commons literally was bought and sold; a few men of wealth controlled the balance of power in the legislature by having many Members "in their pockets" (therefore, the term *pocket boroughs*). Eight Lords are estimated to have controlled fifty-one seats in the Commons.

This indefensible corruption finally caused the British to act. The process of reform, the first step toward mass democracy, began with the Reform Act of 1832. Passage of this statute required a major political struggle. During the preceding year and a half, two other attempts at reform had failed. The struggle produced riots, demonstrations, and an attempted run on the banks to bankrupt the government. In London troops were alerted to defend the government against any attempted revolution. (Many people remembered what had happened in France only forty years earlier.) A great military hero was called to serve as Prime Minister in a short and futile effort to restore order and resist reform. It is no wonder that the result of all this is often included in lists of constitutionally significant statutes.

Did the British, then, install a system of mass democracy at almost the same time as the United States? If you guess yes, go back to Chapter 1 and start reading this book again. Nothing in Britain ever is transformed at a single stroke. Gradual, evolutionary, piecemeal reform is the British way. The Reform Act of 1832 (so significant that historians almost always refer to it as the Great Reform Act) redistributed the seats in the Commons and extended the right to vote. Although representation still was not proportional to population, many rotten boroughs were eliminated and about 150 seats were allocated to the new industrial towns. Uniform voting requirements were established in the towns, and about 200,000 voters were added to the electorate.

Yes, all that uproar for only an additional 200,000 voters. Even after this reform many fewer people could vote in Britain, despite its population being twice as large, than in the United States. Nonetheless, this reform well merited the label of "great." The first bar in the right-hand portion of Figure 7.1 shows how dramatic the change was; the electorate increased by about 50 percent. Perhaps even more important was the fact that a law had been enacted: This provided a precedent for further reform in the future. The British are leery of the unprecedented; they are much more willing to accept change when they can be convinced that it is just an increment to something that has already been done.

As significant as the precedent, the dramatic expansion, and the redistricting were, the most important result was entirely unintended. The increase in the electorate required registering voters for the first time. No voting lists had existed; previously, those enfranchised numbered so few that election officials knew them without having to check names on a list. With reform, droves of new voters would be coming to the polls; a list would be necessary. To cover the cost of paperwork a small fee was charged. Some of the newly enfranchised might not have wanted to pay this or, perhaps, didn't know that they now were entitled to vote. Those wanting to replace the current Member might well succeed if they could get the newly enfranchised registered; handling the paper work and paying the fee was a means of doing so. Those having political ambitions (either to launch or maintain such a career) formed registration societies.

Over the next few decades these societies evolved into political parties. Before then parties had been little more than factions in the Parliament; in the latter half of the nineteenth century modern parties—organized at the grass roots outside the legislature—developed in Britain. The Reform Act had expanded democracy not only through the intended enlargement of the franchise but also through the unenvisioned launching of a channel for popular collective action.

One other significant effect of the Reform Act was to bring a new class into British politics. The newly represented towns were strongholds of the commercial and industrial interests. This class now joined the gentry—those whose wealth was based on landed estates—in running the country. Other classes remained shut out from influence. As the left-hand portion of Figure 7.1 shows, only about 7 percent of the total adult population was entitled to vote even after the Reform Act.

Having worn themselves out with this effort, the British didn't change the franchise again for thirty-five years. Voting rights didn't, however, simply stagnate. The franchise was based on a property qualification. Prosperity during the middle third of the nineteenth century enabled another 400,000

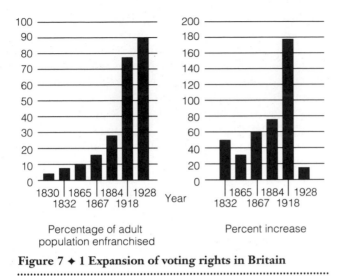

Figure 7 ✦ 1 Expansion of voting rights in Britain

voters — twice the number added by the Reform Act — to qualify. Sometimes you get reform by doing nothing and the British are masters of benign (and, at times, malignant) neglect.

In 1867 a second Reform Act was passed; it created a mass electorate of around 2 million.[2] As you can see from Figure 7.1, this second reform produced a bigger proportional increase in the electorate than had the initial reform. The first reform had disrupted society; the one of 1867 caused little excitement: The precedent of electoral reform had been set more than three decades earlier. Even after this second reform, only 16 percent of the population (less than half the men, to say nothing of the women) could vote. Nonetheless, a new class was incorporated into the system. Many industrial workers were enfranchised, enough so that they became a majority of the electorate in typical towns and cities.

The next step in reform did not have to wait nearly as long as had the second. In 1884 the franchise again was extended; now most men could vote. Again the effect was to grant a role in governing the country to a new class — this time to farm workers. Now about 5 million people could vote. Britain had come a long way during the nineteenth century; yet it still lacked even the universal manhood suffrage widely established in the United States way back in the Age of Jackson.

---

2. Compare this with the fact that 6 million voted, to say nothing of the number eligible, in the U.S. Presidential election of 1868.

Figure 7.1 shows that the first reform of the twentieth century (coming in 1918) truly was a blockbuster. Finally, all men (except that diverse triad of criminals, lunatics, and peers) could vote. And women, who in the United States had to wait nearly two years longer until the Nineteenth Amendment to the Constitution was ratified, received the right to vote. That's not quite true. Never able to do something entirely at once, the British decided that the risk of letting women vote would be more tolerable if granted only to mature females. Frivolous women (by definition, those under 30) weren't included in this extension of the franchise. Nonetheless, the bulk of another social group had been given a share in self-government. The growth in the electorate was the largest ever, soaring from 8 million to over 20 million. Now, finally, eighty years after the process of democratization had started, most adults could vote.

The absurdity of the voting qualification for women couldn't be sustained for long. In 1928, women between the ages of twenty-one and thirty received the vote; the sexes were enfranchised on the same basis. Electoral reform had required five installments spread out over almost precisely a century. No better example of the British approach to political reform—incremental change over an extended period—could be found. Such a way of doing things may strike Americans as silly. Remember, however, that the United States needed a civil war to establish in law the principle that African Americans were human. The simultaneous effort to grant them political rights (again showing the limited effectiveness of written constitutions) was thwarted for about a century. And during that time one would be hard-pressed to argue that the United States made any incremental progress toward the ultimate goal, in contrast to Britain's plodding, but relentless, progress toward reform.

In a comparative study of voting rights in sixteen European countries, Stein Rokkan found that "the stronger the inherited tradition of representative rule, the *slower* [emphasis added], and the *less likely to be reversed* [emphasis added], the process of enfranchisement and equalization."[3] Where this didn't exist, where "continuity in the operation of the medieval organs of representation" was absent, voting rights were granted early and suddenly, but often lost subsequently.[4]

The contrast between Britain and France illustrates the polar extremes. At the close of the eighteenth century both countries were dominated by an aristocratic elite. France, whose medieval representative organ the Estates General hadn't even met for well over a century and a half, had a revolution and instituted universal manhood suffrage. Since then the country has experienced other revolutions and coups and has had at least a dozen different

---

3. Stein Rokkan, *Citizens, Elections, and Parties* (New York: David McKay, 1970), p. 83.

4. Rokkan, pp. 82, 86.

constitutional systems. Frequently, the right to vote has been cut back and has had to be reextended subsequently. The result has been a system tormented by enduring political cleavages.

Far from having a revolution at the same time, Britain did nothing for forty years. The country then embarked on the piecemeal reform that I've recounted: five installments spread out over a century, always expanding the right to vote, never turning back. Each reform incorporated another social group into the political process. Furthermore, except for the struggle at the start of the process, Britain experienced limited social upheaval (although winning the right to vote for women was hard-fought). All in all, it's a pretty impressive achievement.

Although voting rights obviously are fundamental, they are only the first step toward mass democracy. Enfranchising men gave greater impetus to achieving that goal than did extending voting rights to women. For men, gaining the right to vote was the start of a process. Working-class parties began to develop after the reform of 1867 and at the turn of century began to play an important role in the political process. The vote was a means by which working men became able to affect the policies of government. For women, gaining the right to vote was the culmination of a process. Extending the vote to them did not produce new political movements. Even some existing movements withered in the belief that their work was done. Those participating in the contemporary women's movement in Britain — concerned, for example, with correcting the disproportionate number of women among Members of the House of Commons — feel a kinship with their forerunners who fought for the right to vote, but no direct line of organizational activity exists. Incorporating new social classes into the electorate transformed the party system; incorporating the other gender did not. Furthermore, showing an effect on policy output is more difficult in the case of gender enfranchisement than it is in the case of social enfranchisement.

Thus, the process of expanding the franchise reveals a great deal about how political change occurs in Britain, how various social groups acquired a role in the political process and with what effect, and how the party system developed as it did. In the next chapter I'll explain how this process affected Britain's leading parties and their ideologies.

With the enfranchisement of young women, Britain had achieved universal suffrage. Nonetheless, two other reforms still were able to advance democratization. During the 1960s many countries came to recognize a lower age of legal maturity. In keeping with such thinking, Britain lowered the voting age to eighteen in 1969.

The other reform, curiously, made Britain more democratic by *curtailing* the right to vote. As late as the middle of the twentieth century, Britain permitted two forms of plural voting: the business premises vote and university constituencies. Prior to 1918 one could vote in Britain not only where one resided but wherever one owned business property. Thus some people could vote in several different constituencies. Since a single election day was not established until 1918,[5] a businessman could tour his various commercial premises over a period of weeks, voting as he went. After 1918 the business premises vote was limited to only one vote in addition to where one resided.

At its peak in 1929, the business premises vote was enjoyed by nearly 400,000 people, more than 1 percent of the total electorate. Following World War II, it had declined to only 65,000. Nonetheless, the Labour party abolished (you should be able to guess why) this form of plural voting in 1948.

Although also peculiar by American standards, the other form of plural voting was rather more defensible. Beginning in 1603 Britain's institutions of higher learning were granted direct representation in the House of Commons. Oxford University, for example, had two members in the Commons. All told, universities returned twelve Members of Parliament, only a fraction of 1 percent of the House of Commons. Graduates of a particular university could vote for its member(s). Thus, some 229,000 people had two votes: one where they lived and a second for a university constituency. One could argue that university graduates are more intelligent or, at least, better informed than the average person (an argument that may recommend itself to many readers of this book). Nonetheless, even university constituency plural voting offends against the well-known definition of democracy as one person, one vote.

Because university constituencies smacked of elitism (and because few of the university MPs were Labour), the Labour party abolished them along with ending the business premises vote. Thus, as far as the franchise is concerned, Britain obtained political equality at the middle of the twentieth century. Britain had been much more hesitant than the United States to extend the franchise. Yet in 1950, when Britain had instituted political equality, the United States still was far from establishing it, using the poll tax, literacy tests, and other irrelevant legal bars along with illegal intimidation to deny African Americans the right to vote. Slow and steady often wins the race.

The Electoral System and Its Possible Reform

Britain has two types of elections: general elections, in which all seats in the House of Commons are contested, just as occurs in elections for the U.S. House of Representatives, and by-elections to fill individual vacancies. No

---

5. In 1910, for example, voting took place from December 2 to December 19. The officials in each constituency determined when the polls would be opened in their area.

primary elections are held; political parties in the various constituencies designate candidates to contest the elections. Nor do the British voters ever have a chance to vote for the chief executive, since the fusion of the legislative and executive branches confines this responsibility to the House of Commons. And the upper house, you'll recall, is hereditary and appointive, not elective.

The procedure for both general and by-elections is familiar to Americans — a system known as single-member, simple-plurality (SMSP) or (more commonly in Britain) first-past-the-post. This means that each electoral district returns only one member to the legislature and the candidate winning more votes than any other, regardless of what proportion of the total vote that may be, is elected. This procedure attracts little attention in the United States because in almost every district only two candidates, a Democrat and a Republican, receive any significant share of the vote. Typically, therefore, in the United States the person elected will have the support of a majority of the voters, if not of the electorate.

When more than two parties possess appreciable strength, however, some curious — perhaps indefensible — results occur. This is because under the SMSP system the share of the legislative seats a party obtains *has no necessary relation* to the proportion of the popular vote that it received. More crucial than the share of the vote is its distribution. Should a party's support be spread fairly evenly throughout the country, it may be so diluted that it wins few, if any, seats. Success requires concentrating support sufficiently to finish first in some districts. Doing that doesn't require a substantial segment of the total national vote. For example, in October 1974 the Liberal party received over six times as many votes as did the Scottish Nationalist Party (SNP), more than 5.3 million to less than 850,000. Yet the Liberals won only two seats more than the SNP in the House of Commons: thirteen to eleven. The Liberals spread their support across more than 600 constituencies throughout the country and rarely were able to finish first; the SNP concentrated theirs in Scotland's 71 constituencies and in several instances outpolled everyone else.

Table 7.1 shows the effect of the electoral system on the parties in 1992. The Liberal Democrats received more than half as many votes as did Labour and yet won only a fourteenth as many seats. The Liberal Democrats had three times as many votes as all other third parties and independent candidates combined and yet won four fewer seats. One might say that the Liberal Democrats were "shortchanged" nearly 100 seats; they were entitled to nearly six times as many as they received. As you know from personal commercial transactions, when you are shortchanged somebody else comes out ahead. Both Labour and the Conservatives got a "bonus" of additional seats that increased their strengths by more than a fifth. As a result, although the Conservatives were well short of a majority among the voters, they enjoyed a comfortable majority in the House of Commons.

Table 7 ✦ 1 Proportional and Actual Results of the 1992 Election

	Conservatives	Labour	Liberal Democrats	Others
share of total popular vote (%)	42	34	18	6
equivalent share of Commons' seats (#)	274	221	117	39
number of seats won in election	336	271	20	24
difference (#)	+62	+50	−97	−15

The relative magnitude of these impacts is clearly apparent in Figure 7-2. For the Conservatives and Labour, the entire bar represents the number of seats they actually won in 1992. The lower part of the bar shows the number they would have obtained had seats been allocated proportionally to the share of the popular vote received. For the Liberal Democrats and Others the graph shows the reverse; that is, the lower part of the bar is the number of seats that they actually won in 1992 and the entire bar shows what their strength in the Commons would have been had seats been allocated proportionally. Thus, the size of the "bonus" and the "shortchange" is vivid.

A national (as distinct from a regional) third party is at a severe disadvantage under SMSP. That assertion raises an interesting question. From the time that parties (grass-roots organizations outside Parliament) developed to the end of the nineteenth century, the Liberals and the Conservatives were the two leading parties. One or the other always formed the Government and typically controlled a majority of the seats in the House of Commons. By the 1920s this had changed; a new Labour party had grown sufficiently strong that it managed to form two Governments during that decade (although it didn't hold a majority of seats in the Commons). The shift on the left of the political spectrum from Liberal to Labour continued, so that after World War II Labour won a majority in the Commons and the Liberals were pushed almost to extinction.

If third parties are so disadvantaged by the electoral system, how did Labour manage to displace the Liberals as one of the two leading parties? Although part of the explanation lies with factional feuding that weakened the Liberals, the primary reason is that Labour met the requirement mentioned above for success under SMSP: It concentrated its vote. Although Labour wasn't a regional party, like the current Scottish National Party, its support wasn't distributed evenly throughout the country. Remember how the extension of the franchise eventually incorporated the working class. Not

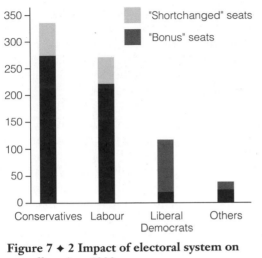

Figure 7 ✦ 2 Impact of electoral system on seat allocation, 1992

only did it become a majority in many towns and cities after 1867, but working-class residences were concentrated in particular parts of these urban areas. In less urbanized areas where coal mining was the main occupation, the working-class vote also was concentrated. Building a national political force takes some time; Labour couldn't sweep to power immediately after the workers were enfranchised. But the new party possessed the necessary base from which to mount an effective challenge to the existing major parties; its concentrated support meant that it could beat all comers in many districts.

I've concentrated on discussing the disproportional aspects of SMSP in anything less than a strict two-party system. Space doesn't permit me to examine in detail the interesting results this system has produced in Britain. For example,

- In 1951 the Labour party won more votes (nearly 14 million) than any other party had before and *lost* the election.
- From 1979 to 1983 the Conservatives increased their seats in the Commons by fifty-eight while their share of the vote declined slightly. However, when their share declined by only 0.1 percent from 1922 to 1923, they lost eighty-eight seats.
- In 1983 28 percent of the vote allowed Labour to win 209 seats in the Commons, while in 1931 31 percent gave it only 52 seats.

Such curious results make considering some alternative to SMSP worthwhile.

Were Britain to alter its electoral system, it most likely would adopt some form of proportional representation (PR). PR is not a single system but a variety of procedures with the common feature that the share of the legislative seats a party receives corresponds fairly closely to its share of the popular vote. Those who advocate PR claim, therefore, that it is fairer than SMSP. Opponents of PR charge that it fractionalizes the party system, encouraging splinter parties to form. Unless some minimum share of the vote is imposed (such as the 5 percent hurdle in Germany), even minuscule parties will obtain seats. Fringe parties will not be weeded out, as occurs with SMSP, and the legislature will consist of a dozen or so parties, as happens in Italy. This, continues the argument, will produce weak, indecisive government; no majority will exist for any policy. The defenders of SMSP can't deny that the system produces disproportional results, but they are willing to pay this price to help the leading party in each election obtain the legislative strength necessary to implement its program. Proponents of PR respond that such power may not be desirable. If parties have sharply distinct programs, then giving first one and then the other control of the Government will result in zigzags as each undoes the work of its predecessor. The result will be adversarial politics in which partisans automatically reject their opponents' policies, regardless of merit. Better, they say, to have a system like PR that forces cooperation among at least some parties.

Whatever the merits of these arguments, how likely is such a change in Britain? Parties are not charitable organizations. You can be certain that few people in either the Conservative or the Labour parties feel guilty about enjoying the benefits that the electoral system confers on their parties at the expense of the Liberal Democrats, the principal third party. You can understand why the Liberal Democrats have been the chief advocates of a switch to PR. Unfortunately for them, however, their small band of Members in the House of Commons has no hope of enacting such a law. So why isn't PR as academic an issue in Britain as in the United States?

From 1979 through 1992 the Labour party lost four successive elections, despite high levels of unemployment that might have been expected to give it a substantial victory. Furthermore, most of the time when it last was in power from 1974 to 1979, Labour lacked a majority in the House of Commons. In fact, for only four of the forty years from 1951 to 1991 was Labour in office with a comfortable working majority in the Commons. Some people in the Labour party, therefore, have come to think that the only means of ending the apparent "normal" Conservative dominance is a shift to PR. Since World War II no party in Britain has received a majority of the vote. If that distribution of the vote were reflected in the Commons, as PR would intend, then even if they were the largest party, the Conservatives would not have a majority. Labour, even if it were only the second largest party, might be able to form a coalition with a third party and get back into power.

Although many Labourites have become more sympathetic to PR, others in the party, especially on its left wing, remain skeptical even after a fourth straight election defeat in 1992. These people (who have been labeled "one last heavers") stress the narrowness of Labour's most recent loss. If fewer than 4,000 people had not voted Conservative in 12 key constituencies, *no party* would have had a majority in the Commons. This Labour faction continues to believe that their party can return to power under the existing electoral system.

Even were Labour united in favor of PR, a change in the electoral system would remain problematic. Labour and the Liberal Democrats aren't in power; they can't pass any legislation. The Conservatives are in power and they have no incentive to make a change. Having won majority control of the House of Commons in four straight elections with little more than two-fifths of the popular vote, why should the Conservatives want to abandon SMSP? Only if Labour and the Liberal Democrats can figure out how to get back into power under the *existing* electoral system will they have any opportunity to alter it.

Many observers thought that the Conservatives might well be driven from power in either 1987 or 1992. A "hung Parliament" seemed a plausible outcome in both elections. This term refers to the situation in which no single party holds a majority of seats in the House of Commons. In such a case the largest party could attempt to form a minority Government; Britain has had those on occasion during the twentieth century. Such a Government, however, is constrained in the policies that it can implement and always is vulnerable to being voted out of office by the Commons. To avoid such weakness, one or the other of the two leading parties might try to form a coalition with the Liberal Democrats. The likely Liberal Democratic price for such support would be a promise to change the electoral system to PR.

Contrary to expectations, however, the Conservatives won majority control of the Commons in both the 1987 and 1992 elections. Therefore, the Liberal Democrats lacked opportunity to strike any bargain for their support. In the absence of a hung Parliament the Conservatives have no reason to agree to alter the electoral system. However, two factors — devolution and the Euro-elections — may impose some pressure upon them to consider a change. Demand for greater autonomy in Scotland may become so great that even the Conservatives have to devolve some powers. Were that to occur, a Scottish assembly probably would be created to enact regional legislation. Many Scots would favor having the members of that assembly elected by some form of PR. Since the Conservatives received only a quarter of the vote in Scotland in the 1992 election, PR likely would give them greater strength in any regional assembly than would SMSP. Thus they would have some incentive to abandon SMSP in Scotland. But were PR conceded there and a precedent thus established, would it only be a matter of time until a similar change had to be made in the electoral system for the House of Commons?

As for the Euro-elections, Britain is the only member of the EC that *doesn't* use PR to select members of the European Parliament. The Greens won 15 percent of the vote in Britain in the 1989 Euro-elections, but because of SMSP received not even one member of the British delegation. The Liberal Democrats with 6 percent also were shut out, although the Scottish Nationalist Party, with only 3 percent, did elect one Euro-Member. The Greens and the Liberal Democrats between them had a fifth of the vote, but were denied any representation in the European Parliament. Continuing to be the only country using an electoral system that produces such results may become increasingly indefensible for Britain. The argument that SMSP is needed to produce Governments with majority legislative support clearly is irrelevant to the Euro-elections. As with elections for a Scottish assembly, however, conceding PR for Euro-elections could be a precedent that eventually would lead to PR for the House of Commons.

To Americans, the British preference for SMSP is unexceptional. To Europeans, the puzzle is that Britain has rejected PR for so long. Most European countries have used PR for most of the twentieth century. The Rokkan study mentioned earlier found that PR was more likely to be adopted in countries with considerable ethnic and religious diversity. (Although I argued in Chapter 2 that Britain is not homogeneous, it is not as diverse as Rokkan's generalization would require.) On the other hand, SMSP has been more likely to survive in larger countries (that is, larger than ones like Belgium or the Netherlands) "with stronger governmental establishments."[6]

Rokkan's comparative study makes clear that Britain's electoral system is not an aberration. However, it cannot be taken for granted, as in the United States, as the only conceivable procedure for calling the holders of governmental power to account. The Liberal Democrats, of course, will continue to press for a change. More important, Labour is becoming considerably more sympathetic as well. While the Conservatives' partisan interests remain opposed to a change, some pressures — most significantly — may push even them to consider revised procedures. As we saw with extension of the franchise, change in Britain, although slow, does occur.

Campaign Regulations and Practices

American elections occur regularly on fixed dates. Not only does the interval between elections vary in Britain, but the date of an election is unknown until about a month beforehand. The only requirement is that elections must not be more than five years apart; beyond that the timing of an election is at the Prime Minister's discretion.

The effect of the British procedure on the regularity of elections is apparent from Figure 7.3. The two horizontal lines indicate the interval between

---

6. Rokkan, pp. 88–89.

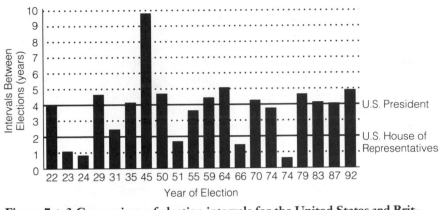
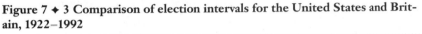

Figure 7 ✦ 3 Comparison of election intervals for the United States and Britain, 1922–1992

elections for the U.S. President or House of Representatives. Sometimes the interval between elections is longer in Britain than in the United States, sometimes shorter — all without any apparent pattern. Britain can even have, as you can see from the dates along the horizontal axis, two general elections in a single year. In February and again in October 1974 all the seats in the House of Commons were up for election.

You may be puzzled why, given what I've said, one of the intervals was nearly ten years. The years of the two elections involved should give you a clue. Since Britain had had a general election in 1935, the next one should have occurred no later than 1940. For Britain, unlike the United States, World War II began in September 1939. Political leaders did not want partisan politics to hamper the country's fight for survival. So, they agreed to postpone elections until the war was over. The five-year maximum can be ignored if *both* the House of Commons and the House of Lords approve doing so. Each year through 1944 both Houses voted to extend the life of Parliament for another year. Since Parliament is supreme, it can do whatever it wants.

Despite these differences in regularity, the result appears to be rather similar. From 1920 through 1992 Britain held twenty general elections; during the same period the United States had only one fewer, nineteen, Presidential elections. Furthermore, the *average* interval between elections in Britain was four years, exactly the same as for U.S. Presidential elections.[7] Is this a distinction without a difference? Does the flexibility in scheduling British

---

7. Four years is the British median; the mean is slightly less (3.7 years).

elections matter? Yes, probably. In the United States regardless of whether circumstances (economic indicators, foreign incidents, and the like) are good or bad for the President's party, an election must be held at the scheduled time. In Britain the Prime Minister can try to maximize support for his or her party by calling an election when things are going well for the country.

How much of an advantage this gives the incumbent party is impossible to say. Obviously, Britain can't go back in time to find out what the results would have been if the Prime Minister had selected a different date for any given election. Many factors affect the outcome of an election and the impact of timing can't be isolated and measured. Beyond that, Prime Ministers, lacking a crystal ball, don't always get the timing right. Many people argued that Prime Minister Edward Heath called the February 1974 election too early; had he waited, the Conservatives might have been able to gain the handful of additional seats (the party won only five seats fewer than did Labour) necessary to maintain themselves in power. The problem is that circumstances may not improve; the Prime Minister who waits may find himself or herself boxed in with no room for maneuver. Prime Minister James Callaghan hardly could have wanted to call an election after the disastrous "winter of discontent" when the garbage piled up and the grave diggers prevented interments, but he had no alternative.[8] Manipulating the timing of elections may well help the incumbent party but can't guarantee success.

Taking a more positive view than possible partisan advantage, the British procedure for scheduling elections makes the mandate theory of elections more plausible. According to this conception, an election presents the voters with a choice between alternative policy programs. Elections clearly become a means of calling those in power to account. Furthermore, whatever party wins can claim to have popular approval — a mandate — for the policies it then implements.

The mandate theory makes an election resemble a referendum. The familiarity of the mandate theory in Britain (along with the traditional preference for limited, rather than mass, democracy) helps to explain why referenda were unknown in Britain until the 1970s. As you may recall from Chapter 3, the first referendum — on whether Britain should remain a member of the EEC — was not held until 1975 with another following in 1979 on Scottish and Welsh devolution.

The EEC referendum was supposed to be a special, one-time only, procedure. Although the devolution referendum refuted that idea, more than a decade has passed without another one being held. As Chapter 3 explained, the British people favor more frequent use of referenda. Many wanted a

---

8. Although the loss of a vote of confidence in the Commons is what forced Callaghan to call an election in May 1979, he could not have delayed beyond five more months even had that vote not gone against him.

popular vote, as the Danes and French had in 1992, on the Maastricht Treaty. Prime Minister Major refused, however, to permit a referendum. He argued that because the Conservative Manifesto for the 1992 election had supported the Treaty, the people had endorsed it by reelecting the Conservatives.

The flaw in the mandate theory is that even if an election can be called when an issue is most controversial, nothing can guarantee that the campaign will focus only, or even primarily, on that issue. Furthermore, people vote as they do for a variety of reasons (class status, housing tenure, parents' politics, and the like), many of which have nothing to do with the issues debated in the campaign.

In practice the mandate theory becomes little more than a partisan argument employed by the winning party to justify its program. For example, Labour argued that it had a mandate to take many privately owned enterprises into government ownership during the 1945 to 1950 Parliament because it had included this policy in its 1945 election manifesto (party platform). Public opinion polls indicated, however, that many people who had voted for Labour in 1945 did *not* support its nationalization policy; they had been won over, despite their opposition to nationalization, by Labour's social welfare proposals. So, although flexibility in timing can matter, this difference between British and American procedures doesn't transform elections into a fundamentally different political procedure.

Although election dates aren't fixed in Britain, the prevailing practice is to hold elections (both general and by-elections) on Thursdays. Once the Prime Minister has decided on a specific day, he or she usually gives a week or two warning that the monarch will be dissolving Parliament to call for new elections. After Parliament is dissolved, candidates have about a week in which to file the papers necessary to appear on the ballot. About two weeks after nominations close, the election is held. The whole campaign consumes only about a month, which is quite a contrast with the United States, where those running for President may start campaigning a couple of years before the election.

The 1992 campaign was as short as the law permits. Prime Minister John Major announced on March 11 that he would ask the Queen for a dissolution. Parliament was dissolved on the following Monday, March 16. The election was held on April 9. Thus polling day was announced only 30 days in advance.

Since the only national officials elected are Members of the House of Commons (Britons can't vote for the office of Prime Minister) and, except for 1979, local elections aren't held simultaneously with national ones, the ballot is quite simple. The voters' only task is to decide which one of the typically three to five candidates they wish to represent the constituency. Until 1969 the ballot carried only a candidate's address and occupation, in addition to his or her name; party labels weren't used. Since then candidates have been permitted up to six words to describe their party affiliation. Some independents use this provision for last-minute electioneering. For example, one candidate during the Vietnam war styled herself "Stop the SE Asian War." Some prefer a lighter touch, like the candidate who labeled himself as belonging to the "Science Fiction Loony Party." Naturally, the press referred to him as the loony candidate.

Such candidates do little harm; few people are willing to vote for them. Nonetheless, some Britons have been concerned that frivolous candidates might make elections a travesty. Getting one's name on the ballot is incredibly easy; all that is required is the signatures of ten qualified voters in the constituency. An electoral deposit, first imposed in 1918, is intended to deter candidates having little prospect of significant support. Candidates had to deposit £150 with their nomination papers. Those failing to win an eighth of the vote forfeited the deposit; the government kept the money. Initially, the deposit was a considerable amount of money; a person's total income for a year might only be several hundred pounds. Over the years, however, inflation so reduced the value of this sum that the requirement of a deposit ceased to eliminate loony or eccentric candidates (some of whom contested more than two dozen elections although they knew they were almost certain to lose their deposit every time). Therefore, prior to the 1987 election the deposit was increased to £500.[9] The proportion of the vote a candidate must win to get the deposit back was reduced to 5 percent. The increased deposit appears to have done little to control the number of candidates. In 1987 the number did drop by about a tenth compared to the previous general election. But in 1992 the number of candidates *rose* considerably to a record level of nearly 3,000.

Whether the British arrangement eliminates not just frivolous candidates but serious, although unorthodox, candidates as well is open to question. The Liberals (now known as the Liberal Democrats) have been adversely affected by the deposit. In 1950 about two-thirds (well over 300) of their candidates lost their deposits. The party teetered on the brink of extinction for the rest of the decade. Although much stronger in the 1980s, the party objected to the increase in the deposit. The Liberal Democrats did not fear losing deposits (they lost only 1 in 1987 and only 11 in 1992), but could ill afford, given their limited funds, having more than £300,000 tied up in deposits when they needed money to buy campaign materials.

The Greens, on the other hand, are unable to meet even the lowered deposit minimum. In 1992 the party offered more than 250 candidates and all lost their deposit. Thus contesting the election cost the party nearly a quarter of a million dollars, entirely apart from campaign expenses. Candidates advocating environmental issues clearly are not frivolous. Penalizing them merely because they win only a few votes tends to constrict discussion of

---

9. The value of the pound sterling (£) fluctuates a good bit from one year to another. For example, in September 1992, £500 was around $1,000 but was around $785 in November 1992.

important issues. The Greens weren't the biggest loser of deposits in 1992. The Natural Law party of Maharishi Mahesh Yogi offered more than 300 candidates and all lost their deposit. Although not frivolous, the Natural Law party (in contrast to the Greens) hardly could be said to have contributed to serious discussion of the issues in the 1992 campaign.[10]

Members of the Commons are not required, either by law or by custom, to live in the constituency they represent. Remember that Britain is a unitary system, not a federal system. Someone who lives in southern England may well contest a constituency in Scotland. Some candidates do promise that if elected they will move to the constituency. And at times candidates with local roots will attempt to discredit opponents who come from outside the area by referring to them as carpetbaggers (perhaps in ignorance of the American origins of this term). Such strategies probably don't win many votes; what matters is the amount of time a Member spends in a constituency and the effort devoted to working for its interests.

Becoming eighteen qualifies one to vote in Britain. You may have heard something about the new tax (the community charge) imposed in Britain at the end of the 1980s, and you may have assumed that, since it was informally called the poll tax, it was intended to be a means of denying some people the right to vote, as had occurred in the American South for years. This is *not* correct. Although you could be sent to jail for failure to pay the community charge, you did not have to pay to be permitted to vote. In any event, the phasing out of the community charge by the middle of the 1990s will eliminate any possible misunderstanding.

Voter registration procedures differ between Britain and the United States. In Britain the government takes greater initiative in trying to register those eligible to vote. Every October each household receives a form on which the head of the household is to list all residents at that address who meet the voting requirements. Failure to return the completed card makes one subject to a small fine, although this is rarely collected. The registration officer in each constituency compiles a list of registered voters from the information returned and posts the list on bulletin boards in public buildings, such as the town hall, or other public places. People not on the list who believe that they should be may protest to the registration officer and, if the decision is unsatisfactory, may appeal to the county court. Similarly, anyone may protest the inclusion of persons he or she considers ineligible.

The importance of the British approach to voter registration is demonstrated by the fact that low participation in U.S. elections is due more to

---

10. The NLP was supported by former Beatle George Harrison. He explained that the party sought "to enhance the individual's life so that collectively we're all enhanced . . . to try to do stuff out of the mould of the old politics." Another former Beatle Ringo Starr commented, "I don't know what they stand for. I saw George this morning in an interview and he wasn't real sure what they stood for either."

people not being registered than to those who are registered failing to vote. Since the British government takes the initiative for registering voters, fewer British citizens are prevented from voting than American citizens.

Nonetheless, British citizens do have to respond to the government's initiative. Although, as noted, the poll tax was unrelated to the right to vote, the law permitted the government to use voter registration records to compile the poll tax lists. Some people who sought to evade paying the poll tax avoided registering to vote—didn't respond to the government's initiative. This behavior was especially prevalent among young people who had just reached the voting age of eighteen. More than a tenth of those who came of age between 1987 and 1992 are thought not to have registered. For all ages, the electorate would have been about 2.5 percent larger than it was in 1992 if people had registered at the same rate as in 1984. The poll tax had a significant impact on reducing voting participation in Britain.

In contrast to its active role in registering voters, the government in Britain has lagged behind the United States on absentee ballots. Until 1985 only those incapable of getting to the polls (such as the physically infirm) were permitted an absentee ballot. Now an absentee ballot is a convenience available to those who are away from home on election day. Rather than ask for an absentee ballot, a voter can authorize another person to cast his or her ballot. The new law also gave the vote to Britons living outside the country. For twenty years after moving away from Britain, expatriate Brits can retain their registration in the constituency where they last lived. Only about 30,000 of the 2.5 million eligible were registered in 1992, no more than a few hundred in any given constituency. Such electors may vote by absentee ballot or by proxy.

Shortly before the election, registered voters receive a card from the government reminding them of the election and telling them where their polling place is located and the hours that it will be open (see Figure 7.4). Here, too, the British government seeks to encourage and facilitate participation in elections. Voter turnout in Britain is considerably higher than in the United States. Only once in the twentieth century—the first election in which women could vote—has turnout fallen below 70 percent. In one post-World War II election, it reached 84 percent. In 1992 nearly four-fifths (78 percent) of the registered voters participated in the election, the highest turnout in nearly twenty years.

During the brief election campaigns, candidates speak at various meetings, sometimes talking to three or four gatherings at schools or other public facilities during a single evening. You can see one such meeting in Figure 7.5. Occasionally a national political figure attends one of these meetings in an attempt to boost attendance. Typically, should forty or fifty people show up, that's a good turnout. Most of those who do come probably have already decided to vote for the candidate, although a few may be trying to make up

ON HER MAJESTY'S SERVICE — OFFICIAL POLL CARD

YOUR POLLING STATION WILL BE:

POLLOKSHIELDS BURGH HALL
70 GLENCAIRN DRIVE
GLASGOW G41 4LL

POLLING HOURS
7 AM TO 10 PM

POLLING DAY

11TH JUN 1987

GLASGOW POLLOCK

CONSTITUENCY

NUMBER ON REGISTER, NAME AND ADDRESS

PK43 / 920

SANDY MACTAVISH
1905 GLENCAIRN DRIVE
GLASGOW   G41 4PR

IF UNDELIVERED RETURN TO RETURNING OFFICER,

PARLIAMENTARY ELECTION

You need not take this card with you when you go to the polling station, but it will save time if you take it and show it to the clerk there.

When you go to the polling station, tell the clerk your name and address, as shown on the front of this card. The presiding officer will give you a ballot paper; see that he stamps the official mark on it before he gives it to you.

Mark your vote on the ballot paper secretly in one of the voting compartments. Put one X in the space to the right opposite the name of the candidate for whom you wish to vote. You may vote for only one candidate. If you put any other mark on the ballot paper your vote may not be counted.

Then fold the ballot paper so as to conceal your vote, show the official mark on the back to the presiding officer and put the paper into the ballot box.

If you spoil the ballot paper by mistake, do not destroy it; give it back to the presiding officer and ask for another.

If you have appointed a proxy to vote in person for you, you may nevertheless vote at this election if you do so before your proxy has voted on your behalf.

If you have been granted a postal vote, you will *not* be entitled to vote in person at this election; so please ignore this poll card.

ISSUED BY THE RETURNING OFFICER

Figure 7 ✦ 4 A poll card

Figure 7 ✦ 5 A constituency campaign meeting

their minds and some may simply enjoy shouting embarrassing comments or raising difficult issues.

Since relatively few people attend these meetings, the campaign must go to the voters. Figure 7.6 shows a party worker at a tube (subway) station greeting commuters as they return home from work. One of the most traditional electoral activities in Britain is canvasing. Candidates and their supporters go door to door throughout the constituency seeking to identify favorable voters. These contacts may require candidates to answer questions about their policies, but they try to avoid lengthy debates on the doorsteps so that they can cover as many houses as possible. All candidates really want to know is who intends to vote for them. On election day party workers can check the official record of who has voted and contact those voters who said they would support the candidate but haven't yet gone to the polls. Canvasing could be dismissed as a fairly marginal political activity. Yet the practice means that British voters have a much better chance than do American voters of actually meeting the candidates face to face. This can only help to give Britons a sense of voting for a real person rather than just a name.

Figure 7 ✦ 6 Campaigning at a tube (underground train) station

The post office delivers free of charge one communication from a candidate to every voter in the constituency. Typically this "election address" includes the candidate's picture, some biographical information, and a statement of the policies he or she thinks are especially important. Portions of election addresses appear in Figures 7.7, 7.8, and 7.9; a Conservative standing in an English constituency, a Labour candidate in a Scottish constituency, and a Liberal Democrat in an English constituency. Despite what I've said about being able to stand anywhere in the country, notice that all three of these particular candidates stress their local connections. Since the Conservatives had been in power nationally for several years in 1987, Parkinson stresses the accomplishments that the party has achieved. Sir William tries to convince voters that although nationally the Liberal Democrats are the third party, in this constituency they are the true challengers to the Conservatives.

Each candidate is required by law to appoint a campaign manager (called an election agent) who must account for *all* campaign expenses (excluding the candidate's personal expenses). No campaign spending for a candidate (or against an opponent) is permitted unless authorized by this agent. Expenditure is limited by law. The maximum varies according to the type of constituency and the size of its electorate, but it usually is less than $10,000. Small as that is by U.S. standards, the typical candidate spent only about two-thirds to three-fourths of the maximum in the 1987 election.[11]

---

11. David Butler and Dennis Kavanagh, *The British General Election of 1987* (London: Macmillan, 1988), p. 236.

Figure 7 ✦ 7 Portion of a Conservative election address

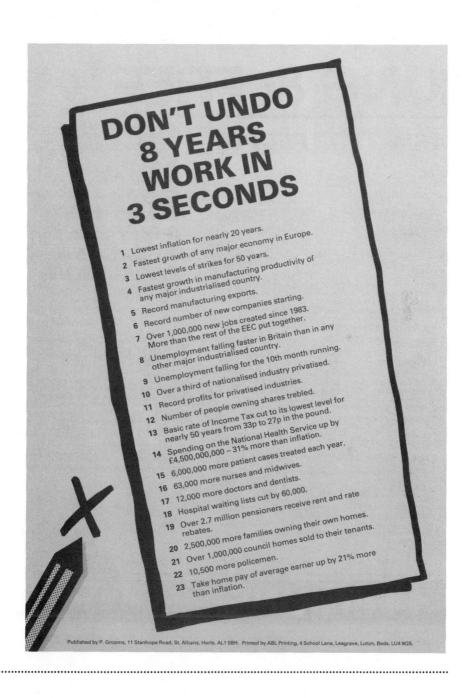

Figure 7 ✦ 8 Portion of a Labour election address

A PERSONAL MESSAGE FROM JIMMY DUNNACHIE YOUR LABOUR CANDIDATE IN POLLOK ...

Dear Elector,

I live with my wife in Pollok and for many years I have represented parts of the Pollok constituency in local government: on Glasgow Corporation, Glasgow District Council and, since 1978, on Strathclyde Regional Council.

I have served on the policy making Executive Committees of the Councils and I am currently Senior Vice Chairman of Strathclyde Region's Social Work Committee.

Throughout my local government service I have at all times been available to my constituents. I work hard and I fight well for the people I represent. I now seek your vote to continue my fight for you at Westminster when Labour wins this election.

I know that the next Labour Government will end the hardships that Thatcherism has imposed on our people because Labour will once more invest in our people. Together we will build a better future.

I will never rest until my fight for the people of Pollok has won a better environment and secured a decent standard of living for everyone in Pollok.

This is my pledge to you.

Yours sincerely,
JIMMY DUNNACHIE

VOTE LABOUR

DUNNACHIE X

Published by: Wm O'Rourke, Election Agent,
259 Peat Road, Glasgow G53.

Printed by: T.F. Dryden Printing Ltd (T.U.)
147 Howard Street, Glasgow G1 4HF.

Focus Special

William Goodhart

Changing Britain for Good

A PERSONAL MESSAGE FOR

FROM

WILLIAM GOODHART
**Liberal Democrat for
Oxford West & Abingdon**

Election Communication

Sir William Goodhart
Liberal Democrats

William and his wife, Celia, have lived in the constituency with their family for more than 20 years. Celia is herself a former Parliamentary candidate and now a headmistress of a girls' school. Their eldest daughter works for the NHS as a child psychologist. Their two youngest children, Laura and Benjamin, are at University.

William Goodhart was brought up in Oxford, where his father was a professor. After National Service in the Oxford and Bucks Light Infantry, William studied law at Cambridge University, gaining first-class honours.

William was appointed a Q.C. in 1979 and is an eminent lawyer. He is Chairman of the all-party human rights organisation "Justice", which works to prevent miscarriages of justice.

William Goodhart is a leading member of the Liberal Democrats and is a member of the Party's Policy Committee, working together with party leader Paddy Ashdown

The contest in this constituency is between William Goodhart and the Conservative. Labour have always done badly here. Labour came third in 1983, 1985, 1987, 1989 and 1991 in local and national elections. Make your vote count!

For more information, to help William Goodhart's campaign, display a poster or for a lift to the polling station, please ring (0865) 204106.

Figure 7 ✦ 9 Portion of a Liberal Democrat election address

"Oxford West & Abingdon urgently needs a change of MP. After a year of recession, we need an MP who will fight for the Health Service, against local education cuts and get more police for our area."

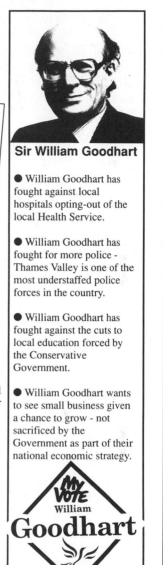

Sir William Goodhart
91 High Street, Oxford
Tel: 204106

Dear Resident,

After thirteen years of Conservative Government the country urgently needs a change of direction. Our Conservative MP has voted for the Poll Tax, the opting-out of our local hospitals and Oxfordshire education cuts – he cannot avoid responsibility for them.

This area needs an independent local voice. We need someone who will stand up for our local Health Service, the education of our children and those who have fallen foul of the Conservative-led recession. Only the Liberal Democrats can provide that voice – <u>Labour have always been third here.</u>

As your MP, I will ensure that local voices, not party dogma, take first place.

Yours sincerely,

William Goodhart

Sir William Goodhart

● William Goodhart has fought against local hospitals opting-out of the local Health Service.

● William Goodhart has fought for more police - Thames Valley is one of the most understaffed police forces in the country.

● William Goodhart has fought against the cuts to local education forced by the Conservative Government.

● William Goodhart wants to see small business given a chance to grow - not sacrificed by the Government as part of their national economic strategy.

MY VOTE
William
Goodhart

It's a Straight Choice

It is a straight choice in this election between local Liberal Democrat William Goodhart and the Conservative. Labour have always been third here, and still are.

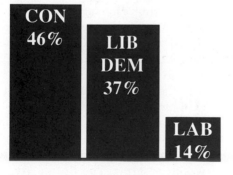

CON 46%

LIB DEM 37%

LAB 14%

Spending by parties at the national level is *not* limited. In the 1987 election the national organization of the Conservative party spent nearly $16 million, Labour spent more than $7 million, and the Alliance about half as much as did Labour.[12] The Conservatives hinted in 1992 that they had a campaign fund of about $36 million, but this probably was a strategic exaggeration. In any event, they owed banks for loans of around $22 million. Labour spent close to $13 million on the 1992 campaign, about 90 percent of which came from the trade unions. The Liberal Democrats had to make their appeal with under $3 million.

The Conservatives had twice as many large billboard sites throughout the country as did Labour and nine times as many as did the Liberal Democrats. On the other hand, on election day Labour's newspaper advertising far surpassed the Conservatives'. Labour had nineteen full-page ads in the national newspapers, compared to only seven for the Conservatives; the Liberal Democrats had none. Furthermore, during the campaign Labour had an ad on the electronic billboard at London's most prominent location.

The national organizations must be careful that nothing in their campaign materials appears to appeal for votes for a specific candidate — including their party Leader and potential Prime Minister. This limitation does not preclude using pictures of the Leader in election leaflets, as Figure 7.10 shows. Notice, however, that the front of the leaflet does not urge the electorate to vote for Major as an individual candidate or mention the name of the constituency he was contesting. Had it done so, the cost of printing it would have had to have been included in the official account of his campaign spending for his constituency. That cost alone might well have exceeded the maximum that he could spend on his constituency campaign.

To avoid the possible legal complications, for many years British parties declined to advertise in newspapers during election campaigns. In 1974, however, the Liberal party broke with this practice. Although none of the expense it incurred for this advertising was allocated to the official spending accounts of any of its candidates, none of these accounts was challenged in legal proceedings. Therefore, during the next election campaign the Conservative and Labour parties followed suit with ads in the national press; such ads have been the practice ever since. (Several examples appear in Chapter 8.)

Television plays a major role in British elections. Of course, the news programs cover the campaign. I say "of course," but, surprisingly, this wasn't true until the 1959 election. Before that, you wouldn't have known from watching newscasts that an election was in progress. The British, you see, wanted to believe that elections are a time for rational choice between policy alternatives; they wanted to avoid the hype and hoopla that they felt had

---

12. Butler and Kavanagh, p. 235.

debased the U.S. electoral process. Furthermore, the broadcast media were worried that no matter how objective their coverage, they would be criticized for favoring one party or another. (This is an especially sensitive issue for a country in which part of the TV and radio media are owned by the government.) Despite such concerns, the British finally recognized that ignoring elections was journalistically absurd. Now, besides news coverage, television provides various public affairs programs commenting on the campaign and discussion or interview programs that give party leaders (and even some less prominent candidates) an opportunity to express their views and respond to questions.

On most weekday mornings during the campaign, each of the main parties holds a press conference at their national headquarters in London. (One of the Conservative party press conferences appears in Figure 7.11.) Various party leaders are present to make short statements on the issues that the party wants to emphasize and to answer questions from the press. The parties hope that clips from these sessions will appear on the evening TV news programs. The parties' leading figures usually spend little time campaigning in their constituencies, preferring to tour the country. Although they may make major speeches on this tour, they are more concerned with visiting a prosperous farm or an efficient factory so that the TV cameras can get some apparently interesting but basically irrelevant footage for the evening news.

For example, during the 1992 campaign Prime Minister Major strolled into a fishmonger's stall in London (the full complement of media types in tow) and observed, "We used to come in and buy kippers." To which the stallkeeper replied, "Well, we still sell kippers." "I'll have some kippers. I'll have some kippers," cried the Prime Minister. This momentous exchange was well covered in the media and, doubtless, won the crucial fish-sellers vote for the Conservative party.

None of this is terribly different from American practices (hamburgers, perhaps, instead of kippers?), but one aspect of the role of television in elections differs considerably in Britain. Neither parties nor individual candidates are permitted to buy any TV time for special programs or ads. Instead, free broadcast time is officially allotted to the main parties. The parties prepare at their expense whatever type of program they wish; these programs are carried by both the government-owned BBC (British Broadcasting Company) and the commercially operated ITV (Independent Television).

Although British election campaigns are short, you'll be surprised to learn that the total time provided for all the parties combined for election telecasts in 1987 was only about two and a half hours. Labour, the Conservatives, and the Alliance each had five telecasts of about ten minutes each. This was the first election in which a third party was allowed as much time as each of the two leading parties. Only one other party (the Greens) offered enough candidates (fifty) to earn any TV time; it was permitted only a single telecast.

Figure 7 ✦ 10 Conservative election leaflet

A MESSAGE
from
John Major

There is a very clear choice at this election. We can go forward - or back.

A Conservative Government will go on cutting taxes. Labour's costly pledges would put taxes right back up again. For everybody.
Can you afford five years' hard Labour?

My Government will go on winning the inflation fight. A Kinnock Government would let inflation go up again.
Can you afford Labour's higher prices?

Our policies will help people to own their homes. Labour's policies would push up mortgage rates and hit the housing market.
Can you afford the cost of Labour?

Our reforms are delivering better health care and higher standards in schools. Labour would throw everything into turmoil.
Can you afford Labour's muddle?

We have brought industrial peace to Britain. Labour would give power back to the unions - and let the pickets loose on our streets.
Do you want to go back to strikes and disruption?

We have made Britain respected abroad, and stood up for Britain's interests in Europe. Labour would throw our strong position away.
Do you want Brussels to rule Britain?

Recently, times have been tough. But we've won through. Britain must reap the reward. We're poised for recovery: more growth and new jobs. Business agrees that what is needed now is the safe re-election of a Conservative government.

Let's get on with building a better life.

Don't throw your future away.

Vote Conservative on April 9th.

CONSERVATIVE ☒

Published by Conservative Central Office, 32 Smith Square, Westminster, London SW1P 3HH & printed by Eyre & Spottiswoode Ltd., Union Crescent, Margate, Kent CT9 1NU

Figure 7 ✦ 11 Press conference at Conservative party headquarters

··

The Scottish Nationalist Party was given two telecasts within the Scottish viewing area, and the Welsh nationalists had one in Wales.

The equality between the three main parties was not maintained in 1992. The Conservatives and Labour each had five broadcasts, but the Liberals were granted only four. The Greens again qualified for a single broadcast, as did the Natural Law party for the first time. All these were national broadcasts; the two nationalist parties retained their regional broadcasts. Given the number of lost deposits, the Greens would have been better off financially with fewer candidates. One could argue that if they had offered only a fifth as many candidates, 10 minutes of TV time would have cost them only $45,000 instead of the nearly quarter of a million dollars they forfeited.

The free TV time, along with the free postage and the shortness of the campaign, does much more to keep down the cost of British elections than does the spending limitation, which applies only at the constituency level in any event. Campaigns also cost less than in the United States because British constituencies have much smaller electorates. Because Britain's population is only about a quarter that of the United States and the House of Commons has half again as many Members as the House of Representatives, the typical English constituency has about 70,000 voters and the typical Scottish and Welsh one about 56,000.

The British have tried harder than have Americans to maintain relatively equal constituencies. Boundaries are updated every ten to fifteen years, the most recent changes having occurred before the 1983 election. Despite these efforts, the size of electorates varies from 24,000 to 100,000. On the other

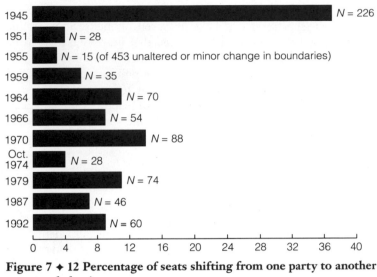

Figure 7 ✦ 12 Percentage of seats shifting from one party to another at general elections

hand, two-fifths of the English constituencies have electorates ranging only from 63,000 to 77,000 and three-fifths of the Welsh and half of the Scottish ones fall within a range of 50,000 to 63,000.

As is true in the United States, incumbency is a big advantage. Figure 7.12 shows that only once since World War II (1945) have as many as a third of the seats in the House of Commons changed hands from one party to another in a general election. (The 1950, February 1974, and 1983 elections are omitted because extensive constituency boundary changes make any comparisons with the previous elections impossible.) Most of the time, fewer than a tenth of the constituencies shift. Furthermore, the shifting constituencies tend to be the same ones, swinging from one party to another and back again over the years. About three-fourths of all constituencies are won by the same party election after election.

What this means is that in the overwhelming majority of constituencies, the result is a foregone conclusion. No matter who the candidates are, no matter what issues are raised during the campaign, the result never is in doubt. Elections appear to offer a procedure for calling power-holders to account; in fact, only those voters in a handful of marginal constituencies have an opportunity to wield such power. Such a charge applies equally to the United States; however, the American system doesn't make accountability as crucial a constraint on power as does the British system.

Although incumbency is major strength in both Britain and the United States, the reason for its potency differs between them. In the United States

Representatives manage to generate some personal loyalty among the electorate through constituency service and extensive self-publicity. Some of this occurs in Britain. A poll early in the 1990s found that more than two-fifths said they were satisfied with the job that their Member did for the constituency, while less than a quarter were dissatisfied. More important, however, is the strong loyalty that most British voters have felt for a particular party. They have tended to vote for their party regardless of who the candidate was. A voter told an interviewer back in the 1950s, "I'd vote for a pig if my party put one up." More compelling evidence supporting this point is a recent poll, which found that although three-fifths knew which party had won the seat in the previous election, only half knew the Member's name. Studies of British voting behavior suggest that this traditional attachment to parties began to decline in the 1970s. Some experts argue that British voters now act less automatically, that issues and party performance influence electoral choice more than in the past. Even with this change in behavior, the personality of a candidate matters only in a very closely contested seat. Few candidates can expect to win even as many as 3,000 votes on a personal basis, that is, other than because of their party affiliation. The result is that party loyalty in voting behavior tends to attenuate accountability.

The type of person elected used to differ considerably between the two leading parties. Many of those elected as Labour had been manual workers, while typical Conservative Members ran businesses. Over the years, however, both parties have elected fewer Members from their traditional class base and have returned more Members from the professions.

Some contrasts remain, however. Nearly half the Conservative MPs elected in 1992 had graduated from Oxford or Cambridge, while only a fifth of the Labour MPs had. On the other hand, three-fourths of *both* groups of Members had higher education degrees. At the secondary education level, in 1992 for the first time a majority (53 percent) of Conservative MPs had been educated in state-supported schools, rather than privately. Despite this shift, the contrast with Labour remained striking since 87 percent of its Members went to state schools. As for the archetypal public school, a tenth of the Conservatives had gone to Eton while only two Labour MPs had.

Turning to occupational background, the largest single group among Conservatives (a third of the total) was company directors; only four Labour MPs held such a position. A fifth of the Conservatives elected in 1992 were lawyers, compared to only 8 percent of the Labour Members. The Conservatives had twenty-nine farmers to only one for Labour. Labour's two largest occupational categories were higher education faculty (forty-eight) and schoolteachers (forty-three). Together they accounted for a third of the Labour Members. Only half as many Conservatives had one or the other such occupation, thus accounting for only a seventh of their party's total membership. An eighth of Labour Members were trade union officials; the Conservatives had none.

The average person elected to the Commons will be in his or her late forties, with little difference between parties. In 1992 more women were elected than ever before — a grand total of sixty, less than a tenth of the total membership of the House of Commons. This is a slightly smaller proportion than women obtained in the U.S. House of Representatives in 1992. Also in 1992 more "coloured" (as the British would say) were elected than ever before — all of six. (The three largest parties had offered only twenty-four such candidates.) One of these six was a woman, who had been initially elected in 1987; it was the first time that a black woman had ever been elected. The 1992 election also had a first occurrence: the first "coloured" person to be elected as a Conservative. Although at 9 percent African Americans are underrepresented in the U.S. House of Representatives, nonetheless the proportion is considerably higher than in Britain.

Summary

More than a century and a half of change, which gradually brought a sequence of social groups into the political process, has produced the current British electoral system. Britain shares the same basic system (single-member, simple-plurality constituencies) with the United States, but in most other aspects campaign practices and electoral regulations differ between the two countries. In some instances the British seem to have the best of it (short and relatively inexpensive campaigns, for example); in other cases the American procedure seems more favorable (for instance, greater citizen involvement is provided by the use of primary elections to select candidates).

The greater opportunity for contact with candidates during the British campaign doesn't appear to have given citizens much sense of participation in the political process. Britons feel they have little control over what politicians do in office; they are searching for some means of enhancing their influence over policy making, perhaps through referenda. Despite British elections being countrywide struggles waged by well-integrated parties for control of the Government, voters don't feel that elections are an effective means of calling power-holders to account.

Such feelings suggest that parties (the subject of Chapter 8) have failed the public in some ways, have not satisfactorily served as channels through which popular desires can be converted into public policy. The assertion that the British public is disillusioned with elections and parties, however, flies in the face of two facts. If elections are thought to be a waste of time, then why is turnout so much better in Britain than in the United States? If British voters are disillusioned with elections, what must this say about American voters? And if British parties are perceived as failing to do their job, then why haven't elections become personalized? British elections don't resemble the American conglomeration of virtually autonomous personal contests. Chapter 8 will need to examine the role of British parties and compare them with American ones.

Little is heard in the United States about changing the electoral system, aside from occasional academic debate about reforming the electoral college used for Presidential elections. In Britain, however, electoral reform continues to produce lively discussion. Concerns about the nature of the leading parties have generated some of this. Alternating control of the Government between parties with sharply distinct programs may not produce consistent or well-conceived public policies. An electoral system forcing cooperation among parties — a less adversarial system — might achieve better results. The relevance of this argument is affected by the nature of the party system. In the strict two-party system of the United States, SMSP works satisfactorily. Where the party system departs significantly from the two-party model, SMSP may not be an entirely appropriate system. The extent to which Britain differs from the United States in departing from the two-party model is the first topic addressed in the next chapter.

8
✦
Parties

The governmental institutions and electoral procedures of Britain and the United States differ in many respects; the two countries' party systems, however, long have been grouped in the same category. Both were considered to be among the world's few two-party systems. The appropriateness of that label for Britain is questionable. Differences with the U.S. party system are so great that saying both countries have the same type only causes misconceptions about British politics. Explaining why Britain has been thought to be a two-party system, but isn't, requires discussing party history and organization. That discussion can indicate how it came about that more than two options were offered to the British electorate. Whether the number of choices offered to the British voters changes depends on whether the parties offer distinctive packages of ideology and policies that appeal to particular segments of society. Therefore, the latter portions of the chapter focus on these matters.

The Party System

Figure 8.1 shows the strength of the two leading British parties in the House of Commons since World War II. The portion of seats they have held has fluctuated little, running

• 185

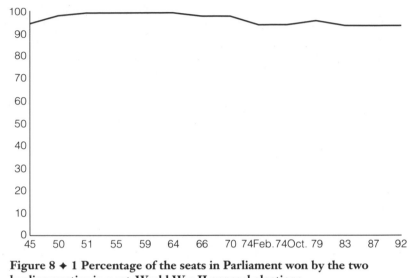

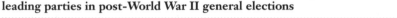

Figure 8 ✦ 1 Percentage of the seats in Parliament won by the two leading parties in post-World War II general elections

consistently well over nine-tenths. For over a half century the Conservatives and Labour have been the only parties with any prospect of winning a majority of the seats in the Commons and, thereby, holding the office of Prime Minister and controlling the executive. How could there be any doubt that Britain is anything other than a two-party system?

Remember how the SMSP electoral system adversely affects nationwide third parties; spreading their support fairly evenly over the entire country results in winning few seats despite their having substantial popular support. Therefore, Figure 8.1 presents only a partial picture of the party system. Figure 8.2 offers a somewhat different view. Two-party dominance is not nearly as great in voting support as it is in Parliamentary strength. Through the 1960s the gap between these two measures of party success wasn't large. This changed, however, in the 1970s: Despite a substantial loss of popular support for the two largest parties, their control of the Commons' seats declined only slightly. From 1974 to 1992 the combined share of the popular vote for the two largest parties averaged 75 percent, meaning that third parties consistently won a quarter of the votes.

That information indicates only the *total* impact of third parties; focusing on how they've affected elections at the individual constituency level is even more striking. If only two parties have substantial support in a given district—if third parties are irrelevant, fringe movements—the winning candidate is likely to receive a majority of the votes. The inability of the winner to attain that majority suggests that, far from being inconsequential, a third

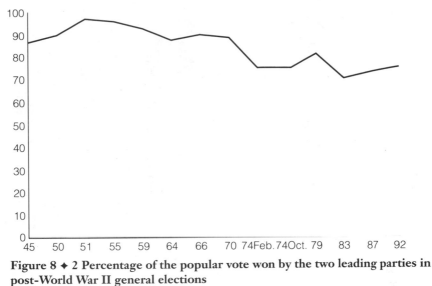

Figure 8 ✦ 2 Percentage of the popular vote won by the two leading parties in post-World War II general elections

party is diverting many votes away from the largest two. With that in mind, look at Figure 8.3. Even when the largest parties were most successful (1970), a fifth of the victors were unable to obtain a majority of the votes cast in their districts. In three of the nine elections included in Figure 8.3, over half the winning candidates were elected with a minority of the vote. In the six elections since 1974, only half (52 percent) of all the Members elected to the House of Commons managed to win the support of a majority of the voters in their constituency.

One other bit of information provides an interesting snapshot of the British party system. In December 1981 a Gallup poll found that more than a third of the public supported the newly formed Social Democratic Party (SDP) and a seventh supported the traditional third party, the Liberals. Together (the two parties were in the process of creating an electoral "Alliance") they were preferred by half the respondents. The two leading parties, Labour and the Conservatives, each had the support of less than a quarter of the public.

The Liberal Democrats (created by the merger of the Liberals and the SDP) aren't the only third party to be organized throughout the country. The extreme right-wing National Front has offered candidates (although it didn't do so in either 1987 or 1992), as does the ecology-oriented Green party. But they have received so little support that they never win any seats. The Greens, however, were amazingly successful in the 1989 elections for the European Parliament. They came in third with 15 percent of the vote, nearly three

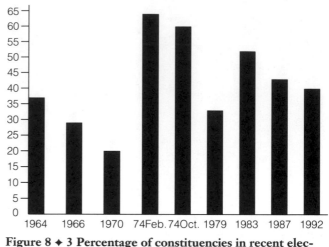

Figure 8 ✦ 3 Percentage of constituencies in recent elections won on less than 50 percent of the vote

times as much as the Liberal Democrats. The British electoral system took care of them, however; they received no seats. As noted in Chapter 7, all of the Green candidates in the 1992 election lost their deposit; that is, none of them received as much as 5 percent of the vote in their constituency.

In addition to third parties that contest elections throughout the country, Britain has several regionally based parties. Although support for the Welsh nationalists (Plaid Cymru, pronounced "plied come-ree") and the Scottish Nationalists (SNP) has declined from what it was in the 1970s, these parties continue to be an electoral factor in these two nations. In six elections from February 1974 through 1992, the SNP's share of the vote in Scotland ranged from 12 percent to 30 percent. In 1992 it received 22 percent. Popular support for the SNP has been greater than for Plaid Cymru, which has ranged from 7 percent to 12 percent in Wales with 9 percent in 1992.

Although in October 1974 the SNP managed to win eleven seats, in elections since then it has won only two or three, just as has Plaid Cymru (PC). In 1992, despite winning a larger share of the vote in Scotland than Plaid Cymru did in Wales, the SNP got only three seats and PC got four. Thus, although these two parties influence the debate on some political and even constitutional issues, their activities hardly transform the nature of the British party system.

The same could be said of the situation in Northern Ireland. No United Kingdom party system exists; Britain has a party system and Northern Ireland has an entirely separate one. One of its most successful parties used to be affiliated with the Conservative party, but that link was severed years ago. Now the only parties able to win any of the handful of seats allotted to

Northern Ireland are the ones that only operate there. Labour and the Liberal Democrats don't even bother to contest any of the constituencies in Northern Ireland. The Conservatives did fight eleven of the seventeen constituencies in 1992. One of their candidates managed to obtain a third of the vote, but nine were under a tenth and four lost their deposit.

The ability of one of Britain's third parties (the Liberal Democrats) to cut into the two leading parties' strength far surpasses the achievements of George Wallace in 1968 and John Anderson in 1980 in the United States. On the other hand, the share of the vote won by Ross Perot in the 1992 Presidential election was quite similar to that obtained by the Liberal Democrats in Britain's 1992 election. Despite this coincidence the British party system differs significantly from the American system; adequately understanding British politics requires going beyond the activities of the largest parties. What makes this difference between the countries' party systems remarkable is the third-party success that exists in Britain despite the impediments. The SMSP electoral system, the electoral deposit, and the limits on radio and TV all hamper third parties. Yet such parties not only continue to exist in Britain, but in the last two decades have played a significant role in British politics. The impediments are not without effect, however. Perhaps the best way to understand their impact and to characterize the British party system is to say that Britain has a multiparty system for elections but a two-party system as far as legislative and executive power is concerned.

Party Development and Organization

In the middle of the nineteenth century the Parliamentary factions of Whig and Tory evolved into modern mass parties of Liberal and Conservative organized at the grass-roots level, as mentioned in Chapter 7. With the growth of the electorate, seats no longer could be bought, especially after the secret ballot was instituted in 1872 and the Corrupt Practices Act passed in 1883.[1] If the voters couldn't be bribed, they would have to be persuaded; candidates would have to promise beneficial policies in exchange for votes. No single candidate, however, could deliver on such promises. Only by cooperating with other candidates advocating similar policies could any prospect of enacting them exist. Obviously, the most efficient procedure was for like-minded candidates to create a national organization to coordinate their constituency-level campaigns. Thus, in 1867 (not entirely fortuitously the year of the second Reform Act) the National Union of Conservative and

---

1. So stringent is British law that were you to visit a candidate during an election campaign, he or she could not even buy you a glass of beer for fear of being charged with violating the law by "treating."

Unionist Associations was founded; ten years later the National Liberal Federation (NLF) was launched.

As this linkage of discrete, constituency-level associations into integrated national parties progressed, a crucial change occurred. The associations ceased to be personal machines and became party organizations. That is, the candidate/Member no longer controlled the association; he (as it then was) became its servant and it, in turn, served the national organization. This is one of the most fundamental differences between British and American politics. In the United States organizations called the Democratic or Republican parties exist in most Congressional districts. The political structure that really matters, however, is the one created and maintained by the incumbent Member of Congress. Typically, Members of Congress owe very little to the formal party organization in their constituencies. In Britain the reverse is true; the constituency association (the formal organization of the party's dues-paying members in that area) is what matters. The association is *not* the candidate/Member's personal machine; he or she lacks the supporting organization that Members of Congress develop as a matter of course.

Despite this crucial shift in Britain, the fundamental functional relation between the party in Parliament and the party in the country did not alter. The mass party existed not to control the Member and direct him in what policies to support, but to provide the time and money needed to elect candidates committed to the national party's goals. This relation was more consistently followed in the National Union (Conservatives tend to be more deferential) than in the NLF; on occasion, national meetings of NLF party members passed policy resolutions opposed by the Parliamentary leaders. Nonetheless, both parties had developed from the national, Parliamentary level to the local, electoral level and, therefore, possessed similar power structures, regardless of whether members were more assertive in one party than the other.

The birth of the Labour party introduced into British politics a party organized in reverse fashion with a very different purpose. Extending the vote to working-class men in the latter third of the nineteenth century further fueled existing social conflict produced by economic and working conditions. Trade unions sought to improve conditions for their members and various socialist societies agitated for reform. Eventually in 1900 several such groups joined to form the Labour Representation Committee (LRC).

The LRC's objective was to get a new class of Member into the House of Commons. The political elite's willingness to incorporate a new class into the *electorate* only wasn't sufficient to satisfy the LRC; it wanted working men to be represented in Parliament by their own type. The LRC did not believe that middle-class Members, however sympathetic to social reform, could adequately understand the condition of the working class. To achieve this goal the labor movement outside Parliament would have to organize to get working class men *in* Parliament.

This electoral function was not to be the party's only purpose. The organization would also instruct those who were elected about what they were to do in Parliament and, should this be necessary, coerce them into doing it. Thus, Labour was, in contrast to the Conservatives and the Liberals, organized out side (the country) in, rather than in side (Parliament) out.[2] And rather than serving primarily as an electoral machine, the party was to provide a channel through which the people could control government to produce the policies needed to improve their living conditions. Labour was to be a grass-roots, rather than elite, dominated organization. Indeed, this is why many of its members prefer to call it a movement (suggesting spontaneous action by the people) rather than a party.

As Labour's strength grew, the Liberals' declined; the party was torn by personal factional feuding and its inability to locate a core clientele once Labour gathered up the working-class vote. In 1922 for the first time Labour polled more votes and won more seats than the Liberals. Never again would the Liberals come second in either; never again would Labour be third in either. Although the Liberals were unable to regain major party status, Britain had a three-party system for much of the 1920s and 1930s. In 1945 Labour won its greatest triumph ever (in terms of share of seats in the Commons). With the increasing enfeeblement of the Liberals, British politics appeared to be returning to its two-party form of the latter nineteenth century.

In the mid-1970s, however, the Liberals revived to poll nearly a fifth of the vote. And parties at the geographic fringe — the Welsh and in particular the Scottish Nationalists — made significant gains. By the close of the decade these inroads seemed to be playing themselves out.

Then, however, the Labour party lurched to the left. Many of its moderate members departed to found a new Social Democratic Party (SDP). The SDP and the Liberals soon formed the Alliance, a means of cooperating in election campaigns while maintaining separate party organizations. At the close of the 1980s the SDP and the Liberals attempted to merge into a single party. A power struggle between the leaders of the two parties resulted in part of the SDP going off on its own while the rest joined with the Liberals to form what eventually became the Liberal Democrats. The rump SDP stumbled on for a short time, only to throw in the towel in June 1990. Thus, going into the 1990s Britain had two leading parties, Labour and Conservative, and a third party of some significance. Not only could the third party poll a sizable share of the vote, but its history extended back beyond that of one of the leading parties to a time when it had been a major party. Although I've pointed out the fundamental difference in organization between the two parties founded in the nineteenth century and the one launched in the twentieth century, the power structure of the parties requires fuller discussion.

---

2. In 1906 the LRC changed its name to the Labour party.

The Conservative Party

The basic organizational unit of the mass or non-Parliamentary portion of the Conservative party is the local constituency association. Party membership is more formal in Britain than in the United States. Declaring a preference doesn't suffice; one has to formally join a local association, which requires paying a small amount for dues each year. The Conservatives have been one of most successful parties in democratic countries in recruiting members. During the 1950s they had around 2.75 million members and even now, with fewer than half as many, their number is substantial compared to other parties in democracies.

The most significant activity of the local association—the function that gives it its only real power—is to decide who will be the Conservative candidate for Parliament in that constituency. The association's selection committee interviews potential candidates and recommends two or three of them to the executive council. After hearing them speak and answer questions, the executive recommends one candidate to a meeting of the association's members, which almost invariably approves the executive's choice. Remember that Britain doesn't have primary elections. To have any voice in selecting candidates one must, at the very least, be a member of a local association and, preferably, be on the executive or the selection committee. This situation greatly enhances the value of party membership in Britain compared to the United States.

Early in this selection process, the chair of the association usually requests Conservative national headquarters to suggest potential candidates from its list of people who have expressed an interest and been found suitable. The selection committee may gather names on its own as well. Although these are supposed to be cleared with national headquarters, that doesn't always happen. The associations are very protective of their power to choose whomever they wish as the candidate. If they feel that national headquarters is trying to impose someone upon them, that is the last person they will select. National headquarters could veto an association's choice of candidate, but never does so. Given the many safe seats in Britain (those consistently won by the same party), the few people on the association's executive and its selection committee wield considerable power in determining who holds national legislative office. Selection as candidate for the party holding the seat is tantamount to election.

Only rarely does an association refuse to allow an incumbent Member to continue as their candidate. Occasionally when that occurs the rejected Member will contest the next election as an independent. Contrary to his or her belief in having a large personal following among the voters, these attempts to buck the system almost always end in disaster for the maverick. In 1992, for example, the Conservatives in one constituency rejected their Member because of questionable ethics in using his position in Parliament for personal financial gain. Not only did he finish fourth in the election, but he also lost his deposit. And he didn't even get the satisfaction of denying the seat to his replacement; the official Conservative candidate won.

At the national level the party's most visible organ is the Conference. This meeting, held each year for about three and a half days, somewhat resembles an American Presidential nominating convention. Like U.S. conventions, the Conference is a gathering of delegates from the local constituency associations. Early each fall several thousand party activists converge on some seaside resort. The Conference meets annually although elections don't occur that often; in contrast to an American political convention, it has nothing to do with nominating anyone for anything; its sole purpose is to discuss policy. Earlier in the year the associations will have sent various resolutions to party headquarters, some of which are selected for debate. After a couple of hours of delegate speeches on a given resolution, it typically passes without amendment and often without dissent.

The volunteer, mass organization outside Parliament was intended to serve, not control, the party's legislators. The channel of communication it provides between the parliamentary elite and the rank-and-file members in the country flows primarily downward; only rarely does what percolates back up have much influence on party policy. Parliamentary leaders see little harm in letting the delegates talk and pass resolutions; these merely express the delegates' opinions and do not bind the leaders in any way. Nonetheless, occasionally the proceedings reveal such enthusiasm for a particular policy that the Parliamentary leaders feel compelled to support it so as not to alienate their followers.

The Conference serves an advisory function, but it is the Central Council that is designated as the mass party's governing organ. The Council is, in effect, a smaller and briefer version of the Conference. Since it does not meet much more frequently than the Conference, however, direction of the mass party's affairs falls mostly to the Executive Committee, which typically convenes every other month. Given its membership of about 150, most of the detailed work is done by subcommittees.

In Parliament the key organ in the party's organization is the Conservative Private Members Committee. No one calls it by that name, however, referring to it instead as the 1922 Committee. In that year a revolt among Conservative Members of Parliament drove the Parliamentary Leader from his position. The committee then was created to help ensure that in the future Leaders would be aware of the views of the average Members of the Parliamentary party and not get so far out of step that they would be forced to walk the plank. (Given the ultimate fate of Margaret Thatcher, one may wonder how effective the 1922 Committee can be in performing its function.)

The 1922 Committee does not make policy but provides Conservative Members of Parliament with a forum in which to question leaders' actions and policies. Votes are rarely taken; the chair of the group must interpret the "sense of the meeting." The chair has direct access to the Parliamentary Leader to be able to alert him or her when views are beginning to diverge. Sometimes the Leader attends a 1922 Committee meeting to answer criticism and to try to convince the legislators that his or her policies are the right ones. Prime Minister John Major addressed the 1992 Committee when seeking to unite Conservatives for the Maastricht Treaty late in 1992.

Through the 1922 Committee, Conservative legislators are organized into subject-matter committees. (These party committees should not be confused with the legislative committees of the House of Commons.) The scope of these committees corresponds to that of the various governmental departments. The committees discuss current political issues and government policies and help to crystalize the party's position on them. Ideally, internal party policy differences can be settled in private through this process.

I've been using a capital *L* to refer to a Parliamentary Leader. The Conservative party (whether in or out of power) is headed by an individual called the Leader. Although the adjective *Parliamentary* makes clear where this person is based, the Leader heads the entire party—the mass, as well as the Parliamentary, portion. The U.S. President and Congressional leaders may disagree even when they are in the same party. Thus, in the United States questions often exist about who really is the head of a party and about who can authoritatively state its position on current issues. In Britain such confusion doesn't arise.

The Conservative Leader is preeminent. To ensure that the mass party organization remained confined to helping to win elections and to publicizing the party's position on public issues, Conservative national headquarters was placed under the direction of the Leader, not under any of the mass party organs (the Conference, Central Council, or, even, the Executive Committee). National party headquarters is his or her personal machine. The Leader appoints the officials who supervise the party's staff, handle its finances, and maintain lists of potential candidates. He or she is the authoritative voice for the party's policies and is not bound by any policy resolution of the mass party. Furthermore, key party policy committees are responsible to the Leader, not to any mass party organ. He or she appoints the chief whip of the Parliamentary party and selects whomever he or she wishes for the Shadow Cabinet (the top leadership group in the party when it is out of power). The Labour Leader has none of these powers. The Conservative Leader also has enormous authority over the party's legislators because, as either the current or the potential Prime Minister, he or she can greatly affect the course of their political careers.

Despite these powers, the Leader is accountable—indeed, vulnerable. Remember that you read in Chapter 4 how Margaret Thatcher was removed from office as Prime Minister by being deposed as Leader of the Conservatives. (You might want to turn back and review the procedure for electing a

Leader; see pages 71–73.) Strictly speaking, the choice of Conservative legislators for Leader must be confirmed by a meeting of all Conservatives in both Houses of Parliament, prospective Parliamentary candidates, and members of the Executive Committee of the mass party. This gathering of about a thousand people, however, is little more than a rubber stamp.

In summary, the Conservative party is very hierarchically structured, with the Leader at the apex. Despite possessing great power even when the party is out of office, the Leader can be driven from his or her post by determined opponents in the Parliamentary party or, perhaps, the mass party as well. In fact, in the twentieth century Conservative Leaders have suffered this fate more frequently than have Labour Leaders. Margaret Thatcher's deposal was by no means unique in the annals of the Conservative party. No one would ever think that the Conservative party is democratic, yet the Leader is responsible to the followers. His or her power ultimately is checked by the need to convince the followers to accept the policies he or she prefers.

Doing so involves more than arguing the merits of a policy. Thatcher's ouster was touched off by her anti-European stance; many Conservatives believed that Britain would be isolated and ineffective in the European Community if her policies were continued. This concern by itself would not have been sufficient to remove Thatcher. What really worried Conservative MPs was the poll tax. They feared that the voters were so angry about the poll tax that they would slaughter Conservative candidates at the next election. Many Conservative MPs voted to get rid of Thatcher because they believed that doing so was the only way to save their skins. A new Leader, willing to jettison the poll tax, was essential to prevent termination of their political careers. Yes, Thatcher's policies did bring her down, but it was the personal good of her followers rather than the best interests of the nation that played the major role in making her accountable.

The Labour Party

You'll recall that the Labour party was organized in reverse sequence to the Conservatives. This has given Labour a very different structure and ethos. The Parliamentary Labour Party (PLP) is to serve the mass party by enacting its principles into law. The Labour party's development has given it a more complex organization than the Conservative party. The mass party not only coordinates the activities of the local associations, but also seeks to integrate various related organizations — primarily trade unions and cooperative societies. These organizations affiliate with Labour at both the national and the local level.

Labour's semifederated structure allows for two types of members: direct and indirect. Just as with the Conservative party, one can join Labour directly by paying dues to a local association. Only about a quarter of a million people (many fewer than for the Conservatives) do this. Most of the Labour party's members, about 5.5 million, join indirectly; they are members simply because the union to which they belong has affiliated with the party and has paid a political levy for each of its members.

Many of the Labour party's indirect members may not really support it at all and may, in fact, vote for its opponents in elections. Indirect members who dislike Labour can "contract out," that is, sign an official form saying that they do not want any of their union dues paid to the party. Very few do so, however; the amount per person that goes to Labour is so small that alienating one's workmates by contracting out doesn't seem worth it. When the small individual sums are multiplied by millions of people, of course, the total involved is substantial. About half Labour's regular operating funds — its non-election campaign finances — comes from the trade unions. In a sense Labour's finances are based on apathy and inertia.

Each local constituency party is governed by a General Management Committee (GMC) composed of delegates from ward committees and the affiliated organizations, primarily local branches of unions. Since the GMC usually meets only once a year, effective power is wielded by the executive committee, which is chosen by the GMC and meets monthly. When a candidate for a Parliamentary election is to be selected, the executive committee prepares a short list (the leading applicants) and the GMC chooses one of them.

Candidate selection is one of the most important powers of constituency Labour parties (CLP), just as is true of the Conservative party. Recently, the exercise of this power has created bitter battles between the left and right wings of the party. The procedure had been that an incumbent Labour legislator couldn't be dumped as a candidate in the forthcoming election unless the CLP passed a motion of no confidence in him or her. The left wing complained that this provided party members too little control over Members of Parliament; the Members just brushed off activists' demands that they should work harder to enact policies that "true socialists" wanted. Left-wingers sought a procedure that would facilitate getting rid of those Members who refused to do their bidding. They secured a change in party rules requiring every CLP to reselect candidates during each Parliament. A sitting legislator no longer was automatically adopted as the candidate in the next election, but had to be specifically approved to seek reelection as the party's nominee. Furthermore, this reselection process had to be open to new applicants.

By American standards this seems a modest reform, but in the Labour party it was shocking because British legislators had been remarkably well insulated from popular accountability. A handful of local party activists decided who the party's candidate would be, and, once elected, a Member of the Commons virtually enjoyed life tenure, never having to fear the bruising

primary election fights that have ended the careers of some American politicians. The change in the rules made Labour legislators more accountable,
but not, as one would expect in a democracy, to the voters. The power was
entrusted to local party officials, who are not representative of the electorate
or even of that portion of it voting Labour. Remember that the change was
sought by the left wing of the party. Although it could legitimately employ
democratic rhetoric in advocating this change, the real objective of this wing
of the party was to get people sharing its views into office, both in the
legislature and in the party. This was a power struggle, not just a debate over
democratic values. Two to three dozen Labour legislators had their careers
ended prior to the 1983 election because of the new procedures. Only seven
were "deselected," that is dumped by their CLP, but many more retired
rather than try to win reselection. (Some of them joined the new Social
Democratic Party.)

The widespread fear that Labour was being taken over by extremists led
to another rule change in 1987. An electoral college that was composed of all
party members in a constituency along with delegates from local trade unions
was given the power of selecting candidates. By enlarging the group that
makes the choice, the party leaders hoped to dilute the strength of extremists
and field candidates acceptable to the electorate. Simultaneously, the leaders
worked to purge the party of the Militant Tendency (or Militants, a radical
group willing to go beyond elections and Parliamentary activity to direct
action in its pursuit of social change). Although the combined effect of these
measures has been to reduce the influence of extremists in candidate selection
(and in policy formulation, as well), it has not eliminated this entirely. Disputes over candidate selection continue to crop up, particularly around Liverpool, which has been a Militant stronghold for some time.

In 1992 three left-wing Labour MPs who had been ousted by their CLP
stood for reelection as independents. Two finished third and one fourth with
24, 14, and 9 percent of the vote respectively. In each case the new, official
Labour candidate retained the seat; the dissidents failed to siphon off enough
votes to penalize their CLPs for having rejected them.

Although the CLPs have the power to select candidates, the national party
organization is more involved in the process than is true in the Conservative
party. National headquarters must be given an opportunity to comment on
the short list before the CLP makes its choice. Furthermore, the choice isn't
final until endorsed by headquarters, which doesn't always do so. In by-
elections the local party must share the power of selection with headquarters,
which means they may have little to say about the matter.

The body that governs Labour's national mass organization is Conference. Well over a thousand delegates from local parties and affiliated organizations attend these annual gatherings to discuss and vote on various policy

resolutions submitted by their groups. Voting strength is allocated according to the number of party members an organization has, so a total vote of 6 million on some issues is not uncommon.

The power of Conference is a matter of controversy. Various party documents and leaders have said from time to time that Conference is the ultimate authority and controls Labour legislators. If this were true, Members would be accountable not to the voters but to a party organ, which would seem to short-circuit democracy. Conference is prohibited, however, from telling Labour legislators how they must vote on a specific bill. Principles endorsed by Conference are to be carried out as soon as practicable, but (major loophole) the party's constitution doesn't say who determines what is practicable. Labour Leaders can't openly defy Conference (behavior that Conservative Leaders normally could get away with in their party), but they have some freedom in deciding when and how to implement its decisions; in practice, "when" may turn out to be never. Procrastination is risky, however, since the Leader must report to each year's Conference on the work of the PLP. During the debate on this report, delegates may challenge the Leader if Conference resolutions have been ignored.

Between Conferences the mass party is run by the National Executive Committee (NEC), which can expel party members and disaffiliate local parties. National headquarters and its professional staff are directed by the NEC. Thus, in contrast to the Conservative party, Labour's headquarters is not the Leader's personal machine but the servant of Conference and the NEC.

The Leader, Deputy Leader, and Young Socialist delegate are ex officio members of the NEC. The remaining twenty-six members are chosen at Conference. Delegates from trade unions elect twelve, delegates from constituency parties elect seven, and delegates from socialist and cooperative organizations elect one. Five places are reserved for women, and all Conference delegates vote on these. The same is true for the party treasurer, who is ex officio on the NEC. Since the trade unions always have a huge majority of Conference votes, they are able to select the bulk of the NEC: eighteen members (the twelve union seats plus the five women plus the treasurer). Furthermore, by longstanding Conference procedure, each delegation casts all its votes as a single block. The combined block votes of the four largest unions comprise well over a majority of Conference's total voting strength. Thus, when the main unions agree, they determine what policies Conference supports and who controls the NEC.

During the 1940s and 1950s, union leaders usually were politically moderate and not very assertive. They accepted the Parliamentary leaders' policies with little question. In fact, the Parliamentary leaders found the union leaders useful allies in fending off attacks by extremist delegates from the constituency parties. Furthermore, since most union leaders were interested in industrial relations and not in a political career, the majority of the NEC's members were Members of the House of Commons, not union officials.

Beginning in the 1950s, the PLP was so split on key policies that even though most of the NEC were from the party's legislative elite, that didn't guarantee that the Parliamentary leaders could control it. More important, the new generation of union leaders was less deferential than its predecessors had been and often leaned to the left on policy. Britain's economic troubles further worsened relations between union and Parliamentary leaders; at times Labour Governments were forced to pursue policies that the unions opposed. Instead of being able to count on the union block vote to save them from defeats at Conference, Parliamentary leaders found some unions giving aid and comfort to left-wing enthusiasts from the constituency parties. Leading the Labour party—a difficult job in the best of circumstances—became an even more onerous task.

Getting Conference to vote for left-wing policies accomplishes little, however, if party leaders simply ignore these policies during election campaigns. Thus, the left was determined to gain control over the party's manifesto (what American parties call a platform). The tide of victory in this destructive battle flowed back and forth in the early 1980s; eventually a truce was called with nothing having been resolved. A new Leader and a commitment to winning combined to produce little conflict over the 1987 manifesto, although it was much more moderate than the 1983 one.[3] Nor was much protest heard about the contents of the 1992 manifesto, at least not until after Labour lost yet again. If future Parliamentary leaders treat Conference resolutions as cavalierly as they did in drawing up the manifesto in 1979, however, the conflict is likely to be renewed. On the other hand, Parliamentary leaders do have some room for maneuvering and can soft-pedal some policies they think will alienate voters.

As for Labour organization in Parliament, the PLP has two overlapping sets of committees. Area groups help to ensure that Labour legislators attend important debates and vote as the party wishes. Subject groups resemble the Conservatives' subject-matter committees, giving the rank-and-file Labour legislators some input into policy making. These committees' influence is rather marginal when the party is in power (the Cabinet dominates the policy process then), and even when it is not, a committee's influence depends to a considerable extent on its chairperson's status within the party.

The PLP chooses a chairman [sic], whose function is similar to that of the chair of the 1922 Committee. When Labour is in power, this person heads a

---

3. So out of touch with the interests and desires of the average voter was the 1983 manifesto, which went on at great length presenting a host of nostrums, that one of Labour's moderate leaders termed the document "the longest suicide note in history."

specially created liaison committee intended to keep the Labour Government informed of the views of the average Labour legislator. When Labour is out of power, the PLP elects a Parliamentary Committee each year. Its twelve members—along with three Labour members from the House of Lords, the PLP chairman, the chief whip, the Deputy Leader, and the Leader—are in effect the party's Shadow Cabinet. The Leader may add others to the Shadow Cabinet but has to work primarily with advisors chosen by the party's legislators more than the Conservative Leader does.

Given its self-image as a democratic movement of the people, the Labour party was slow to designate a Leader. The PLP had a chairman in its early years, but this was simply because someone had to preside at meetings. The chairman was not to exercise any special authority or power. During the party's first two decades, the post passed among six men, with four years being the longest unbroken period of service. Eventually the party reconciled itself to having a Leader only to experience one of its greatest traumas: In 1931 James Ramsay MacDonald (the first Labour politician to be called Leader) replaced his minority Labour Government with a coalition Government dominated by the Conservatives. The bulk of the Labour party refused to follow MacDonald and excoriated him for betraying his followers.

The combatants in that conflict are long dead, but the idea that one can't trust the party's leaders—that they are scheming to sell out the movement— continues to flourish within the Labour party. A taste of power is thought to so besot leaders that they will jettison principle for personal gain and glory. One of the ways a Labour Leader can try to counteract these suspicions is to demonstrate that he or she is a true socialist. Usually this means strident advocacy of government ownership of key enterprises. Unwavering support for unilateral nuclear disarmament also can serve to establish one's left-wing credentials. As he was managing to moderate a number of Labour's policies in the late 1980s, Leader Neil Kinnock resolutely maintained his lifelong unilateralism. (Both he and his wife were long-term members of the Campaign for Nuclear Disarmament.) In response to the new international situation created by the INF Treaty between the United States and the former Soviet Union, Kinnock seemed to suggest that he might be willing to consider changes in this policy, and all hell broke loose within the Labour movement. Kinnock had to beat a quick retreat as Labour's left-wingers denounced him as another case of MacDonaldism. Nonetheless, he eventually succeeded in swinging Labour away from unilateralism in what proved to be a vain attempt to make the party more attractive to the electorate.

When Labour is out of office, the Leader is supposed to be elected annually. Because in most years no one stands against the incumbent, no election is held. Until 1981 only Labour legislators could vote for the Leader. Here again the left wing sought to expand its power within the party by depriving the PLP of this power. Now, when an election is needed, it is held during Conference.[4] The PLP is granted only 30 percent of the votes. The same proportion is allocated to the constituency parties, and the remaining 40 percent, the largest share, belongs to the unions. Having to please the electorate every few years is likely to make Labour legislators somewhat moderate or at least realistic. Denying them the sole power to select the Leader by bringing into the process people not subject to such a constraint seems likely to produce Labour Leaders more inclined to the left; that, at least, was the left wing's goal in securing this change in procedure.

Despite the similarity in title, the Labour Leader's position differs from that of the Conservative Leader in several ways:

1. The Labour Leader does not choose the bulk of the Shadow Cabinet or appoint the chief whip; the Labour legislators do.
2. Party headquarters is not the Labour Leader's personal machine; instead, the NEC directs it.
3. The Labour Leader can't make policy on his or her own authority.
4. The Labour Leader must report to Conference annually on the work of the Parliamentary party, whereas the Conservative Leader doesn't.
5. The Labour Leader is elected by a diverse group, only a minority of which has any experience of serving with him or her in the legislature.

Nonetheless, the Leader is the most powerful single person in the party. When Labour is in power, the Leader, who is then Prime Minister, functions essentially as a Conservative Prime Minister would. A Labour Prime Minister picks the Cabinet members he or she prefers and, along with the Cabinet, runs the country. A Labour Prime Minister can't ignore strongly held views in the party, but neither can a Conservative Prime Minister. Finally, if the most distinguishing evidence of power is the ability to retain one's office, then the Labour Leader is stronger than the Conservative Leader. In the twentieth century intraparty revolts have driven Leaders from power more often in the Conservative party. The Conservative party provides for annual election of the Leader even when the party is in power and the Leader is serving as Prime Minister. This, you recall, is what brought Margaret Thatcher down. Labour is more protective of its Leader. When the party is in power, the Leader can be challenged only if a majority of the votes at Conference are cast in favor of holding an election.

---

4. This may require calling a special Conference. Immediately following Labour's defeat in the 1992 election, Kinnock announced that he would resign as Leader. To avoid having a lame-duck leader for half a year (and, according to some, to give his preferred successor a leg up), he insisted that the election not be delayed until the regular fall meeting of Conference. Therefore, a special one was convened in July 1992.

In trying to make Labour more attractive to the voters, Kinnock moved the party back to the center, although he himself had been on the left for years. Not only did he shift its policies on both government ownership and unilateral nuclear disarmament, but he directed an internal purge of Militants and others on the left. Those holding key positions in party headquarters became "his" people, rather than servants of the NEC. Many Labourites asserted that he had become just as imperious in running Labour as Thatcher had been in dominating the Conservatives. The formal contrasts in powers between the Leaders of the two parties proved not to be so great in practice. Such convergence required a significant departure from party history and values for Labour. The desire to get the Conservatives out of office was so great, however, that most Labourites were willing to stomach this.

When in 1992 this remedy failed to restore Labour to robust good health, complaints about the bad taste of the medicine were quickly voiced. The question is not the stance of the party's new leaders; they certainly wish to continue Kinnock's efforts. What is crucial is the attitude of the rank and file, since the views of party members matter so much more in Labour than in the Conservative party. Will the members insist on a return to traditional party values or, at the least, impede any effort to build a united left with the Liberal Democrats?

The Liberal Democrats

As the once-great Liberal party declined further into minor-party status during the 1950s, its national organization almost disappeared. A national headquarters was still maintained, but it employed only a handful of people. Most of the work was done by members volunteering a few hours. Although some of these people were capable, the party's amateur operation was obvious. The party attracted a number of idealists; they entered with bubbling enthusiasm, but soon became disillusioned and left. Many of these people were politically naive or even, in British terms, a bit dotty. Because one could rise to the top much more rapidly in the Liberal party than in either the Labour or the Conservative parties, it also appealed to calculating, ambitious people whose backgrounds were curious, at best. Several of these later went on to even more marginal political movements or business ventures than the Liberal party had become. At the core, the old guard remained — out of sentimental links with the past — and it usually ran party affairs. The party went through several reorganizations that changed the names of various party organs but that did little to alter power relations.

Like the other two parties, the Liberals held annual meetings (known as the Assembly) to discuss policy resolutions, although there wasn't a prayer that any of these could be enacted by Parliament. Like the other party meetings, the Assembly's structure was supposed to be composed of representatives from the various constituency Liberal parties. However, party organization had deteriorated so much that one could walk in off the streets, join the party, participate in the discussions, and vote on the resolutions. Assemblies became increasingly ill organized and disorderly. Contradictory votes (not unknown at Labour Conferences) were the least of it; at times few of the participants knew what motion was being discussed and voted upon. This state of affairs would have been serious if the party had had any power; as it was, the chaos mattered little.

Because national headquarters was so weak and could provide almost no assistance, local party organization was mostly autonomous. And because the few people who did manage to get elected to the House of Commons as Liberals relied to a considerable extent on a personal vote (the Liberal party label, unlike the Conservative or Labour one, wasn't worth many votes), constituency organization came closer to being the Member's personal machine than was the case in the other two parties. As a result, it often was difficult to say just what the Liberals stood for. The Assembly's resolutions were inconsistent, when not obscure, and Liberal candidates from one constituency to another offered widely differing, even contradictory, policies.

Liberal Members of Parliament enjoyed a good bit of autonomy. Even when their numbers had declined to half a dozen, they remained the only people entitled to vote for the Leader. The Liberal party shared the Conservative party's course of development (from Parliament out to the grass roots) and, therefore, was unlikely to embrace the views about party power structure that Labour held due to a reverse course (grass-roots into Parliament). On the other hand, the party had a tradition of assertive members calling the leaders to account, which grew stronger because the Liberal legislators' lack of power and the weak national party organization meant that nothing could be done to whip party members into line.

The Liberals benefited from having a series of very capable Leaders with personal magnetism and the ability to use television effectively. They recognized that to be taken seriously by the voters, the party must be better organized. Such efforts, which already had progressed considerably, were assisted by the merger with the SDP in the 1980s. Most of the SDP leaders had been career politicians (some quite prominent) in the Labour party. They were unwilling to accept the rather casual indiscipline that characterized the Liberal party. Although they didn't seek to centralize all power in the hands of the elite (that is, the Members of Parliament), they wanted to be certain that any radical fringe elements among the rank and file couldn't control the party. Avoiding that, after all, was their reason for leaving the Labour party.

These trends have produced the current Liberal Democratic party. Annual party meetings are much more organized and businesslike than in the past. Party policy is more consistent throughout the country. So far has the change progressed that some of those preferring the almost anarchical freedom of the past have broken away from the Liberal Democrats to revive the Liberal party (which formally was abolished when the merger with the SDP occurred). Despite continued differences in ethos and contrasts in detailed procedures, the Liberal Democrats' organization does not now differ fundamentally from the other two parties.

One contrast, however, is sufficiently major to be more than a matter of detail. The Liberal Democrats have a popular, or mass, election to select their Leader. All party members are eligible to vote. A mail ballot in 1988 elected Paddy Ashdown (who had led the Liberals before the merger) as the new party's first Leader.

✦ ✦ ✦

Each of Britain's three main parties has a different organizational ethos. Not only is the Conservative mass party intended simply to serve the Parliamentary elite, but most of its members accept this role and behave deferentially. The Liberal Democrats' forerunner (the Liberal party) was founded on a similar basis as the Conservatives, but the party possesses a well-developed tradition of member assertiveness and desire to participate in shaping party policy. From its founding Labour intended for the Parliamentarians to serve the mass party, which was to be the vehicle for involving the average citizen in public affairs. Despite these differences and the contrasting arrangements that they produce, all three parties are organized basically the same in that Parliamentarians, not mass members or their officers, are in command. Given the absence of primary elections in Britain, members of all three parties do wield significant power in selecting candidates. Their influence on party policy, however, is considerably attenuated. Thus, British parties are only marginally more successful than American ones in providing the citizens a means of directing government.

Ideology and Policies

As just explained, British parties' differing developmental paths produced sharp contrasts in organizational ethos. These differing paths also caused the substance of partisan appeals, the programs the parties offered to the public, to vary distinctively.

The Conservative Party

Despite what the main title of this section might suggest, the Conservative party lacks an ideology. It doesn't possess an integrated set of doctrines flowing from a coherent worldview of politics and society. Conservatives would deny that their party lacks anything. They see the absence of ideology as an asset, not a flaw. They fault the Labour party for having an ideology that, they believe, makes its activists unthinking fanatics.

Conservatives wish to respond to events not in conformity with some abstract, probably irrelevant, idea, but pragmatically in accord with the unique set of relevant facts. They would concede only that they have an attitude toward society, an outlook on life. They present themselves as the party of government, the party composed of those people best suited by heredity and experience to run the country. At times the essence of their electoral campaigns seems only to be: Never mind our policies. Simply trust our capable leaders, who will know what's best to do, whatever may happen.

British Conservatives seek the middle way, trying to avoid the extremes of either individualism or collectivism. They tend to be more moderate than are many Americans who describe their political views with this label. British Conservatives prefer individual freedom to bureaucratic direction, of course, and they believe that widespread private ownership of property is essential to a healthy democracy. They recognize, however, that social considerations often necessitate modifying these beliefs in practice. It was the Liberal party, not the Conservative party, that espoused the doctrine of laissez-faire in the nineteenth century. The idea that the government may need to act to correct economic abuses or stimulate the economy is not foreign to a Conservative. British Conservatives aren't as automatically or as extensively antigovernment as are American conservatives.

Part of the reason is that the Conservatives have been in power much of the time in modern Britain. One need not be antigovernment when one controls the government and decides what actions it will take. Furthermore, as traditionalists the Conservatives support the sources of authority in British society: the monarchy, the established church, the military, the police. Since these make up the government, how could any good patriot oppose it?

Not being antigovernment doesn't make the Conservatives proponents of big, interventionist government. In the first place, they see little that needs reforming. Beyond that, they hold a rather limited view of government's ability to deliver benefits. Social inequality, for example, bothers them little and, in any event, can't be eliminated. People contribute to society in various ways; it's only natural that their rewards and political influence should vary as well. Government should seek to improve the quality of life (although a little adversity is good for people), but not try to create a heaven on earth.

Despite their support for the existing social structure and for one of the major factors helping to maintain it—the public school system—Conservatives traditionally have stressed community. The party isn't collectivist, as Labour has been. Its individualism, however, has been tempered. The intellectual eighteenth-century godfather of Conservatism, Edmund Burke, regarded society as an organism, growing over the years just as does a human being. England, as a whole, was more than just the sum of its individual citizen parts. In the nineteenth century many landed gentry, which provided the backbone to the Tories (the Conservatives' forerunners), held a paternalistic attitude toward the less well-off. The gentry were not self-made men — such people were in the Liberal party — but had for the most part inherited their wealth. They felt obliged to use their riches responsibly for the benefit of society.

Prime Minister Benjamin Disraeli added to Conservative traditions the idea of One Nation. He sought to make the British Empire a source of pride for all citizens. Whatever your station in society, he proclaimed, you are all British. Thus, the Conservatives emphasize national unity. They regard themselves as the only truly national party, and they seem almost to feel that they are the only true patriots. The British flag is often displayed prominently at Conservative party meetings.

Although the Conservatives have been the party of the social elite, they regard themselves as representative of all interests, rather than of just a single section of society, as they charge Labour is. Conservatives berate socialists for emphasizing class divisions and needlessly stirring up divisive feelings. In contrast, they say, Conservatives seek the national interest. This concern with national community affects the process of Conservative politics, as well as the substance. While willing to fight for what they favor, Conservatives search for broad-based consensus. The process of reaching an agreement should unite, not divide, the nation.

Although the Conservatives have been the party of the status quo, they should not be dismissed as unthinking reactionaries. Were that the case, they, rather than the Liberals, would have been unable to maintain their position as a major party in the twentieth century. The Conservatives have flourished because they have been able to adapt to change. Lacking an ideology, they have pursued pragmatic policies. Sometimes they have opposed their opponents' reform measures, other times they have introduced some themselves. Rather than denouncing welfare policies and socialized medicine, they have claimed that they can operate such programs more efficiently and effectively than other parties can.

When the Conservatives returned to power in the 1950s, they sold back to private ownership few of the enterprises that Labour Governments had taken over from 1945 to 1951. In fact before 1945, the Conservatives, not Labour, had brought some enterprises into government ownership. Despite their emphasis on patriotism and the glories of the nation, the Conservatives, not Labour, arranged for British entry into the Common Market. Labour, traditionally the more internationalist party, became increasingly hostile to this step. Ironically, Labour was more worried than the Conservatives about what would happen to the Commonwealth (the contemporary descendant of the British Empire, which always made Conservative hearts quicken with pride). Although not every Conservative is willing to embrace British membership in an increasingly tightly integrated European Community, yet Thatcher's strident hostility toward Europe was a major factor in the party's revolt against her Leadership.

The issue of Europe is only one instance of how Thatcher departed from Conservative tradition during the decade and a half that she was Leader. In both her style and the substance of her policies Thatcher broke with the past. Thatcherism was not traditional Conservatism. She came from the small business middle class (the daughter of a grocery story owner), not from the traditional social elite, and had to work for everything she obtained (although she did marry a wealthy industrialist). Since no one had given her anything, she wasn't about to give anything to anyone else. Unlike most Conservative Leaders of the past, she was not patronizing in either the positive or the negative senses of that word. Under her the Conservative party became more doctrinaire, if not ideological, and, much more than in the past, adopted what Americans would regard as a conservative stance.

She and her close associates were heavily influenced by the theories of American economist Milton Friedman, accepting his argument that the money supply was the key element in controlling inflation. To prevent a return to the disastrous situation of 1975 when the annual rate of inflation under a Labour Government had skyrocketed to 27 percent, government had to stop expanding the money supply by borrowing huge sums. This could be avoided only by cutting government spending. Spending cuts also would permit lowering income tax. That, in turn, would restore the incentive for hard work and business competition because people would keep more of what they earned. Furthermore, a tight money supply would force employers to make more efficient use of their workers and to resist excessive wage demands, since they couldn't easily borrow money to finance their businesses. Thatcherites believed that the free enterprise system, along with unfettered collective bargaining, could be relied upon to limit wage demands and to avoid the need for the government to intervene to control prices and wages. The problems of low productivity, inefficiency, and international lack of competitiveness that had bedeviled the British economy would thereby be solved.

The short-term cost for this long-term solution was the worst unemployment in Britain for half a century and widespread business retrenchment and bankruptcy. Thatcher's willingness to pay this cost set her apart from her predecessors at the head of the party. An additional contrast to the four men who had led the Conservatives during their previous extended period in power (1951 to 1964) was that she launched a major program of privatization. One government-owned enterprise after another was sold back to the public, including services like the water works, for which even antisocialist Americans could accept government ownership. So great a departure was this from past Conservative practice that Harold Macmillan, who had been Leader of the party from 1957 to 1963, likened it to a rich family having fallen on such hard times that it had to sell off the family silver.

She labeled herself a "conviction politician" who had no interest in trying to seek consensus. Compromise was not for her (see the discussion in the latter part of Chapter 1). Contrary to Burke, Thatcher declared that society didn't exist. The term simply was an abstraction made up by ivory tower sociologists. The only reality she could see was a conglomerate of discrete individuals, each seeking their interests.

The Conservatives fought a double-barreled campaign in 1987, as Thatcher sought her third term in office. On the one hand, they stressed their accomplishments over the previous eight years—in particular, the strengthening of the economy. They had kept inflation lower than in most other countries, and the economy was growing at a higher rate than in France or Germany. Best of all, unemployment was beginning to decline. Indeed, opinion polls showed that people were much more optimistic about the state of the British economy than they had been only a couple of years earlier.

The other prong of the Conservative campaign in 1987 is summed up in their slogan "Britain is Great Again. Don't Let Labour Wreck it." (Figure 8.4 shows a newspaper ad featuring this slogan.) The Conservative argument was that the Labour party was not only incompetent, but so dominated by extremists that it was downright dangerous. In foreign affairs Labour could not be trusted to keep Britain's defenses strong; in domestic matters its support for libertines, homosexuals, and minorities was destroying all aspects of British society that right-thinking people held dear. As one remedy, the Conservatives indicated that they would pass a law permitting schools to secede from the state-supported education system to escape from the clutches of left-wing local governments.

Under Thatcher's direction the most traditional of British parties seemed in the process of creating some new basic principles. Her overthrow did not entirely reverse this process. The new Leader, John Major, was her preferred successor. Furthermore, many members of the Cabinet he formed were Thatcherites. Nonetheless, Conservative policies did begin to shift. The hated poll tax, which she had seen as a means of pressuring people to stop demanding ever-increasing services from local government (everyone had to pay the tax and the more local government spent in an area the more tax one owed), was dropped. A more conciliatory attitude toward Europe was adopted. And Major exhibited greater sensitivity to the needs of the common people and interest in what government might do to aid them. He spoke with conviction of wishing to create a classless society. (Major's social origins are more humble even than Thatcher's and, although he, like she, could be called self-made, the experience seems not to have hardened him as it did her.)

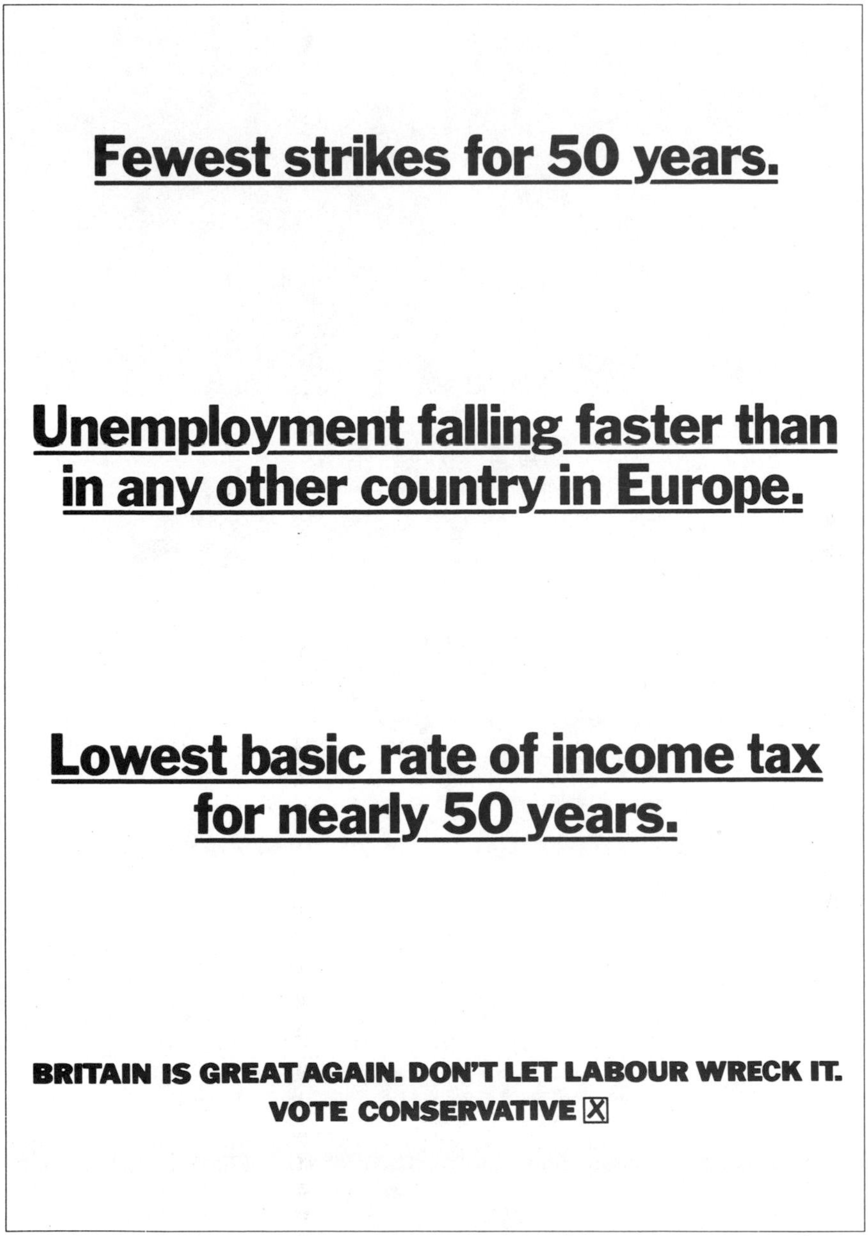

Fewest strikes for 50 years.

Unemployment falling faster than in any other country in Europe.

Lowest basic rate of income tax for nearly 50 years.

**BRITAIN IS GREAT AGAIN. DON'T LET LABOUR WRECK IT.
VOTE CONSERVATIVE ☒**

Figure 8 ✦ 4 Conservative newspaper ad for the 1987 election campaign

Published by Conservative Central Office, 32 Smith Square, London SW1P 3HH

VOTE
FOR RECOVERY.

NOT THE
START OF A NEW
RECESSION.

Just as recovery is under way, Labour would start a new recession. A Conservative win will end uncertainty, raise confidence and speed Britain ahead. Labour would put taxes up, mortgages up, inflation up and strikes up. That's why 90% of business leaders say that Britain needs the Conservatives to keep Britain moving forward.

VOTE CONSERVATIVE ⊠

Figure 8 ✦ 5 Conservative newspaper ad for the 1992 election campaign

Strident doctrinaire certainty was giving way to the old pragmatism of negotiation and compromise. Cod liver oil was being replaced with sugar pills. Much of the rhetoric remains vague. Does a classless society mean an American-type social system — certainly a major transformation of Britain?

Or is it simply a return to one-nation doctrines of the nineteenth century, which sought to bridge class differences with patriotic nationalism? Were Major's Conservatives just turning their backs on Thatcher's laissez-faire to return to the older noblesse oblige tradition?

Despite the change in Leader, the Conservatives' 1992 election campaign didn't differ dramatically from its 1987 appeal to the voters. Again they pictured Labour as too inexperienced and erratic to be trusted with running the economy. They claimed that they alone knew how to keep inflation from getting out of control. (See Figure 8.5 for a newspaper ad on this theme.) The economy currently was in recession and unemployment was rising, but this was due to world factors. Conditions in Britain were no worse than elsewhere.

In contrast to Labour, they would control government spending so that taxes could be cut. Labour's proposed tax changes, the Conservatives alleged, would cost the average person well over $2,000 a year more than they currently were paying. Such a threat to incentives, along with Labour's proposed minimum wage, would cripple the economy.

At the close of the campaign Major did stress an issue that had not received much attention when Thatcher was Prime Minister. He warned that electing Labour would throw Britain into a constitutional crisis. Labour was too willing to devolve power to Scotland. Once that process began, according to Major, the United Kingdom soon would break apart. In warning against devolution, Major was emphasizing the national unity tradition of Conservatism.

Once voters considered what the Conservatives had done and would do, contrasted with what Labour would do, they should recognize that "The Best Future for Britain" was under a reelected Conservative Government. This slogan appeared on many Conservative billboards, along with the picture of Prime Minister Major and smiling schoolboys seen in the ad in Figure 8.5. In short, it was the traditional Conservative electoral appeal: Only we have the experience and knowledge to be trusted with running the country. We'll do whatever needs to be done; don't worry about the details.

The Labour Party

In contrast to the Conservative party, the Labour party has an ideology: socialism. That ideology's content, however, is as vague as the basic principles of Conservatism.

A variety of socialist groups had been active in Britain during the latter part of the nineteenth century, and some of them were among the groups that founded the Labour party. However, the Marxist type of socialism has had little influence on Labour doctrine; the party's intellectual heritage is rooted instead in the Christian socialism of the social gospel school. As one of the party's Leaders once wrote about its forerunner, its "socialism was derived far more from the Methodist Church and a Christian approach than from Continental revolutionaries."[5] Keir Hardie, who more than anyone else deserves to be called the father of the Labour party and who was a working-class Member of the Commons even before the party existed, observed, "Socialism is at bottom a question of ethics or morals. It has to do mainly with the relationships which exist between a man and his fellows."[6]

As for secular socialists, the main influence on the Labour party was the Fabian Society. This elite group of intellectuals wanted nothing to do with Marxist revolutionaries; the Society's statement of purpose begged "those socialists who are looking forward to a sensational historical crisis, to join some other society."[7] Sidney Webb, one of the most influential Fabians and a Labour activist during the party's formative period, asserted that four conditions were essential if political and social reform were to occur in Britain: (1) Change must occur democratically; (2) change must occur gradually, causing no dislocation; (3) change must not be regarded as immoral; (4) change must be achieved constitutionally and peacefully.[8] Hardly a cry to man the barricades against the capitalist oppressors! Fabians believed that sound factual research would convince all reasonable people of the need for socialism.

Fabians were living proof that you could be a socialist without using Marxist jargon or swallowing an abstract, elaborate theory of history. They made advocacy of reform respectable by showing that they favored extensive change without revolution: Their enormous influence upon the development of Labour reinforced the practical bent that the party derived from the other groups involved in its founding. Besides socialist intellectuals, those who launched the party included representatives from the trade unions. These people cared little about some future millennium when the state would wither away; they wanted to improve living conditions for the average person now. By providing money and organizational muscle, the unions made Labour's success possible. In the past middle-class, socialist splinter parties had made little progress; they could not have hoped to be a mass movement.

Although Labour developed in a distinctively British fashion, a comparative study of European parties provides further insight into the party's

---

5. Hugh Gaitskell, *Recent Developments in British Socialist Thinking* (London: Cooperative Union, n.d. [circa 1960]), p. 4.

6. Quoted in Socialist Union, *Twentieth Century Socialism* (Harmondsworth, England: Penguin Books, 1956). Despite the fact that his statement may now seem sexist, Hardie was quite supportive of women in politics.

7. Quoted in Margaret Cole, *The Story of Fabian Socialism* (London: Mercury Books, 1963), p. 92.

8. *Fabian Essays in Socialism*, edited by G. Bernard Shaw (Garden City, N.Y.: Doubleday, n.d.), p. 51.

moderate tradition. Rokkan observes that in Britain and Scandinavia, elites resisted the claims of workers for political and economic rights but did little to directly repress these movements. (We saw something of this process in Chapter 7.) As a result, the largest and most moderate of European labor parties developed in these countries. In France, Germany, Austria, and Italy — where various attempts were made to repress unions and socialism — the working class tended to become isolated from the national culture. Here left-wing, reform politics developed as strong ideological movements with a ghetto mentality.[9] To some extent the British Conservatives are right to claim that their party stressed national community. Twentieth-century British politics derived considerable benefit from that crucial choice.

Labour began, then, simply with the goal of getting working-class men into Parliament, without specifying in great detail what they would do once they got there. Not until 1918 did the party officially adopt an explicit socialist goal: "to secure for the workers . . . the full fruits of their industry . . . , upon the basis of the common ownership of the means of production, distribution, and exchange. . ."[10] This statement clearly opposed capitalism, but, beyond that, what did it mean? Surely, the party didn't intend to expropriate some individual's fish and chips shop. To indicate that the party's attack was directed only at large, corporate business, the doctrine developed of focusing on control of "the commanding heights of the economy." Leaving aside the vagueness of those words, what form was control to take? Would the government become the owner or would each enterprise be owned by its workers, as the guild socialists advocated?

Because Labour is a democratic party (a "broad church" as its members like to say, before denouncing members who disagree with them as traitors to the cause), these issues never have been resolved. The left wing, which believes that it alone is true to Clause IV, sees the essence of socialism as nationalization: government ownership. It argues that any government claiming to be democratic must control the large concentrations of economic power so that social ends, rather than the benefit of a few, are served. The working class, through its representatives, must control all forms of power.

Labour moderates, who also see themselves as true to the party's principles, do not regard nationalization as a panacea for social ills. They point out that the extensive program of nationalization that the party implemented from 1945 to 1951 did little to promote greater equality by redistributing wealth; this result will necessarily occur unless a government seizes private enterprises without compensating their owners — action the moderates would

---

9. Stein Rokkan, *Citizens, Elections, Parties* (New York: David McKay, 1970), p. 110.

10. Clause IV of the Labour party constitution lists "Party Objects." The portion quoted is from subsection 4. Somewhat confusingly, these words sometimes are referred to as Clause IV and other times as Clause 4.

reject as tyrannical. For them, socialism is not a matter of government own-ership of the means of production, distribution, and exchange; rather it is a quest for social justice (not that the left wing is uninterested in this). Govern-ment's task is to maintain a floor of basic benefits for all, as a right, and to ensure that everyone really has equal opportunity to rise above that floor to the maximum of his or her ability. The quest for equality is not just a matter of correcting disparities in wealth and income. The values of British society must be transformed to eliminate snobbery and privilege. Class barriers and social inequalities that prevent people of differing status from associating easily with one another must be destroyed.

The conflict over the true nature of socialism has carried over into La-bour's foreign policy. The party has been internationalist, taking the view that workers share a common bond whatever their nationality. Why, then, have many in the party been so hostile to European unity, protesting the loss of British sovereignty to the EC? (This would seem to matter only to the superpatriotic nationalists in the Conservative party.) The explanation is the EC is perceived as an alliance of capitalists and faint-hearted socialists; British membership prevents the country from controlling its own economy and thereby forecloses socialist reform.[11] Furthermore, the EC's Common Agri-cultural Policy penalizes the British working class with higher food prices. In 1980 the Labour party conference voted for Britain to be pulled out of the EC once Labour returned to power. The party's manifesto for the 1987 election said it would "reject EEC interference with our policy for national recovery and renewal."

One of the changes in Labour policies brought about by Neil Kinnock was to swing the party around to acceptance of the EC. Part of the reason for his success was Labour's desire to reverse its isolation from strong socialist parties in France and Germany. Even more important was the EC's Social Charter. This outgrowth of the Single European Act enumerated many employee rights that the member countries were supposed to respect.[12] Thatcher's hostility to the Social Charter meant that it must be a good thing. Labour came to see tighter integration into the EC as a means of protecting programs and services that Thatcherism might weaken. Should Labour man-age to return to power, the EC would provide support for actions that Labour would wish to implement. Since the EC had come to benefit the worker, as well as the employer, it deserved support.

Although never a majority position, pacifism traditionally has been strong in the Labour party. (If all workers are family, regardless of nationality, then

---

11. This oversimplifies a bit since some on the party's right wing also have opposed British membership in the EC.

12. For a study of this aspect of the EC see Beverly Springer, *The Social Dimension of 1992: Europe Faces a New EC* (New York: Praeger, 1992).

they should not kill each other in wars, which only enrich the capitalists, anyway.) At times such feelings combine with the left wing's distrust of the capitalist United States to produce neutralist sentiments. In the early 1980s the party conference opposed any defense policy based on nuclear weapons and not only wanted all cruise missiles withdrawn from Britain, but also the closing of all U.S. bases there. Nonetheless, a proposal for Britain to withdraw from NATO (North Atlantic Treaty Organization) was defeated.

Labour's effort to return to power when Thatcher sought her second term in 1983 was one of the most disastrously and incompetently waged campaigns in the history of British politics. The party's policies were extreme on both domestic and foreign issues, completely out of touch with most of the electorate's concerns (see footnote 3). The party's Leader and, therefore, candidate for Prime Minister — a former darling of the left wing — was so far past his prime that almost no one could take him seriously as a possible replacement for Thatcher.

For the next election in 1987 Labour had a new, young leader (see Figure 4.5). Although few thought he possessed much intellectual depth, Kinnock had a winning personality; people liked him a great deal better than they did nanny Thatcher. So slick and inspiring was Labour's first party political broadcast during the campaign (Kinnock's life and values, stressing his rise from humble origins) that, virtually by popular demand, it was broadcast again.[13] This is just one example of Labour's highly professional campaign in 1987, a campaign widely regarded as having outshone the Conservatives' efforts. Labour charged Thatcher with being insensitive and uncaring. Figure 8.6 shows the punch line to a four-page sequence of ads. Each of the first three pages pictured a person such as a teacher and said, "Try telling him that education [or whatever government service was relevant to the picture] is adequately supported"; the last page thus attacked Thatcher's inflexibility. Labour argued that government services were deteriorating under the Conservatives and that even if unemployment was declining (which was uncertain since the methods by which it was estimated had been changed by the government), it still was far beyond any acceptable level.

Despite its excellent campaign, Labour suffered from two great liabilities. First, the economy had improved. If you weren't one of the unemployed — and even at 3 million the unemployed were only a fraction of the electorate — you didn't have much to complain about. Second, there was the albatross of Labour's defense policy. The party was committed to unilateral nuclear disarmament, that is, getting rid of Britain's nuclear weapons regardless of what the former Soviet Union did. Although Kinnock was moderating Labour's other policies, on defense he remained unilateralist.

---

13. It was so good that U.S. Senator Joe Biden plagiarized some of it for his 1988 campaign for the Democratic Presidential nomination.

Figure 8 ✦ 6 Labour newspaper ad for the 1987 election campaign

During the campaign a TV interviewer pressed Kinnock on how Labour could defend Britain without nuclear weapons. If the Soviet Union said it was going to invade and Britain resisted, then it would nuke Britain. How could Kinnock protect the country if he had gotten rid of its Polaris missiles within two weeks of coming into power (as he had said he would)? Kinnock gave one of his usual rambling answers and seemed to say that in the end passive resistance and guerrilla warfare from the hills was all that could be done to make such an invader decide to withdraw. To the Conservatives this sounded like surrender. They quickly prepared a classic ad that knocked Kinnock out of the ring (see Figure 8.7). From that point on everything Labour said to clarify its position on defense only made matters worse.

Defeat in 1987 resulted in fewer internal recriminations (than had been typical in the past) and in greater determination to correct those flaws remaining in the party's appeal. Kinnock continued to push the purge of the left wing and he himself abandoned his long-term commitment to unilateralism. Those party leaders in charge of formulating Labour's economic policies met with bankers and business leaders to assure them that a Labour Government would not be radical. It would not take back into government ownership all the enterprises that Thatcher had sold to the public. It would not impose a siege economy with control on investment abroad and high taxes. And it would not give in to every desire of the trade unions, although it obviously would not be as hostile to them as Thatcher had been.

By the start of the 1990s Labour had been transformed. It resembled only slightly the party of 1983. This shift wasn't so much a new departure as it was a return to the type of party Labour had been in the 1940s and 1950s. Thus the revival of traditional party values had progressed farther in the Labour party than in the Conservative party, where change had to await the toppling of Thatcher.

In 1992 the Labour party stressed that it had gotten its house in order and now "It's time for change. It's time for Labour." You can see one of the variations on this slogan in Figure 8.8. Labour was concerned that the Conservatives' reorganization of the National Health Service would result in worse health care, that care might cease to be available to all citizens as a matter of right. Labour would spend more on the NHS. It also would improve other social programs, such as increasing pensions and child benefit, the payment going to every family regardless of income.

Labour pointed out the many flaws, such as recession and rising unemployment, that existed in Britain. They hammered their case home with the constant refrain, "If the Conservatives can't get it right after 13 years they never will." However, the alternative that Labour presented—the mix of policies that sought to make Labour the trustworthy, caring party of the 1940s—failed to win the electorate's acceptance. How a fourth straight defeat would affect the evolution of Labour policy remains to be seen.

Figure 8 ✦ 7 Conservative newspaper ad on Labour defense policy for the 1987 election campaign

It's time to save the NHS.

This election is a referendum on the National Health Service.
Labour will stop the privatisation of the NHS
and invest an extra £1 billion in modernisation.

TO JOIN LABOUR OR TO MAKE A DONATION TO HELP OUR CAMPAIGN, PHONE 081 200 0200.

Figure 8 ✦ 8 Labour newspaper ad for the 1992 election compaign

The Liberal Democrats

The preceding discussion should have demonstrated that although one major party has an ideology and the other doesn't, in practice policy differences between them usually haven't been great. This partisan consensus reached its height during the 1950s, the period of Butskellism. During that time differences between Labour and Conservatives were no greater than between Democrats and Republicans in the United States. Clearly, this no longer was true in Britain of the 1980s; Thatcher had shifted the Conservatives to the right, and the left wing had become dominant in the Labour party. Although Butskellism had not returned at the start of the 1990s, the major parties were moving toward it again.

These movements are of great significance for third parties, especially those at the center of the political spectrum. They have a much greater opportunity to make a distinctive appeal to the electorate when the major parties are moving toward the fringes than when they are battling for center ground. During Butskellism one prominent politician dismissed the Liberal party with the assertion, "We're all Liberals now." Most voters agreed that the Liberal party had ceased to serve any useful function; less than three-quarters of a million voted Liberal.

One of the main factors in preserving the party was Britain's worsening economic condition. As the prosperity of the 1950s gave way to stagflation (high inflation combined with little or no economic growth), many voters began to swing between Labour and the Conservatives, hoping to find some group of leaders who could figure out how to run the country effectively. As this search came to seem increasingly futile, some voters began to think that perhaps the Liberals should be given a chance to see what they could do. Then, with the advent of Thatcherism, some space opened up at the center of the political spectrum, offering fertile territory for Liberals to plow.

Early in the 1980s, however, the Liberals found an interloper also trying to make headway in this territory. Labour's lurch to the left had driven many of its moderates to depart, forming the Social Democratic Party (SDP). Accommodation was necessary or these two center parties would destroy each other just at the time that the political situation offered a chance of success for parties in that position on the spectrum. Since most people in both parties were unwilling to give up their organization's separate existence, an Alliance was formed and contested both the 1983 and 1987 elections.

Given the polarization of the major parties, which appeared to be alienating many voters, the Alliance sought to offer a middle way, combining the best of what the majors were offering with those needed measures they had been too doctrinaire to consider. The ad in Figure 8.9 is a good example of how this appeal was expressed. If voters were turned off by the two major parties' confrontational politics, then, presumably, they would find appealing

ONLY THE ALLIANCE CAN SATISFY YOUR HEAD AND YOUR HEART.

THE HEAD.

1. We will maintain trades union legislation.
2. We will retain a minimum nuclear deterrent.
3. We will support and increase the police force.
4. We will introduce a fair voting system.

THE HEART.

1. We will cut unemployment by 1 million within 3 years.
2. We will invest more in education.
3. We will cut hospital waiting lists.
4. We will increase pensions and benefits for the elderly.

Vote Alliance and you don't have to choose between head <u>and</u> heart – you can have them both.

Figure 8 ✦ 9 Alliance newspaper ad for the 1987 election campaign a program of consensus policies offered by a party willing to play a balancing role in the political process. The Alliance would spend more money on creating new jobs than the Conservatives were willing to spend, but not as much as Labour urged. Those trade union reforms that the Conservatives had enacted that were reasonable, such as requiring secret ballots for strike votes, would be retained.

The distinctive element in the Alliance campaign was reform of government. Government secrecy (much more pervasive than in the United States) was to be cut back, power was to be decentralized by devolving various functions to regional governments, a written bill of rights defending basic liberties was to be established, and the electoral system would be altered to proportional representation. (It just so happened that such an electoral system would greatly increase the number of seats the Alliance would hold in the House of Commons.) All this was expected to give Britain better — more effective, fairer — government.

Although officially the Liberal party supported Britain's nuclear deterrent, the party, like Labour, had a unilateralist wing. The Social Democrats (in particular their Leader David Owen) who had left Labour in part over this defense issue were determined not to be saddled with unilateralism in their new political organization. Some Liberals would have been content for Britain to phase out its nuclear weapons by letting them gradually become obsolete, but Owen demanded that Alliance policy provide for modernization of Britain's Polaris missiles to maintain their credibility.

The eventual merger after the 1987 election of the bulk of the SDP with the Liberals to form the new Liberal Democratic party did not produce any great change in policies. In 1992 the party continued to stress its proposals for constitutional reform. As in the past, it asserted that adversarial politics resulted in a slanging (name-calling) match between the two largest parties. This caused the election campaign to become bogged down in trivialities; the real issues weren't being debated. The ad appearing in Figure 8.10 develops this theme. At each side of the page are copies of billboards used by the Conservatives and Labour. In the middle are the issues ignored by these billboards — issues that the Liberal Democrats were discussing.

Heading this list was education. As the 1992 campaign developed, this came to be the primary Liberal Democrat policy. Not only did the party commit itself to such actions as reducing class size, buying more books and equipment, and building new buildings, but it also said precisely how much it would increase taxes to pay for these measures. Polls appeared to indicate that the electorate liked both the proposed actions and the party's honest explanation of how they would be financed. However, such positive feelings failed to induce many people to vote for the party.

Although the Liberals often argued that they were a radical party (because they went to the roots of the system and were willing to consider reforms that

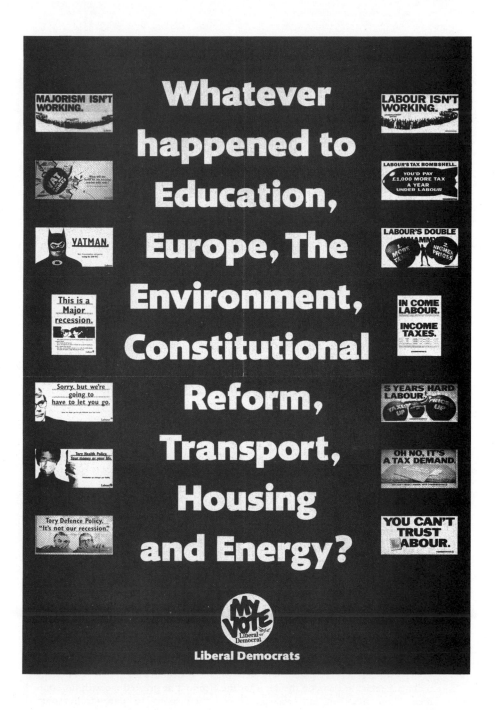

Figure 8 ✦ 10 Liberal Democrat newspaper ad for the 1992 election campaign

the major parties ignored), the Liberal Democrats are best understood as offering a centrist alternative to the programs of the two major parties. Whether the Liberal Democrats can maintain a distinctiveness as the two major parties converge on the center remains to be seen. If, as their only hope of removing the Conservatives from power, the Liberal Democrats and Labour begin discussing how they might cooperate, then maintaining a distinctive center alternative may become less desirable.

Strength and Supporters

Figure 8.11 shows the results of recent elections in Britain. The impact of the SMSP electoral system is notable in the contrast between share of the popular vote and share of the seats in the House of Commons. Thatcher and the Conservatives came to power in 1979. Notice that the Conservative share of the vote was only slightly larger then than in the three subsequent elections. Support for the Conservatives has remained almost constant for well over a decade.

Labour's popular support dropped dramatically in 1983. Although its share of the vote increased at both of the subsequent elections, by 1992 the party had not regained its level of 1979. The Liberals (under whatever name) show the reverse pattern: a striking gain in 1983 and, despite declines in both subsequent elections, higher support in 1992 than in 1979.

As for seats in the House of Commons, the two elections in the 1980s saw the Conservatives at their highest point and Labour at its lowest. Although the figures do not correspond exactly, party strengths after the most recent election resemble those following the 1979 election.

Labour was happy to see the back of Margaret Thatcher. The party made the mistake of thinking that John Major lacked backbone and would be a pushover. Beyond that, antipathy to the poll tax had made the Conservatives quite unpopular. At the start of April 1992 Neil Kinnock (along with most objective observers) was certain that a week later he would be kissing hands at Buckingham Palace.[14] The outcome of a twenty-one–seat Conservative majority was a bolt from the blue.[15] How did Labour yet again manage to snatch defeat from the jaws of victory?

---

14. This is the formal procedure for initiating a new Government. The satirical puppet TV program, "Spitting Image," on election night showed Queen Elizabeth having a nightmare. She feared that kissing hands would mean that Roy Hattersley, Labour's deputy Leader and possessor of rather moist lips, would be slobbering all over her.

15. When I walked into the office of the head of one of Britain's top public opinion polling agencies at noon on the day after the election, he greeted me with the comment, "You are looking at an absolute disaster." In response to queries from reporters, he conceded that the outcome was the worst result for polling since opinion surveys had been invented.

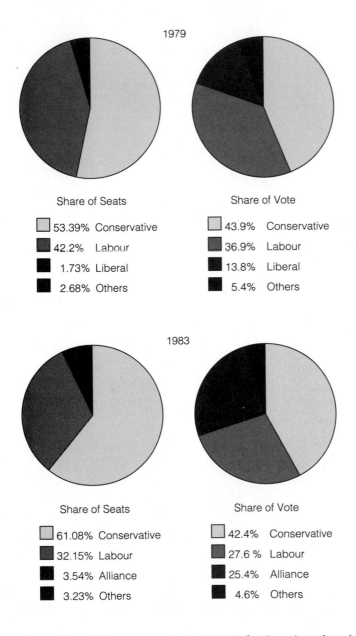

1979

Share of Seats

- ☐ 53.39% Conservative
- ◼ 42.2% Labour
- ◼ 1.73% Liberal
- ◼ 2.68% Others

Share of Vote

- ☐ 43.9% Conservative
- ◼ 36.9% Labour
- ◼ 13.8% Liberal
- ◼ 5.4% Others

1983

Share of Seats

- ☐ 61.08% Conservative
- ◼ 32.15% Labour
- ◼ 3.54% Alliance
- ◼ 3.23% Others

Share of Vote

- ☐ 42.4% Conservative
- ◼ 27.6 % Labour
- ◼ 25.4% Alliance
- ◼ 4.6% Others

Figure 8 ✦ 11 Party strengths in recent elections (*continues*)

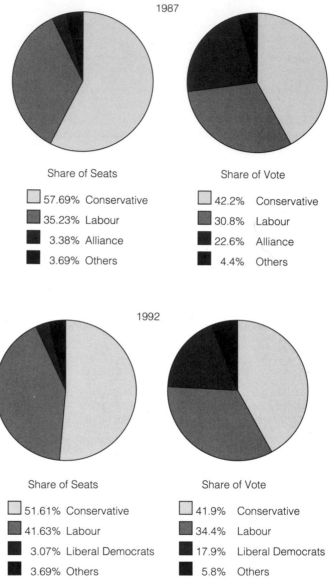

Figure 8 ✦ 11 Party strengths in recent elections (*continued*)

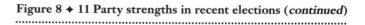

Preliminary postmortems suggested that taxes were a crucial issue. Although the public claimed to be willing to pay higher taxes to preserve a full range of public services, when it came to casting their ballot, they lacked the courage of their convictions. An exit poll (one that surveys voters as they leave the voting stations) found that half the electorate reported that taxes were the most important issue in deciding how they voted. Labour had tried to argue that they would increase taxes only for the rich; those in the top 10 percent, people with incomes in excess of $70,000. What Labour failed to understand was that although few people had such incomes, many in the middle class *aspired* to them. If they ever got there, they didn't want a huge tax bite to deny them the joy of substantial income. Labour had claimed that their tax changes would make eight of every ten Britons better off. Other calculations (widely publicized by newspapers hostile to Labour, as most of the press was) maintained that six of ten would be *worse* off.

Besides the risk of paying more taxes, many people worried that putting Labour in charge of the economy would produce stagflation again. Would business distrust of Labour slow down investment and growth, while trade union links with the party permitted inflationary wage demands? A poll conducted on the two days prior to election day found that only a third believed that they and their family would be better off under Labour, compared with two-fifths who anticipated being worse off (a quarter thought any change in control of the Government would make no difference).

Finally, the question of leadership was a crucial factor. Kinnock was a more plausible Prime Minister than had been Labour's Leader in 1983; however, he still wasn't plausible enough. One poll found that two-fifths regarded Major as the best person for Prime Minister, compared to little more than a quarter who thought that Kinnock was. Many people who had seriously considered voting for the Liberal Democrats voted Conservative to avoid the risks of a Prime Minister Kinnock.

The Conservatives did their best to develop this asset, as you can see in Figure 8.12. Their staff must have worked long hours going through the photo files to find such an awful picture of Kinnock.[16] Raising the issue of who would be Foreign Secretary (the equivalent of the American Secretary of State) was especially appropriate because Britain was scheduled to take over for six months the presiding position in the European Community's Council, beginning only three months after the election. Douglas Hurd, who had spent fourteen years in the foreign service before entering electoral politics, is the perfect embodiment of the British diplomat. Labourite Gerald Kaufman, despite a fondness for American musical comedies, is extremely

---

16. Making the contrast even greater is the fact that in the original both Conservative pictures are in color and both Labour ones are in black and white.

JOHN MAJOR AND DOUGLAS HURD **OR** NEIL KINNOCK AND GERALD KAUFMAN

WHO:

- have turned Britain into a real world power again.

- negotiate firmly and constructively on Britain's behalf. Their skills are widely respected and admired.

- are working to halt the spread of nuclear weapons in an unstable world. They are helping Russia through these uncertain times.

- acted decisively to eject Saddam Hussein from Kuwait.

- are pledged to keep an effective British nuclear deterrent.

- are leading international efforts to protect the environment, help the Third World, promote human rights, and wage war on drugs and terrorism.

WHO:

- have been wrong about every crucial issue affecting Britain's interests, from defence to Europe.

- change their minds on every vital issue. On Europe, they have changed it six times. They cannot negotiate effectively for Britain.

- will sign up to any idea which comes out of Brussels - and at any price.

- would have left our troops sitting in the desert while waiting for sanctions to dislodge Saddam Hussein.

- reject the fourth Trident submarine which we need to keep our defences effective.

- have announced a new defence review which would destroy thousands of jobs and cripple our armed forces.

WHO DO YOU WANT RUNNING BRITAIN
AND REPRESENTING US AROUND THE WORLD?

Figure 8 ✦ 12 Conservative leaflet from the 1992 election campaign

IT'S TIME TO CHOOSE

THE GENERAL ELECTION

IT'S A TWO-HORSE RACE

All the national polls show that the General Election is a two-horse race.

On April 10th either John Major or Neil Kinnock will be the Prime Minister.

IF YOU WANT JOHN MAJOR, VOTE CONSERVATIVE

Published by Conservative Central Office, 32 Smith Square, Westminster, London SW1P 3HH
Printed by Waddie & Co. Ltd., City Cloisters, 188-196 Old Street, London EC1V 9BP   GB42

3 THINGS TO REMEMBER BEFORE YOU VOTE

1 The General Election is about far more than just electing a local Member of Parliament. It's about **deciding who runs Britain for the next 5 years**.

2 This General Election is the closest for years. **Every seat the Conservatives don't win, is one step closer to Downing Street for Neil Kinnock and Gerald Kaufman**.

3 During the last Parliament, **Liberal Democrat MP's voted with Neil Kinnock and the Labour Party on 85 out of every 100 occasions**. Given the choice they sided with Neil Kinnock - not John Major. Given the chance they would do the same again.

CONSERVATIVE ☒

acerbic. To use a popular British cliché, he does not suffer fools gladly. At no other position in the Cabinet did the Conservatives have such an edge in popular perception of the abilities of potential office holders.

As a result of such considerations, support began to shift back to the Conservatives in the last few days of the campaign. On election day typical newspaper headlines read "Polls put parties neck and neck" (two papers), "It's too close to call," and "Election poised on knife-edge." In the end the last-minute surge to the Conservatives not only denied Labour victory, but prevented a hung Parliament as well. A Conservative majority, which almost nobody other than John Major had foreseen, was the result. Almost immediately Kinnock indicated he would be resigning as Leader. The following Monday he officially announced his departure and the process of selecting his successor got underway. In mid-July John Smith was elected as Labour's new Leader.

Party prospects are only slightly linked to the coming and going of particular Leaders. The great advantage of the Conservatives, in particular, and Labour is money. Despite its financial link with the trade unions — the main source of its income — Labour can't match Conservative spending. In a non-election year Labour's income at the national level is only about two-thirds of the Conservatives' and at the constituency level only about one-third. Labour lacks the funds to operate a national headquarters as well organized as is the Conservatives'. Conservative party headquarters is only a short walk from the Houses of Parliament; Labour's is located in an obscure spot south of the Thames. (Conservative Central Office appears in Figure 8.13.) Indicative of Labour's problems are its staff's complaints that it is a bad employer, paying substandard wages. If the party that is supposed to represent the workers' interests fails to remunerate its employees properly, then financial constraints must indeed be severe.

The Liberal Democrats would be only too happy to have Labour's financial problems. During the late 1950s the Liberals had to run their national party machinery on an annual budget of only $50,000; the party nearly went bankrupt. By the 1970s, the party had managed to get its budget up to around a third of a million dollars. The enthusiasm associated with the SDP's founding enabled it to raise a good deal of money initially, but funds soon declined to a level all too similar to that of the Liberals. So financially constrained was the Alliance between the two parties in 1983 that it could afford no national press advertising and after the election had to cut back an already small staff at national headquarters.

Although the Alliance managed to buy some ads in 1987, its total spending at the national level was about the same as it had been in 1983, which means, given inflation over those years, that less actually was spent. While the Alliance was not even successfully treading water, Labour nearly doubled its spending and the Conservatives increased theirs by two and half times. Not

Figure 8 ✦ 13 Conservative Central Office

....

being able to rely on either unions or big business for major contributions, the Liberal Democrats face an uphill battle in trying to become a major party. The other major hurdle the party has to clear is the lack of a core clientele. Understanding this obstacle requires examining British voting behavior.

The traditional, nineteenth-century core Conservative support was the landed interests, the gentry. The Liberals relied then on support from the business sector of society. Increasingly toward the close of the century as the Liberals adopted social reform policies in a futile effort to head off the threat of a working-class party, many industrialists left the Liberals for the Conservatives. To the two segments of society it had attracted, the Conservatives added professionals and farmers. Having been the employers' party, the Liberals experienced great difficulty, even after adopting reform policies, in competing with Labour for working-class support. Thus, the Conservatives could count on strong support from the middle class and Labour could rely on the loyalty of the workers; the Liberals weren't similarly linked with any segment of society. The sharp class cleavages discussed in Chapter 2 helped to reinforce such voting behavior and make success difficult for any party lacking a base in the social structure.

Social class remained the strongest influence on partisan preference in Britain well into the post-World War II period. In the 1970s, however, Britain entered a period of dealignment; attachment to parties became much less automatic and feelings of class solidarity didn't affect voting as they once had. Voters became more inclined to weigh the issues in a campaign and to assess party performance. Election campaigns became not so much a matter of parties getting their voters to turn out on election day as a matter of convincing uncommitted or wavering voters to choose them. A more volatile electorate made the outcome of elections less certain. Nonetheless, nearly three-fourths of those eligible to vote in both the 1983 and 1987 elections did vote the same way each time.

On the other hand, the 1992 election campaign saw a good deal of what opinion pollsters call churning, that is, shifts in voting intention. About 11 million people, around a quarter of the electorate, changed their voting intention between the start and the end of the campaign. That is a considerable amount of change during only a month. The bulk of this change, however, involved people shifting to or from "don't know." A more stringent test of party loyalty might consider shifts in voting intention only among the three main parties. Shifts of this type involved approximately 4.5 million people, about a tenth of the electorate. This suggests a fairly high level of partisan loyalty, but hardly automatic support.

The impact of social class has weakened to the extent that party loyalty has declined and the motivation for voting has altered. In 1992 just half the *unskilled* workers voted Labour. Labour could not win a clear majority even among those whose social class could be expected to make them most supportive. As for *skilled* workers, although Labour was well short of a majority, it managed (barely) to nose out the Conservatives. This was an improvement over 1987 when the Conservatives won more votes among this segment of the working class than did Labour.

Such voting patterns would be unremarkable enough in the United States; given Britain's sharper social cleavages, however, they are a striking departure from past behavior. Why should this have occurred? Several elaborate theories have been proposed. One fairly straightforward argument is that as manual workers become more prosperous they can afford middle-class consumption patterns. Becoming like the middle class in this regard might affect political attitudes and thus party allegiance. Whatever the validity of this theory, certain elements of lifestyle clearly are related to political behavior.

Housing is a good example. More than half again as many home owners voted Conservative in 1992 as voted Labour. More than twice as many people living in council housing (government owned and operated) supported Labour as did the Conservatives. The interaction of social class and housing is striking. Nearly a third of the electorate is working-class home owners. In

1992 they were as likely to vote Conservative as to support Labour. A fifth of the electorate are working class living in council housing. They went for Labour in 1992 by more than 2.5 to 1. Perhaps the working-class home owners are adopting middle-class aspirations and changing their politics to coincide with their new values. Alternatively, buying a home may have involved moving. Therefore, many working-class home owners may no longer be as tightly integrated into a working-class residential community as they once were. They may be coming in contact with more diverse political views. Thinking about these alternative opinions, rather than imitating another social group, may explain any change in voting behavior. Finally, the issue of self-selection shouldn't be overlooked. Those members of the working class who choose to buy a home rather than continue to live in council housing may be the ones who were less integrated into the working-class community in the first place. *Both* behaviors — home buying and cross-class voting — may derive from preexisting core values.

Although perhaps not a lifestyle factor, trade union membership is worth mention as an influence in the direction opposite to home ownership. I noted above that Labour's support among both the unskilled and skilled working class is less than one would anticipate were British politics still pure social class politics. In 1992 Labour's support among the unskilled was about half again as large as was the Conservatives'. Among unskilled trade union members, however, Labour's support was two and a half times as great. Among skilled workers Labour's edge over the Conservatives was only a few percentage points. For those skilled workers belonging to unions, however, Labour's support was double that of the Conservatives. Union membership among skilled workers increased support for Labour by about 25 percentage points.

Whereas in the past social class was the crucial determinant of British voting behavior, now it is class in conjunction with other key attributes that matters. The declining effect of class gives other demographic characteristics an opportunity to influence voting behavior. In 1992 gender had a modest effect.[17] The proportion of women supporting the Conservatives was about 10 percentage points greater than the share voting Labour. For men, the gap in support for the two main parties was only half as large. Support for the Conservatives tends to increase with age, while the reverse is true for Labour. Labour was slightly preferred to the Conservatives by those under 25 in 1992, but lagged behind with other age groups. Here, again, interaction effects are interesting. Women over 65 are more likely than any other gender and age combination to favor the Conservatives, more than half again as likely to vote for them rather than for Labour. Retired men are only slightly more likely to vote Conservative than Labour.

---

17. This was in contrast to 1987, when men and women were exactly the same in their partisan preferences.

At the other end of the age spectrum, the situation is reversed. Men under 25 slightly preferred the Conservatives in 1992. Their female cohorts were almost half again as likely to prefer Labour over the Conservatives. Women of this age may be young mothers who are especially interested in education and other social services, and they are thus inclined to Labour. And/or they may be employed outside the home and be especially likely to suffer from unequal pay. Given gender discrimination in employment, young men are more likely to obtain jobs that not only offer better prospects for advancement but higher entry wages as well. Young women are more likely to have to settle for menial employment. Thus at this age women may be more "radicalized" than are men.

Party support varies a good deal by region. For many statistical purposes England is divided into nine standard regions. To these nine can be added Wales and Scotland for a total of eleven in Britain. In 1992 support for the Conservatives ranged from 55 percent in the southeast to only 26 percent in Scotland. (The latter was sufficient to beat out the SNP for second place.) Labour's vote varied from 51 percent in the north of England to only 19 percent in the southwest. In the latter region it was a distant third to the Liberal Democrats. (The Liberal Democrats also beat out Labour as second party in the southeast, although by a more narrow share of the vote.) The Liberal Democrats looked like a major party in the southwest with nearly a third of the vote. Their low point was Wales with little more than a tenth. The Welsh result was a significant change from the past; the Liberal Democrats' vote declined by about a third. The party suffered a similar major decline in Scotland.

Given the operation of the SMSP electoral system, the distribution of seats in the House of Commons suggests a starker contrast in partisan support. Leaving aside London, the Conservatives dominate England up to north of Birmingham in the midlands. In 1992 the Conservatives won nearly four-fifths of the seats in these regions with Labour obtaining nearly one-fifth. In the three northern English regions plus Scotland and Wales, Labour predominates. In 1992 Labour won two-thirds of these constituencies with the Conservatives getting a quarter of them. As for London, there the Conservatives had the edge with not quite three-fifths of the seats while Labour had slightly more than two-fifths.

The handful of constituencies in which the Liberals managed to concentrate their support sufficiently to win tended to be located primarily in the Celtic Fringe — Scotland, Wales, Devon, and Cornwall. This changed little with the formation of the Alliance. About two-thirds of the seats that the Alliance won in 1987 were in the Celtic Fringe, and the same remained true for the Liberal Democrats in 1992, despite losing some seats and gaining others. The Liberal Democrats appear to be marginalized not only in regard to support by major social groups, but geographically as well.

Further understanding of the party's difficult position as well as some additional insight into the nature of the British party system can be obtained from examining candidates' position of finish in 1992. More than nine-tenths of the candidates that the Conservatives offered either won their constituency or were second. Nearly three-quarters of Labour's candidates were first or second. Little more than a quarter of the Liberal Democrats' candidates managed to do that well. Furthermore, nearly two-thirds of the Members elected as either Labour or Conservative obtained more than half the vote in their constituency. Only 15 percent of the Liberal Democrat Members were that popular. The party's small band of legislators remains vulnerable.

The Conservatives clearly can be seen to be a major party and the Liberal Democrats a third party. Labour's pattern of candidate position resembles that of the Conservatives much more than that of the Liberal Democrats. Nonetheless, the fact that a quarter of a major party's candidates could finish third or worse in 1992 indicates a significant weakness. On the other hand, since two-thirds of the Members of Parliament that Labour elected in 1992 won a majority of the vote, the party is not going to collapse to the level of the Liberal Democrats overnight. If Labour is dying, it will be a long terminal illness.

Until Labour can demonstrate an ability to win an election, however, the Liberal Democrats will remain more than an irrelevancy. The next general election in Britain probably won't occur until 1996. By then Labour will have been out of office for seventeen years, nearly as long as the longest twentieth-century period of futility in American politics — the Republicans' inability to control the White House in the twenty years from 1933 to 1953 (and that involved a world war). If one searches for the last time that Labour had a firm working majority and did not have to depend for its survival in office on the whims of third parties, then the period covers more than a quarter of a century. The perpetual optimism of the Liberal Democrats may seem quixotic, but perhaps the party that really is deluding itself that it just can keep plugging away as in the past is Labour.

The evolution of the British party system into the next century remains uncertain. The situation is not so different from what it was a century ago. In 1890 some political observers may have recognized that change was afoot, but few would have predicted that Labour was about to replace the Liberals. History doesn't repeat itself, but twenty-first–century British politics is likely to be as different from the current relations as twentieth-century politics was from its nineteenth-century forerunner.

Summary

The British parties differ fundamentally from American parties in that they are mass, rather than caucus or cadre, parties: They have an integrated organizational structure from the national headquarters all the way down to the grass roots. A constituency party isn't the personal machine of an incumbent legislator; it is one element in a nationwide organization. Local party members, rather than the electorate at large, control the nomination process. While constituency parties raise some money, national headquarters disburses the big sums. Elections are not as much several hundred skirmishes between individual candidates as they are a battle for control of the Government between national parties, each presenting a programme of integrated, cohesive policies. The winning party then proceeds to implement its proposals by maintaining tight discipline in the legislature.

The British party system also varies considerably from the American system, despite the two countries' sharing the label "two-party system." Britain departs markedly from that model. This is not due simply to occasional successes by several regionally based parties. More important has been the persistent electoral strength during the last two decades of a countrywide third party or alliance of parties. Only the single-member, simple-plurality electoral system, which Britain shares with the United States, has prevented this third force from converting its popular support into significant legislative strength. With a different electoral system Britain would have the multiparty, coalition government politics of the European continent.

The interesting question is whether that might occur even without a change in the electoral system. During the 1980s the two leading parties moved apart on the political spectrum; British politics became much more polarized than it had been during the period of Butskell consensus in the 1950s. This opened up a space at the center of the spectrum where a third party might be able to win an impressive number of supporters. Voter disillusionment with the inability of either the Conservatives or the Labour party to run the economy effectively reinforced this possibility. Then, however, the Thatcher Government did manage to reduce inflation and eventually unemployment as well. Her toppling from the Leadership of the Conservative party and Kinnock's rise to dominance in the Labour party set the leading parties on a course for convergence at the center of the spectrum. The political space for a third force began to contract; it became a good bit more difficult to make a distinctive appeal.

Traditionally British voting behavior had been motivated to a great extent by social class. This was an asset for the two leading parties since they each had a natural core clientele. A third party lacking this clientele was at a considerable disadvantage. The Liberals attempted to make the best of this by claiming that, unlike their big rivals, they weren't beholden to any segment of society. Their pattern of electoral support bore this out. Whether one analyzed the electorate by age, sex, union membership, or social class, the level of support for the Liberals did not vary much. Although the Liberals' claim may have been self-gratifying, it failed to win many votes.

Recent elections in Britain, however, have seen a decline in the ability of social class to motivate voting behavior. Perhaps in the near future *no* party will have a core clientele. If the political habits of a lifetime are deteriorating, if new voters are entering the electorate without being socialized into the class conflicts of the past, then the Liberal Democrats' ability to appeal to a wide variety of people—its classless characteristic—may, indeed, prove to be an asset.[18]

And yet the party still runs smack into that unyielding wall of money. If the electorate is becoming increasingly volatile and must be wooed, then constrained financial resources are a serious impediment to success. The Conservatives can count on money from big business and the Labour party has the unions. Neither source provides as much as the recipient party wants, but both can offer a great deal more than the occasional financial angel, which is what the Liberal Democrats must rely upon.

So, not only is it unlikely that the British party system will return to its nineteenth-century form of Liberal versus Conservative, it is also unlikely to return to its 1920s' form of three approximately equal contenders for power. And yet . . .

---

18. Support for the Liberal Democrats varied in 1992 by only a few percentage points from one social group to another. For example, 22 percent of the professional and managerial class voted Liberal Democrat, 19 percent of white-collar workers, 17 percent of skilled workers, and 15 percent of unskilled workers. Among home owners 19 percent voted Liberal Democrat, compared to 15 percent of council tenants. The Liberal Democrats' support among trade unionists was 19 percent, only 1 percentage point different from their share of the total national vote.

Part IV

◆

Conclusion

Photo on previous page: A military band marching down the Mall away from Buckingham Palace.

9
✦
Prospects for Stability and Change

The French have a phrase — *plus ça change, plus c'est la même chose* — "the more things change, the more they remain the same." Perhaps the British version should be: The less things change, the more they differ. Change in Britain is imperceptible. Only when one looks back over an extended period, say a century, can one see that the country has moved on from where it had been. The British have a talent for making it appear that everything is just as it always has been while they are quietly transforming the fundamental elements. It is as though a venerable building had been remodeled *inside*. New heating and cooling, new lighting, new communications, and the like have been installed, but the outside is unaltered. Looking at the structure's stone, iron, and wood, one would never know that inside business was being carried on just as it would be in a glass and steel high rise.

Change proceeds in this fashion because almost never do those in power say, "Right, we need to devise a plan for transforming things." Remedial action is preferred to preventive programs. And the remedies tend to be of the take-two-aspirins-and-call-me-in-the-morning nature. As a result, some of the most momentous change in Britain has been fortuitous. No one realized that adding 200,000 people to the electorate in 1832 would produce registration societies and that these would evolve into political parties that would transform the operation of governmental institutions.

Fortuitous, imperceptible British change may be; nevertheless, it does proceed apace. The country has been stable, not stagnant. A strong case can be made that Britain has been stable precisely *because* change has been fortuitous and imperceptible. By the latter part of the nineteenth century this unique approach to change seemed to have brought Britain to a golden age. For about six centuries England had been developing limited, constitutional government. The process that had begun with a group of barons trying to protect themselves from the king had culminated in extensive protection of citizens' basic rights from arbitrary government.

Not for Britain the American system that fractionalized power among various branches of government at the national level and between various levels from the national to the subnational. This concentrated power was constrained in Britain not by a written constitution or checks and balances (again, the American options were rejected), but by accountability. The greater the power a governmental institution possessed, the greater its accountability had to be. Ultimately, all streams of accountability flowed into the House of Commons. There the Government not only had to justify its actions, but had to live each day under the shadow of the Commons' ultimate weapon of accountability: the vote of no confidence. Whenever its handling of public affairs failed to satisfy the Commons, whenever its account of its behavior failed to measure up, the Commons could discharge the Government from office, replacing it with new officials in whom it did possess confidence. To ensure that the constraint of accountability didn't negate the benefits of concentrated power, didn't interfere with expert administration of public affairs, the constitutional conventions of individual ministerial responsibility and collective responsibility were developed. Britain had squared the circle: A country could enjoy the benefits of concentrated power without having to suffer its pains.

Having solved the primal problem of government so skillfully (the difficult we do immediately, the impossible takes a few centuries longer), in the latter part of the nineteenth century Britain began work on developing its model constitutional government into a model democracy. Gradually over the coming decades (if not centuries) an increasing share of the population would be allowed a voice in government. Citizens could look forward (if not they, then, perhaps their children) to influencing public policy by selecting those who would speak for them in the decision-making process and supervise the Government's actions. Although the day-to-day task of calling power to account would continue to reside with the House of Commons, the stream of accountability now would flow onto the citizens. They could replace those Members of the Commons who were not up to performing their essential task and periodically (in addition to the Commons' ability to do so directly at will) could indirectly remove the Government from office, thereby sharing a portion of the power to call it to account.

This promising bud never fully flowered, however; the development of democracy in Britain mutated, veered off (fortuitously) on an unforeseen tack.[1] If politicians were to be able to deliver the policies they had promised to the people, then parties would have to field a unified slate of candidates. Everyone on this slate would have to make the same campaign appeals and, if elected, act in concert in the Commons. Furthermore, the leaders would have to be able to bind their followers to the promised policies despite any doubts that might arise during the policy-making process. The Cabinet would have to be empowered to override any obstructionist tactics that could thwart implementing the mandate that the people had bestowed — the program they had endorsed — in the general election.[2] Thoughtful consideration of bills gave way in the legislature to automatic party-line voting. Legislators' function shifted from formulating public policy to supporting the policy proposals of a small group of leaders. Instead of the legislators calling the executive to account, the executive called dissident legislators to account. The leading holders of executive office also led the governing party and, therefore, usually could rely on the support of the party activists in the constituencies. Since the growth of democracy hadn't progressed to the extent of letting the public select candidates (and still hadn't even in the last decade of the twentieth century), the activists wielded a fearsome power. When those executioners turned thumbs down, only the rarest gladiator emerged from the arena alive. A word in the ear from the legislative whips usually was sufficient to determine the crucial digit's direction.

The House of Commons came to be organized into highly disciplined, cohesive parties. Up through the middle of the nineteenth century, voting behavior in the House of Commons justified detailed analysis (just as it continues to do in the U.S. Congress). By the end of the century such study was largely a waste of time. Everyone knew exactly how all the Members would

---

1. A few people had some inkling of what might happen. M. Ostrogorski's *Democracy and the Organization of Political Parties,* published in 1902, was a prescient warning of the likely impact of disciplined mass parties on British democracy.

2. The whittling away of the Commons' power through procedural changes in the late nineteenth century is another excellent example of fortuitous change. All of Ireland then was part of the United Kingdom. Most of its large delegation of legislators favored independence for Ireland and was willing to filibuster Parliament to a halt to try to get it. To prevent this, the Cabinet obtained greater power to control the Commons' business and to override minority opinion. Were it not for the Irish Nationalists, the British Cabinet would be weaker or would have dominated for a much shorter period of time.

vote: the straight party line. Exceptions were so rare as to be unforgettable. Why did Prime Minister Neville Chamberlain, despite winning a division in the Commons by eighty votes, resign in 1940? Because, had all his nominal supporters voted for him, he would have won by over 200. Some legislators from his party had had the temerity to abstain, while others had become such berserkers as to vote against their party. Only a bungled military operation during an increasingly futile struggle for national survival could produce such behavior. Even with such inducement to break ranks, *most* of Chamberlain's followers continued to vote the party line.

The paradox that had diverted the actual course of development from the anticipated one was that expanding self-government had reduced its effectiveness. Broadening the franchise permitted more people to participate in the political process. But it was as though money had been printed without backing; the greater the supply of the currency, the more debased became its value. Instead of being able to select someone to advocate the needs and interests of their particular area of the country, voters in each constituency simply were being permitted to place a drop of sand in the scales to tilt the balance toward one unified bloc or another. Although a representative might sympathize with the concerns expressed by the local people, he or she could justify doing nothing about those concerns with the explanation that the party in the Commons demanded absolutely loyal support for the leaders. The structures that had evolved to effectively handle an expanding democracy had undermined the basic purpose of democracy. All the streams of accountability seemed to have dried up.

Accountability to the electorate? Voters, even groups of them, could do little to change their representatives. The great bulk of seats was safe, always won by the same party. Without primary elections, a handful of party activists (not the electorate) decided which individuals would enjoy this secure tenure. Members of the Commons had to assiduously court the favor of this handful, but the Members had little reason to bother with the concerns of the public at large. Governments were barely more accountable. True, elections did remove them from office on occasion. But, in the quarter century from 1964 through 1987, a period of eight general elections, the percentage of the electorate supporting the party gaining control of the Government ranged from only 29 pecent to 36 percent—hardly a majority mandate for action.

Accountability to the House of Commons? Although legally Parliament remained supreme, in practice party cohesion produced Cabinet supremacy. In the half century since 1941 only once did the Commons vote a Government out of office and that was a minority Government defeated by a single vote. Muscles flexed that seldom atrophy. As for challenging the Government through questioning (without resort to the ultimate sanction of no confidence), the power of the Commons had sunk to the point that a public affairs program staged a mock debate among some Members of the Commons on the topic, "Are MPs too ignorant to do their job?"

Accountability to the Cabinet? Although Labour politician cum academic Richard Crossman had formulated his theory of Prime Ministerial Government before his party returned to power, the workings of the Wilson Governments provided him and his colleague John Mackintosh considerable evidence to flesh out the idea in a compelling fashion.[3] Had Crossman and Mackintosh lived through the Thatcher era, they doubtless would have regarded her performance in office as the apotheosis of their analysis. Increasingly during her term of office, the "vegetables" showed little ability to constrain her dominance of the Government, which had destroyed most elements of collective policy making. True, Thatcher's concern about whether key civil servants were "one of us" was a type of accountability. But it was a personalized form that threatened to jeopardize the traditional partisan neutrality of the civil service.

Optimists might concede these points and argue that the costs were worth paying to obtain effective and efficient government. Increasingly, however, this claimed benefit proved to be a chimera. In an evermore interdependent world, many problems are insoluble by a single government, however strong. Even a government like the British one, unimpeded by the roadblocks to action that characterize the American system, came to seem ineffective, unable to cope successfully with the country's basic problems. Inflation, lack of economic growth, international balance of payments deficits, unemployment: No Government of whatever political complexion seemed able to ameliorate these problems. What point was there in going to the polls every few years to choose between alternatives, neither of which could improve the quality of life?

Although voting turnout in Britain has remained high, evidence that citizens are disillusioned (perhaps even alienated) isn't difficult to find. A Gallup poll late in 1990 reported that only two-fifths of the respondents thought that "most Members of Parliament have a personal moral code," while nearly as many disagreed. Half believed that "most Members of Parliament make a lot of money by using public office improperly," while only a quarter didn't think so. Two-thirds agreed that "to win elections, most candidates for Parliament make promises they have no intentions of fulfilling," and nearly four-fifths thought that "most Members of Parliament will tell lies if they feel the truth will hurt them politically." But perhaps it's all in a good cause? No, because only a third believed that "most Members of Parliament care deeply about

---

3. Harold Wilson was Labour Prime Minister from 1964 to 1970 and again from 1974 to 1976.

the problems of the ordinary citizen," while two-thirds thought that "most Members of Parliament care more about special interests than they care about people like you." It's all just self-serving behavior; nearly three-fourths said that "most Members of Parliament care more about keeping power than they do about the best interests of the nation."

Americans don't think highly of their politicians, but many had assumed that things were better in Britain. Such a belief contains a good bit of irony. The founders of the American system were determined to devise a new form of government that would avoid the flaws that they believed had made Britain a tyranny; it was the last country they wanted to copy. The corruption of American government following the Civil War, however, led many to conclude that Britain (at the time of the golden age of Parliamentary government) was the superior system.[4] Not surprisingly, many Britons concurred.[5] Not until well after World War II did a more balanced view emerge. Scholars came to recognize that neither was superior; each had its flaws and its strengths. This might suggest, given a good deal of shared history and many common values, that the two countries could look to each other for policies and procedures to improve governmental performance. Many differences in detailed characteristics, however, counseled against jumping to that conclusion. Transplanted institutions are as likely to be rejected as transplanted organs; government and politics form a system just as much as the human body does. Seeking to incorporate a foreign entity always is a risky process. For example, as an American, I would be inclined to argue that British democracy would be enhanced by the adoption of a system of primary elections. The unforeseeable effect of that step on party cohesion, legislative–executive relations, and the party system is potentially so momentous, however, that it truly would be what opponents of the Reform Act of 1832 charged it was: "a leap in the dark." The potential benefits of primary elections can easily be envisioned; unfortunately, so can the harms. Predicting what mix of these Britain might actually obtain is impossible.

So, the end of this discussion can't be to present a list of reforms that the United States might import from Britain to improve its government, along with a similar list for Britain to import from the United States. Studying British government and politics can help Americans to perceive their system's strengths and weaknesses, to recognize that alternative arrangements are feasible, and to understand the choices involved in doing things as they do. But to unthinkingly advocate grafting onto American government some

---

4. A leading example of this thinking was political scientist, later turned university president, turned state governor, turned President, Woodrow Wilson.

5. A twentieth-century example would be Lord Bryce, Member of the Commons and, later, British ambassador to the United States.

institution or procedure simply because it works well in Britain would be a mistake. Imports shouldn't be automatically rejected, but should be welcomed only if their systemic role in both the donor and the recipient nation has been fully examined.

Therefore, the proper conclusion is to summarize the condition of the British system in the final decade of the twentieth century. Fundamental change is more in the air in Britain than it has been for half a century. The Liberal Democrats, of course, have been advocating such change for years. More recently they have been joined by interest groups such as Charter '88. The Labour party has progressed from merely threatening to abolish the House of Lords to advocating a fundamentally reformed upper house of Parliament. Labour also is willing to devolve some power to Scotland and is devoting serious study to changes in the electoral system. The Conservatives have been least receptive to constitutional change. But even here some movement has occurred. Prime Minister Major has started a process of reducing secrecy in British government by announcing the membership and responsibilities of hitherto secret Cabinet committees and by acknowledging the existence of Britain's foreign espionage agency and naming (!) its head.

However, so far actual reform has been slight, in keeping with tradition. During the last couple of decades Parliament has been experimenting with select committees. This reform is notable not only because it is a conscious attempt to redress the balance of power between the Commons and the Cabinet, but it is also one of those rare instances of importing from the United States. The British hoped in this way to tilt the balance of their legislative–executive relations back toward that existing between the President and the Congress. In keeping with what this chapter has argued about the differing impacts of conscious and fortuitous change and the uncertain benefits of imports, this transplant has failed to produce the hoped-for benefit although it hasn't done any great harm. As was only to be expected, the British executive branch has done everything possible to thwart the Commons from using the select committees to strengthen the link of accountability. Nevertheless, a weapon has been fashioned that Members could potentially use, had they the will to do so.

Willingness is the key factor. Fortuitous personal motivation and behavior are more likely to produce significant reform than is deliberate institutional change. Beginning in the 1970s party cohesion declined a bit in the Commons, although still not coming close to Congressional levels of partisan indiscipline. Although scholars differ on the reason this occurred, most explanations tend to cite fortuitous developments. For example, the Commons' membership used to be characterized by retired military officers, elderly former trade union officials, and bored landed gentry. Now, regardless of party affiliation, the typical Member is well-educated with professional credentials. These new Members have entered politics not in search of a spare-time hobby or an activity to occupy them during retirement, but in search of a career. In short, the amateurs have been replaced by the professionals — the gentlemen by the players, as the British would say.

The validity of this explanation is disputed because the potential effect of the change in Member background can be projected in contrary directions. On the one hand, given their training and skills, these new Members aren't content just to be lobby fodder, as were their predecessors. They want to be effective, to have a role in policy formulation. Such a desire suggests that they will be much less willing to toe the party line, more inclined to call their leaders to account. On the other hand, since they are careerists, they must take seriously the advice that "to get along, you must go along." Having your service terminated for stepping out of line is no great disaster for an amateur; he or she always can find another activity to occupy the time. For a career professional, however, suffering this fate is a crushing blow; he or she, feeling a failure, must start over from scratch in another occupation. The new-style Member may be more highly motivated and properly trained to assume an active role in the policy process; actually playing that role, however, may involve such costs, require such courage, that many forgo the pleasure.

Courage can be contagious and, paradoxically, can be generated by fear. Perhaps the most dramatic and momentous lesson of recent British politics is that revolts can succeed. What the House of Commons as a whole couldn't do, its Conservative Members managed: calling Margaret Thatcher to account. Much of the courage needed to try to topple her was generated by fear of the voters. Although they recognized that their careers would suffer from a vengeful Maggie if the coup failed, they could see that if she wasn't deposed, the voters would terminate, not just damage, their careers. Despite the sizable margins by which most seats are won, no politician ever feels safe. They all run scared. And a good thing it is, too, because that does provide a measure of accountability to the electorate.

So, Thatcher's fall showed that followers *could* call a Leader to account (and if a Leader like Thatcher could suffer this fate then all future Leaders would be well advised to behave so that the ranks didn't mutiny). But the event's significance extended well beyond that for it also demonstrated that the public could play a role in the policy process. If it were willing to raise a major ruckus, the public could rid itself of a hated policy: the poll tax. No one could gainsay that the Government had been accountable to the people. And yet this was a troubling precedent. Riots and deliberate flouting of the law (even by some Members of Parliament) to change policy isn't the way the democratic process is supposed to operate. It is like trimming your fingernails with a meat cleaver — it could be done but is too exciting to be attempted regularly.

The more traditional form of accountability to the electorate appeared to be reviving as well, despite the absence of any event of similar drama. The decline of class voting strengthens accountability because parties can't count on the automatic support of a core clientele to the extent that they formerly did. Parties will have to do more than just get *their* voters to the polls. With greater possible flux in voting behavior, fewer seats seem safe; Members will be more inclined to give high priority to responding to the public's policy concerns. This priority may help to reinforce any inclinations generated by background characteristics to relax party cohesion.

Thus, in the early 1990s accountability to the people was more vital than it had been for some time, just as was true for accountability to the Commons (or at least to Government party portion of it). Accountability to the Cabinet also appeared to enjoy a rebirth. With Thatcher's replacement by John Major, Britain retreated from Prime Ministerial Government toward the more traditional practices of Cabinet Government. Policy making became more collective than it had been for nearly a decade. All the Prime Ministerial powers that Crossman and Mackintosh identified remained in place, but Major lacked the authority to wield them.

The election of 1992 did much to legitimize his position. Now he could claim a popular mandate of his own. No longer was he just "son of Thatcher." (From his standpoint, perhaps the best aspect of this was that he now could tell her to butt out.) Only when he stood on a soapbox (literally) in the closing days of the election and campaigned from the heart did the surge of the electorate back to the Conservatives begin. His sincerity and cool confidence, his assertiveness without abrasiveness, won much praise. The Conservative victory of 1992 truly was his victory; his authority had been enhanced. And yet he was not full of himself. His verdict — "Overall, the result is satisfactory" — perfectly embodied the low-key nature of his leadership. In reiterating his goal of developing "a truly classless society" in Britain, he commented, "That's the sort of society that *my colleagues* [emphasis added] and I will be working hard to build." Major, unlike his predecessor, seemed satisfied to be the traditional *primus inter pares.*

Not only were the various forms of accountability being reinvigorated, concentrated power was also being reexamined. Were its effectiveness limited, then, perhaps some policy decisions should be made at a level nearer to the citizen. Perhaps power needed to be devolved, to be less concentrated. The people of Scotland, Wales, and Northern Ireland might be able to run their nations' domestic affairs better than could be done in London. (Although the politicians of Northern Ireland have shown in the past no ability whatsoever to do so.) Even a relatively small nation like England might have sufficient regional diversity that it would benefit from decentralization. Fully achieving accountability to the electorate might require changing the governmental, as well as the political, structures.

Thus, in the final decade of the twentieth century Britain appears poised to reverse the dominant trend of the century, appears ready to start making concentrated power more fully accountable. Efforts to do so, however, are likely to conform with British tradition, that is to be incremental and gradual. Furthermore, fortuitous side effects of other actions can be expected to have greater impact than deliberate reform efforts themselves. If you want a summary slogan, you can chalk up "Edmund Burke rules, OK."

Index

✦